The Third Career

The Third Career

Revisiting the Home vs. Work Choice in Middle Age

MILICA Z. BOOKMAN

Westport, Connecticut
London

Library of Congress Cataloging-in-Publication Data

Bookman, Milica Zarkovic.
    The third career : revisiting the home vs. work choice in middle age / Milica Z. Bookman.
      p. cm.
    Includes bibliographical references and index.
    ISBN 0–275–96811–1 (alk. paper)
    1. Middle aged women—Employment. 2. Age and employment. 3. Home
economics—Social aspects. 4. Women—Social conditions. I. Title.
HD6056.B66 2000
331.3′94′082—dc21   99–045992

British Library Cataloguing in Publication Data is available.

Library of Congress Catalog Card Number: 99–045992
ISBN: 0–275–96811–1

First published in 2000

Praeger Publishers, 88 Post Road West, Westport, CT 06881
An imprint of Greenwood Publishing Group, Inc.
www.praeger.com

Printed in the United States of America

The paper used in this book complies with the
Permanent Paper Standard issued by the National
Information Standards Organization (Z39.48–1984).

10 9 8 7 6 5 4 3 2 1

I dedicate this book to my sister Jelena who has been my role model since early childhood. In her endeavor to raise children *and* participate in the workforce, she has been a source of inspiration and guidance in both my personal and professional life.

In my *first career*, I was unmarried, childless, and working full time as an attorney. Then I became a full-time homemaker, tending to my home, raising my children, and volunteering in my community. That was my *second career*. Now I look forward to yet one more career, my third, in which I hope to fuse the previous two. I'd like to go back to work, but I don't want to have a full-time, demanding career as I had before; I'd still like to tend to my home, but my children will be grown up or gone so I won't be as needed as before. My *third career* will, I hope, be a balanced combination of so many things I enjoy in life.
—Elise Troy, age 42

Contents

x   Contents

Preface

Throughout my academic career, each book I wrote followed directly from the previous one in a logical sequence. Indeed, research on Third World economic development in graduate school led to an analysis of regional economic competition, which led to the exploration of regional secession, which in turn led to a study of the economic elements of nationalism, and finally to nationalistic demographic engineering. Yet, a book on women, especially privileged, middle-aged women in Western societies, had nothing whatsoever to do with my formal training nor the direction of my academic interests over the past two decades.

The idea for this book came from a source that was thus far new to me: personal experience. Due to circumstances in my personal life, two activities in the early 1990s brought me into consistent and sustained contact with women who were middle-aged, upper-income, and outside the labor force. The first of these activities was involvement in parents' groups at a private school in Miami. When my daughter enrolled in middle school, I began participating in numerous school activities in order to learn about the environment in which she would be spending her teenaged years. Over time and after countless hours working side by side with numerous volunteers, I learned that so many unemployed mothers had above-average stamina, untapped creativity, and boundless energy. Some also had a very strong desire to "do something new". I learned that some women, despite their privilege and their material comfort, had outgrown their past choices and were increasingly feeling confined by the current boundaries of their lives.

The second activity that offered me a glimpse of the lives of unemployed, middle-aged women was a part-time catering service that my friend and I established. Our excursion into the business world in the form of a dessert company was motivated primarily by a desire to give concrete vent to a hobby that we shared, namely, baking (we both had other "real" full-time jobs). As word got around of our endeavors, a relatively uniform response flowed from many of the middle-aged women with whom I had contact. My unemployed female friends, my children's schoolmates' mothers, and female dessert clients all wanted a part of the action. They wanted in! Women began asking me if there was anything they could do in our company. They sought to partake at any level and in any form whatsoever. They were not deterred when I told them that I barely covered my expenses and that the company was perpetually hovering on the brink of bankruptcy. It was clear that it wasn't the financial remuneration they were pursuing. They were amazed that my friend and I had had a potential money-making idea, had formulated it into a concrete goal, and had pursued that goal until it was attained. I, in turn, was amazed that women were offering to deliver my cakes in their luxury automobiles!

I was thus exposed to a large number of full-time homemakers who seemed enviable in their comfortable life circumstances yet who harbored an obvious dissatisfaction. I picked up on a turbulence in their souls and their minds that belied the seeming order and peace of their bucolic and perfectly manicured environments. I witnessed pent-up energy bubbling to the surface in effervescence. I detected an unmistakable desire to "do something else" before it was too late. I recognized a desire to grab another chance at life, against the background of the clicking age clock. I saw the search for an opportunity to start over again. It was clear that these women were groping for something to provide their days with new meaning while giving vent to their intelligence, energy, and creativity. Thus, a coherent and consistent voice was emerging from middle-aged and financially secure women.

Given that I am trained as a social scientist, I began to analyze this voice, and I attempted to put it into the larger context of economic and social conditions of late twentieth-century America. I was fascinated by my accidental findings because they proved erroneous my superficial assumption that advantaged women were complacent and had no inclination to change. In order to understand what seemed illogical to me, I began to read about women. I began to research the literature on middle age, on high-income women, on volunteers, and on full-time homemakers. I tried to learn about women's aspirations, expectations, goals, and dreams. I soon realized that despite the overabundance of literature on women's issues, there was no satisfactory explanation for the behavior I witnessed, and, therefore, no answers to the questions I had.

So I set out to fill the gap. I probed further, conducted a survey, and wrote a book about advantaged middle-aged women. This book, however, is different from others I have written. As a member of the academic world, I have always published solely for academic audiences. Instead, this book is meant to reach beyond the ivory towers of academe. While scholars in economics, sociology, and gender studies will find it of interest, hopefully it will also be useful for the layperson, the person interested in understanding a current phenomenon of importance to women and to our society at large. This book is meant to raise many questions and offer some answers. It is meant to describe. It is meant to elucidate. It is also meant to be practical and useful. With that end in mind, I have purposefully kept the text simple and readable, relegating explanations that may be overly academic to the notes. My preference for a readable style is also reflected in the sources I have used for research: in addition to academic texts, I have relied on the insights of journalists who report from the front lines of social change.

THE LITERATURE ON WOMEN

Perusal of library stacks and bookstore shelves reveals an overabundance of literature on women and women's issues. There is clearly no other subject, with the possible exception of computing, that has undergone such phenomenal growth over the past two decades. However, in the academic literature, the emphasis is certainly neither on middle-aged women nor on advantaged women. Indeed, women's studies have focused on race, disadvantage, poverty, struggle, resistance, empowerment, domination, and exploitation. Alternatively, studies have dealt with the superwoman, the professional career woman, and the traditional mom. The trade publications are a mixed bag, although the emphasis seems to be on career women, educated mothers, the struggle and juggle between work and home, women in the labor force, and women's feelings. Feminist writing has largely ignored the advantaged woman except to disparage her in condescending tone. In turn, criticism of feminist writing has focused on its inability to consider the common and mainstream woman. Thus, both feminist writings and their criticism overlook the aging woman with financial advantages.

An overview of the literature by disciplines also reveals disinterest in middle-aged, advantaged women. Economists have on the whole considered them irrelevant because their contribution to the economy is perceived to be limited to shopping and volunteering (both of which are all too often perceived to be economically insignificant). Sociologists have largely ignored them because they are unrepresentative of the female population at large. Yet, while the advantaged woman is on one fringe of the bell-shaped curve and bag ladies are on the other, the latter have generated more interest in the literature. Gender studies have mostly overlooked advantaged women because they do not have to work, and such privilege has not been rewarded by scholarly attention. Historians tend to focus on important individual women who produced social changes over the past few centuries. Thus, middle-aged women who chose to be out of the labor force held the fascination of no one.

Yet, these women are fascinating. As most people, they want that which they don't have. As most people, they fail to put in perspective what they do have. As most people, they are confused about the unfamiliar. Yet, they are different from other women because they had the capacity to choose to stay out of the labor force. They are also different because in middle age they once again have the capacity to reevaluate past choices, make new ones, and act on them. In exercising that choice in midlife and in responding positively to their inclination to change, they have the potential to benefit themselves, their immediate families, and the economy in general.

They are the women with choices!

ABOUT THIS BOOK

This book strives to explain the curious phenomenon of why many middle-aged women with choices fantasize about joining the labor force (while women who are in it often fantasize about leaving it). It describes the push to change their lives as well as the pull of the labor force; it points out the incentives women feel and the capacities they believe they have. Will their husbands and children understand and support their desire to be employed? What skills do they think they have to offer to the labor market? What kind of work do they hope to do?

These questions and similar others are answered by women during in-depth interviews. In the course of these interviews, women explained why they had originally chosen to be full-time homemakers and why the labor force has subsequently become a magnet that draws them. Despite their often conflicting aspirations, motivations, and goals, these surveyed women provided the insight necessary to identify patterns of choices among middle-aged women.

This book is about more than just numbers from the survey and it contains more than just anecdotes from the interviews. It describes the changes in social perceptions, as well as in labor conditions, that affect women with choices. It explores the possibilities in the labor force for middle-aged women, specifically with respect to the occupations most suited for their particular circumstances. It assesses the skills women have acquired during the years they juggled children, home, and volunteering commitments. Finally, the book offers a new perspective on how middle-aged women with choices contribute to the economy while simultaneously pursuing their personal fulfillment.

The concept of the third career is introduced to describe the unique labor demand and supply characteristics of middle-aged women with choices who are revisiting their home vs. work choices. While women varied in the specific descriptions of their employment aspirations (i.e., opening a flower store, practicing law, or teaching an art class), all envisioned their future work as a hybrid of their previous two careers: in their first, they were unmarried, childless, and employed full time; in their second career, they were full-time homemakers and volunteers, performing their duties with the same skill, dedication, and organization as in their first career. In their third career, women want to be employed, but only on their terms: first, they don't want just any job and second, they don't want a demanding, full-time, and stressful career. Specifically, women want to do something for which they have a passion. They want to do what they love and they want to love what they do. Moreover, while they are willing to work very hard and take on a lot of responsibility, they have also come to value flexibility and free time, and they want their future work to embody it. Thus, the message from these middle-aged women was coherent and clear: they want meaningful work, usually part time and with ample flexibility. Interestingly, these characteristics of work are significantly more important to them than the size of their paychecks. The tradeoffs they are willing to make define the parameters of their particular labor supply. These tradeoffs also affect the employer's demand for their particular labor.

This book is organized as follows. The first part describes the *realities*, consisting of the demographic profile of the women with choices, as well as a description of the expectations that they face from their social environment. The second part describes the *incentives* they have for entering the labor force, incentives that are born from the reinterpretation of their leisure activities and the reevaluation of their volunteer activities. Next follows a study of the labor-market *conditions* in order to understand the nature of the labor market that middle-aged women face. The *capacities* of these women are then assessed. This is done by determining what it is that they really can do and understanding how their skills and abilities might enable them to overcome the obstacles they are likely to face. Finally, the book explores the *benefits* of entering the labor market, including benefits accrued to the individual women as well as to the economy and society as a whole.

Finally, it is noted that this research has implications that are of relevance to more than the small subset of advantaged women it focuses on. This book is about identity, change, expectations, control, and pressures. It is about work and family and the economy. These are issues that all women think about, not just upper-income or professional women. Moreover, to the extent that social change has a source in any group of people, it is those who are the risk takers, who seek change, who take the challenge. This group includes women with choices who are trying to change their lives in middle age. Finally, when husbands of upper-income women see what their wives are trying to do, they will become more accepting and accommodating in their own workplaces and thereby contribute to social and economic change.

Acknowledgments

I am grateful to so many women who have participated, sometimes unknowingly, in all stages of this project. The first group of women whom I want to thank are those who provided the original idea for this book. They are the friends and casual acquaintances who talked to me about their life choices. In our conversations, they revealed their current dilemmas, reviewed their former decisions, and formulated their future aspirations. Over numerous lunches, they bounced off their fears, vented their frustrations, and tested their ideas on me. Thus, many of them unknowingly contributed to this project by providing me with much food for thought. Initial ideas germinated over many more cups of coffee with more women than I can name here. However, two friends stand out for the enormous contribution they made to this project. I want to thank Ann Cortes for her honesty and her insight—first about her own life choices and later about this project. She listened, she contributed, she questioned, and she criticized, for all of which I am very grateful. I also want to thank Bobbi Wald who candidly discussed her life dilemmas as well as those of other women in her age group. Through her exceedingly broad contacts in the Miami area, she gave me an invaluable initial insight into the mind-set of middle-aged women, unemployed women, and women who do not have to work but want to. Both Ann and Bobbi provided the initial stimulus necessary for this research project.

Another group of women helped me locate and organize respondents for the survey. As it was conducted by the snowball method, it was imperative to have at least a dozen potential respondents as a starting point in the hope that they, in turn, would provide leads for others. I would like to thank Pat Cox, Carol Lynn Foster, Elayne Furst, Marisella Lacayo, Any Muench, Melody Roadman, Ellen Steiner, Bobbi Wald, and Carol Walpole, for their assistance in locating respondents who fit the profile I was searching for.

The third group of women consisted of those who agreed to participate in this study and who enthusiastically offered me their hearts and minds. They are the ones who this book is about and the ones without whose participation this book simply would not have been! While I cannot name them in order to protect their privacy, I take this opportunity to thank each and every one of them. These women gave of their time and their energy and thereby added yet one more commitment to their busy lives. I am most grateful for their willingness to talk to a stranger and to reveal sensitive emotions. I thank them for trusting me and for believing in this project. I was thrilled when they said the interview actually helped them clarify their ideas. For all they have given to me, I sincerely hope this book will be helpful to them in formulating strategies for achieving their future goals.

Dori Pappas transcribed the taped interviews just before she was faced with her own home vs. work choice. Nancy Starr, having already made her choice a few years ago, assisted me by completing citations and checking references. Dori and Nancy worked quickly and efficiently, and I am very indebted to them both. Thanks go to Samantha Quan from the Bureau of Labor Statistics for her efficiency and helpfulness in locating obscure data and sources. Elizabetta Linton, my first editor at Praeger, has been a friendly source of guidance through our extensive e-mail correspondence. I am grateful to Suzanne Staszak-Silva and Nancy Hellriegel for their assistance in the publication process. I would also like to acknowledge St. Joseph's University for the allocation of funds that offset the costs of this study.

My daughters Aleksandra and Karla deserve special recognition because they helped keep me focused on what is basic and important by asking elementary questions about the project. Although the issues of middle age addressed in this book are still irrelevant for them, they will all too soon encounter the work vs. home dilemma, and I hope they find this book useful.

Finally, amidst all the women in my acknowledgments there stands one man who has provided the invaluable assistance, support, and love that has enabled me to begin, progress, and complete a project of this magnitude. Without my husband's consistent encouragement, his eagerness to listen to my frustrations, and his willingness to read, comment, and discuss with me, this project would certainly not have been completed as rapidly nor as happily. Thanks, Richard!

Part I

REALITIES

Chapter 1

The Profile of Middle-Aged Women with Choices

Brigitte Kelly, 48 years old, sat comfortably on her plush sofa during our interview. Dressed in an oversized shirt, gym pants, and sneakers, she exuded an air of energy, health, and confidence. While passionately describing her life choices, she pushed her abundant blond hair off her face with a precise gesture of her hand. Throughout the interview, I kept recalling that hand movement. Her personality was so clearly reflected in that gesture: controlled, efficient, unerring. Her life choices were also embodied in that gesture. Everything she had done was clear, logical, and carefully premeditated. She reviewed choices, she made decisions, and if she needed to reevaluate and reorient, she did so swiftly, efficiently, and without looking back. No, Brigitte did not cry over spilt milk. Her most important life choices were made with clarity and determination. Didn't she ever waver, I wondered. Apparently only once, when she made a home vs. work choice.

Brigitte grew up in the Northeast. Early on, she developed an interest in business and fashion. She studied retailing at a major university and upon graduation moved to New York to search for work. Due to a combination of factors (not in the least of which was her drive and enthusiasm), she landed a wonderful job as a buyer for a major department store. There she worked for some ten years, successfully building a major department and overseeing numerous workers. Her job entailed a lot of travel: as a buyer, she had to spend time in Hong Kong, China, and other Asian centers of retail. As an employee in the fashion industry, she had to attend shows in Milan and Paris. Exciting, yes, but also exhausting! Then she fell in love. She married after a short courtship and came to believe she had an ideal life. Her husband was already a successful businessman and together their incomes were sufficient to sustain a lifestyle they both enjoyed. Brigitte wanted to have children right away, never doubting that she could manage career and family. She had the right conditions to do it all, to be a modern superwoman: she had a great career, a supportive husband, a reliable housekeeper, and she would have a loving nanny. So naturally she worked during her first pregnancy. An unexpected miscarriage burst her bubble and forced her to reevaluate her choices. She wanted to ensure that when she conceived again, she wouldn't have to travel as much, nor work as many hours, nor bear as much responsibility. When she expressed her thoughts to her employer, his response couldn't have been clearer. There were no appropriate sounds of compassion, no words reflecting sensitivity, and no understanding gestures. He was unmoved when he explained her limited options: continue working at the same job (with the same amount of traveling) or take a significant backstep (with no travel and less responsibility). Brigitte agonized over her choices. She had invested so many years in her job, she had trained to become exactly what she was and now she was supposed to give it all up. How could she? On the other hand, she wanted a baby desperately. She wanted several, in fact, and she wanted to be there for them: for their soccer games, for their ballet lessons. She wanted to be a room-mother for their classrooms and to drive carpools in a van packed with kids. She wanted a home in the suburbs with a swing set in the backyard. Brigitte's agonizing came to an abrupt end when she conceived again. That was it! She immediately resigned from her job! She gave up stimulating conversations with colleagues, she gave up trips to exotic lands, she gave up the hefty paycheck. She became a stay-at-home mom, out of choice. While it was a hard decision, it was one she never regretted. However, it is a decision she is reevaluating some 20 years later.

Brigitte is now bracing herself to choose again, to once again change her life in a fundamental way. The background for her choice is similar to what it is for hundreds of thousands of women in her age group. Her children are in high school, one is about to go to college. Her husband is urging her to do something, something that she enjoys, something for herself. Many of her friends have gone back to school or have joined the labor force—they are no longer available for the lunches they used to enjoy and the children's activities they used to share. Her world is changing and her needs are responding to those changes. It's time to choose again. But choose what? Go back to school? Go back to retailing? Do something completely new? The options seem vast, the choices virtually endless. Over time those choices narrowed and her ideas crystallized—yes, she will now do what she loves, she will work with flowers. She will use her past skills: business and retail. She will retrain and learn new skills: take a course in floral design. She is creative, energetic, and bright, why not go for it? Brigitte made her choice: she will open a flower shop!

CHOICES

From the moment people wake up in the morning, they make choices. Explicitly or implicitly, they ask themselves, Shall I sleep a few more minutes or shall I jump right out of bed? They continue to make choices throughout the day; choices pertaining to their work, their children, their social lives, their homes, their exercise, their entertainment. At the end of the day, they choose when to collapse into bed at night, and whether to read, watch TV, or simply turn off the light. And so day in and day out.

All people, men and women alike, make choices throughout their lives. They must make choices because there are always more options than means to pursue those options ("Do I watch channel 2, 10, or 34 on TV?"). The resources at their disposal are always too scarce relative to the competing ways to spend them ("I can only watch one channel at a time!"). Indeed, it seems there is never enough time, money, or energy, yet there are always so many ways to spend that time, money, and energy ("I can only afford to buy one dress, yet I want four!"). This imbalance between human wants and the capacity to satisfy those wants forces all individuals to make choices: big choices, small choices, choices all the time. It's the same kind of imbalance that is faced by businesses, planners, and policymakers on a daily basis. Indeed, it is the imbalance that mainstream economists consider the backbone of neoclassical economic analysis.

Just as all people are not created equal, so too there is no equality in the nature and the number of choices people have.[1] Life circumstances limit people's range of options; life conditions act as constraints on their behavior. Inequality in choice permeates social cleavages such as class, race, income, gender, and age. The factors that increase the options and choices of individuals include physical attributes, intellectual capacity, wealth and education, among others. Over time, economic progress and development have greatly increased the choices that all people have, although they have not increased them equally. With respect to women, there is no doubt that choices available to them have increased in the twentieth century. Today, women face more open doors and are protected in more fundamental ways than they ever were before. The feminist movement has undoubtedly contributed to enlarging the options for Western women in numerous ways (especially by granting them legal rights, reproductive rights, and opportunities in jobs and politics). Today women can vote, own property, get an education, and control their fertility. They can make a wide array of choices in each of those areas.

Indeed, the lives of all women are replete with choices. The daily, trivial choices include what to eat for breakfast, what to wear, which road to drive on, and which television show to watch. The life-determining choices pertain to marriage (if, when, and whom to marry), children (if, when, and how many children to bear), education (if, when, and what to study), and employment (if to work and what kind of work to perform). All these choices are interrelated. A choice in one area predisposes a woman to particular choices in another. For example, women who choose to pursue higher education tend to choose to marry later in life and to have children later than women who do not study. Moreover, their choices in education and spouse will often determine their choice of lifestyle and, therefore, also the outcome of some daily choices such as which road to drive on and where to shop.

While all women have choices in all spheres of life and while the range of those choices has increased over time, not all women believe they have the luxury to choose whether (and when) to enter or leave the labor market. They are bound by a variety of constraints. Indeed, their home vs. work choice takes into account psychological factors such as personality and emotional makeup as well as family experiences and history, cultural factors that determine and dictate social norms, and economic factors that determine their reality with respect to life standards.[2] As a result, their home vs. work choice is rarely made easily or quickly. Rather, it usually entails a gradual process during which conflicting issues and emotions percolate over time until either they mature into a conscious decision or life circumstances force a decision.

Women's employment choices are rarely permanent for the duration of their life span. As life conditions are often dynamic, so too are women's perceptions of those conditions. As a result, women flow between jobs. They also flow in and out of the labor force. Some women make the choice to remain out of the labor force at one point in their lives only to reconsider the choice and enter the labor market at a later date. These women are the focus of this book.

WHO ARE WOMEN WITH CHOICES?

Women of varying ages, socioeconomic backgrounds, and religious orientations ponder, evaluate, and worry about their work choices. Irrespective of their marital status, the age of their children, and the amount of money they have, women everywhere question their existing work choices, wonder about other people's work realities, and fantasize about alternative employment options. Only one subset of the general female population believes that it really has the choice not to work for pay. This subset doesn't only consist of wealthy women or only of married women who have a spouse to support them. While it is likely that women with the home vs. work choice have above-average wealth as well as working spouses, there are in fact women from a variety of socioeconomic backgrounds, with and without husbands, who have made the choice to stay home. How is that possible? How can they survive if they don't earn? Don't all households need more than one income in order to sustain a decent standard of living? These questions obscure the fact that survival, decent standards of living and sufficient income are all subjective concepts. Since the nature of the home vs. work choice is subjective as well as objective, it is possible for a broad range of women to stay at home. An objective assessment of the number and the range of choices women have is very difficult in all cases except those at either end of the advantage spectrum: at one end of the spectrum are the wealthy or highly skilled and highly educated women, usually married to employed and successful (read: earning a "good" salary) husbands, living in urban Western societies. These women have more options in general and more choices pertaining to employment than most people. At the other end of the spectrum are the low-income, unskilled, single mothers whose circumstances limit the outcomes of their home vs. work dilemma.[3] Indeed, the vicious cycle of poverty and the concomitant daily focus on satisfying their basic needs tends to obliterate numerous possibilities for choosing fundamental life changes.

Between those two extremes lies the vast majority of the population. That population falls within a wide band whose borders are not clearly demarcated.

Within that band, only the subjective perception of the employment choice is relevant. How a woman perceives her financial reality and her social constraints will affect not only what choices she may make but also whether she even attempts to realize her employment preferences. Because of subjective perceptions, two women under similar conditions may perceive their choices to be entirely different. They may feel differently about those choices. For example, a woman with a total household income of $66,000 (double the national average) may feel that she simply cannot afford to leave her job (in which she earns $25,000) in order to be a full-time homemaker, while another, with identical household and personal income, may view it as a viable option. Thus, while the cultural norms facing both may be the same and their financial realities may be identical, their subjective view of their overall financial conditions may predispose them toward different home vs. work choices. In other words, their subjective views of what constitutes a decent standard of living and adequate survival may vary.

So women of different socioeconomic backgrounds have different perceptions of their necessity and may subjectively perceive themselves to have a choice about employment. In reality, just how much wealth or income must a family have in order to afford the luxury of an adult whose contribution to the household is nonpecuniary? A recent article in the *New York Times* estimated that it was necessary to earn well over half a million dollars per year in New York City in order to feel financially secure and by implication to release the wife from the labor force![4] Yet, a study of millionaires by Thomas Stanley and William Danko states that roughly one-half of wives in millionaire households (namely, those with a net worth of one million dollars or more) are employed.[5] What about the less wealthy population? In her book about middle-aged women across the socioeconomic spectrum, Gail Sheehy identified $30,000 as the family income below which women won't take risks, make major life changes, and otherwise escape from the restrictions of their traditional roles and attitudes.[6] While Sheehy's results indicate a relationship between income and changing one's life circumstances, they do not pertain specifically to entering the labor force. When women make their home vs. work choice, it is in fact very difficult to identify a single universal cutoff income level applicable to all households. The household wealth necessary to release the woman from the workforce depends on a variety of factors, including her expected standard of living.[7] As mentioned above, households vary in their perception of the minimum threshold of living standards that they are willing to tolerate; they vary in what they are willing to give up and they vary in what they will trade off in order to ensure that one of the two adults in the family can remain outside the labor force. Moreover, as Elizabeth Perle McKenna said in her book on work, it is all a question of how we define necessity. Most of us, she says, work not to support our basic survival needs but rather our lifestyle choices.[8] While there is evidence that families have been defining "economic necessity" upward, the variation across income groups has largely remained unchanged.[9]

Fran Leibowitz, an anthropologist who studies the wealthy, writes about people who have money and how they are different from those who do not. She says "rich people can have what they want, whereas [others] usually can't." Also, "being rich is like being an adult: you get to do whatever you want."[10] By implication, being rich means having more choices and that includes choosing whether to work. While many middle-aged homemakers with choices are upper-income, they are not necessarily of the upper class. Class status is described by more than money. It is described by occupation (the nature of the work that the woman or her spouse performs) and education (the nature of the degree obtained and the university that granted it). Those characteristics are embodied in the concepts of exclusivity and power. Susan Ostander described the upper classes by stating that: "the most important factors are the ownership of wealth, the exercise of power, and membership in an exclusive social network."[11] In her research, she has also found the importance of birthright in defining class, as well as cohesiveness in personal relationships and shared outlook.[12]

Other scholars have focused on other definitions. Digby Baltzell has argued that the foremost characteristic of the upper class is that they exert power within society,[13] while William Dornhoff focused on the political dimension of their power in society.[14] All this is to say that the definitions of class are unclear, and the borders that delineate the ranks of the upper class are fuzzy at best. For women with choices, the relevancy of the distinction between upper class and upper income lies in the existence of social pressure not to work. To the extent that they feel strong bonds to the upper class and to the extent that they partake fully in the class "shared outlook," they will have more difficulty breaking out of the confines of acceptable behavior than women who are just plain rich.

WHO ARE MIDDLE-AGED HOMEMAKERS WITH CHOICES?

Women with choices then are those who believe they have real options in the home vs. work dilemma and who act upon those options. However, this subjective definition of the parameters of the cohort yields a very broad and varied group of women. Indeed, women with choices may be young or old, rich or poor, skilled or unskilled, with or without children, married or single. It seems that any female can be a woman with choices if she has the appropriate expectations to suit her financial, cultural, and family circumstances. Studying all these women is simply too ambitious an endeavor. Therefore, in order to limit the breadth of the cohort under study, one particular subset of women with choices has been selected for observation. This cohort is described by the example below:

Denise Bentley is 49 years old. She has spent most of her adult life tending to her home, raising her children, and volunteering in the community. She made a decision some 18 years ago to leave her career as an attorney to become a full-time homemaker. Recently, her youngest son went off to college and now Denise doesn't know what to do with herself; she is confused and disoriented. Her life rolls on without meaning, and she is desperate to find a new focus. In her search for something interesting to fill her days, she is consistently drawn to the idea of returning to work.

There are millions of women like Denise across America. They are between 40 and 60 years of age, college educated, and married with children well beyond infancy (they are at the tail end of their "second careers," which consisted of homemaking and childcare). Some had professional careers before they became homemakers, others flowed between jobs (this was their "first career," in which they were working women). Most have sufficient household wealth to enable them not to work. As young adults, they were able to make the choice to stay home; in their forties and fifties, they have outgrown their roles as homemakers and are revisiting their employment choices. As such they are part of a very small group of women, a minority both from a historical perspective as well as across cultures. The characteristics of middle-aged homemakers with choices are described in detail below.

Age

Middle age is defined roughly as the period between 40 and 60 years. It is a time when women are neither old nor young. In this age group, women are in the third phase of their lives: they have more or less completed the goals and activities that sustained them during their second quintile of life (including bearing and raising children, pursuing higher education, working in the labor force, or any combination thereof).

The years of middle age have been described as the "second maturity" by Maryvonne Gognalons-Nicolet in her study of menopause.[15] Kathleen Rowntree wrote about this period as the time when women "come into their fullness."[16] This concept of coming into their fullness may be extended into a positive feeling about oneself. Indeed, a survey conducted by *Family Circle* shows that more than half of women over 50 are delighted with their lives in middle age.[17] Another survey by *Good Housekeeping* and Clinique found that women said they enjoyed greater confidence as they aged and only one in six associated beauty with youth.[18] Such a celebration of middle age and its concomitant maturity is rooted in changes that women undergo after age 40. In addition to physical attributes, women's emotional, intellectual, and social characteristics undergo transformation. For example, age often provides women with a self-confidence and social ease that they heretofore lacked. By their midforties, they have become less concerned with pleasing others; they have a stronger sense of who they are and what they want.[19] While this portrayal of middle age obviously doesn't apply to all women, those who have felt good about how they spent their past two decades and those whose long-term future outlook is not dismal tend to feel good about their middle years also.

Irrespective of their subjective feelings about age, the objective profile of middle-aged women today is different from what it was even half a century ago. A 50-year-old woman in the 1990s is healthier and has a longer life expectancy than before. That fact alone means that middle-aged women today can look forward to more years of physical and intellectual activity than their mothers and grandmothers could.

Marital Status

Most women with choices are married while a smaller number are divorced, widowed, or never married. Marriage is an integral part of women's employment choices because it represents the principal form of financial security that enables women not to participate in the labor force. All too often, full-time homemakers who become divorced or widowed lose the choice of not working and are driven into the labor force out of financial necessity. Alternatively, women may be independently wealthy and thus do not depend on a spouse or ex-spouse to sustain their lack of employment.

Children

Most women who have chosen to stay out of the labor force have done so in order to raise their children. It is the desire to nurture, guide, and provide love and support that has motivated women to become full-time mothers. Professional women who chose to stay home in order to raise superbabies were concerned with the quality of the education and the values they were transmitting to their offspring. Women who were traditionalists and chose to stay home with their children were equally concerned with the environment they were providing for their little ones. Women who were of the upper classes were motivated to gear their children for participation in their class culture by ensuring that their children went to the "correct" schools and participated in the "correct social activities."[20] Whatever the particular background they brought to bear on childrearing, stay-at-home moms felt that the task of raising their children was too important to be left entirely in the hands of hired help. Therefore, while child-related assistance was employed, it seemed to be a minor supplement to the care provided by mothers.

However, not all homemakers with choices are mothers: some have chosen not to be mothers while others have been unable to become mothers.[21] In the absence of children, full-time homemakers have chosen not to be employed because they wanted to care for their husbands, to engage in volunteer activities, to pursue hobbies, or to take care of their homes.

Employment

A common denominator shared by middle-aged homemakers is their hiatus from the workforce for a significant portion of their adult lives. Some of them may have worked before marriage or before having children and then dropped out of the labor force; others may have never been in paid employment. Some worked only full time, others worked part-time, some experienced both kinds of work. Some had successful careers in which they attained recognition and earned a high income; others flowed between jobs that provided little pay and even less satisfaction.

Wealth and Income

Women who don't work are the ones who can afford not to work. That does not mean that all women who can afford not to work don't work. On the whole, women who have chosen not to be employed and have exercised that choice for a sustained period of time have tended to belong to middle- or upper-income households. It is the financial security derived from household income or wealth that provides them with the opportunity to exercise their choice not to work for pay. In other words, either income or wealth or both plays a role in the employment decision.

PROGRESSIVE AND TRADITIONAL HOMEMAKERS

Combining all the above characteristics of homemakers with choices fails to produce a single, homogeneous group of women. There are simply too many diverse women who fit the description of unemployed, middle-aged, upper-income, married mothers with choices. The size of such a category is too large to encompass a single set of views, aspirations, employment goals, and expectations about achieving those goals. The category of women with choices thus warrants a further subdivision.

Middle-aged full-time homemakers who chose not to work for pay during their adult lives fall into one of the following two categories. One is the progressive avant garde, consisting of women on the cutting edge of social change. In their youth, these women were highly educated, professionally trained, and worked in their professions until they had children. They were usually married to equally highly trained professional men whose incomes were relatively high. They left the labor force in order to raise children.[22] Some thought they might go back, others weren't so sure. Their motherly duties were approached in the same organized and efficient fashion as their careers were in the past. These mothers perceived their current job to be the raising of their children and transforming them into high achievers. They micromanaged the lives of their children and expected perfection in return. They also expected perfection of themselves in their mothering roles. These women were very courageous; they broke ranks with their peers and they embarked upon something different from what they were trained to do and what society expected them to do. They stayed at home! Ironically, society has made a full turn where they are concerned. Relative to their educated cohort, they are the ones who took what Robert Frost characterized as "the road less traveled."[23]

The second group of women who exercised their choice to stay out of the labor force includes the traditionalists. These women chose to be at home with their children or to be available full time to their husbands. Within this group, the quantity and quality of education varied, although generally it tended to be lower than among the professional women described above. Most worked at least for some time, although they tended to flow in and out of jobs without serious commitment to a career. Many worked only part time. Those who were wealthy, whether independently or through marriage, lived in a subculture in which female employment was considered less acceptable than it was for the population at large.

Women with choices who became homemakers thus represent a very complicated cohort insofar as their motivations are not uniform, their backgrounds are not simplistically singular, and their perceptions of their role in family and society are diverse. They are at once a very heterogeneous and homogeneous group of individuals. They are at the forefront of their peers and simultaneously represent the traditionalists. When compared to the general female population, some are innovators because they stayed home while others are traditionalists also because they stayed home. Some women deviate from acceptable behavior within their social circles, although the definition of acceptable female behavior varies from circle to circle. Whatever their particular circumstances, they have shared the luxury of choice with respect to the home vs. work dilemma, as staying home is indeed a luxury.

Whether they are progressive or traditional, women with choices have difficulty fitting into predefined social categories. This is very clear, for example, with respect to class. Indeed, the cleavages between the sexes and the classes tend to converge and overlap in women with choices in ways that they don't in women of other social classes, because women with choices are often defined by class as much as by gender. By virtue of the fact that they often have household help that relieves them of the mundane and boring chores in the house, their identification with their class overshadows their sense of female solidarity. By virtue of the fact that they do not have to work for a living, they again identify with class rather than the general pool of women. Finally, by virtue of the fact that they tend to be more educated than average, they identify with professional women (a classification that also tends to overlap with class).

NEW ASPIRATIONS IN LIGHT OF PAST CHOICES

Women with choices made their original home vs. work decision on the basis of a rational cost-benefit analysis.[24] Such an analysis entailed the (explicit or implicit) weighing of homemaking benefits against the costs of staying home. The benefits of staying at home are psychic (watching ones children grow and transforming one's house into a home) as well as economic (saving on daycare and housecare costs). Costs are measured with the same criteria: psychic costs refer to, for example, the pain of separation from children and the boredom of solitary homemaking. Economic costs refer to the income forgone by not working for pay, in other words, the opportunity cost of their time.[25] Since all rational individuals attempt to maximize the satisfaction (or utility, as economists prefer to call it) that they derive from any course of action, it can be inferred that by becoming homemakers, women derived benefits in excess of the costs they incurred. Some two decades later, middle-aged women are repeating the cost-benefit analysis they performed in the past. The criteria they use to measure costs and benefits have changed over time. Women are vigorously assessing where they are, where they have been, and where they want to go in the upcoming phase of their lives. Middle age offers them a myriad of new possibilities. Some are searching for a new purpose, for a new compass, and for a new direction. They are changing, their points of reference are changing, the society in which they make their choices is changing. These women are reevaluating their decisions because they are dynamic and respond to changes in their lives. They change as their life circumstances change. Conditions change and events occur that make them change their minds. They respond to foreseen and unforeseen developments by assessing their alternatives. They review actions that will lead to other actions and choices that will lead to other choices.[26] The choices they make in middle age with respect to home vs. work will entail different challenges, different struggles, and ultimately yield different gratifications from those they had in the past.

The direction of change for middle-aged women with choices seems to be along one of two paths. Some decide to "do something new with their lives," which may simply entail developing a hobby or embarking upon a course of study. It does not necessarily involve working for a paycheck, not even as a long-term goal. Others are quite specific about joining the labor force. They are drawn to paid employment for many reasons, including the desire to explore new worlds, to gain independence, to earn money, and to acquire status and respect. Whether they are returning workers or first-time entrants, many middle-aged women with choices are turning to the workforce to fulfill their needs. They are thus revisiting their previous employment choices and reconsidering their employment options. Middle-aged women look forward to the next two decades in which to pursue their interests in the working world before they embark upon the golden years of retirement. For these women, there is roughly a 20-year span that needs to be filled. Many believe that the right job can fill it.

By aspiring to enter the labor force, these women are not negating the value or importance of their homemaking activities over the past decade or two. Their families still hold their primary interest and provide them with their primary focus. However, the role they had during their twenties and thirties has expired, and they can move on and feel good about the phase they passed as well as the phase they will enter.

CAPACITY AND INCENTIVE

Middle-aged women with choices have both the capacity and the incentive to realize their new goals. The components of their capacities and incentives are described by the participants in this study and presented in their own words throughout the following chapters. They are merely summarized here.

Women's capacity stems from various sources. First, women in their forties and fifties have greater overall self-awareness (compared to what they had in their early twenties), and specifically, they tend to be more cognizant of their potential, as well as their limitations, than they were at a younger age. Second, they have the capacity because they have been freed from pressing responsibilities. Their children are older and therefore no longer acutely dependent. Their time and energy is no longer needed in the same comprehensive way as when their children were young. Thus, the role of mother has been transformed, and their daily mothering duties have been altered. Third, they have the capacity to enter the labor force because they have the financial means to ease the entry. In other words, they can afford to repackage themselves to become old wine in new bottles, or to retool and reeducate. They have the financial capacity to engage in experimental jobs and businesses that are high risk or that may entail a long payback period. They also do not have to take the first job that comes along. Moreover, their wealth enables their absence from the home since their family can be under the daily care of paid household help. In other words, women with choices can, as can professional women working full time, afford to engage in "domestic outsourcing" for a large variety of daily chores. Fourth, middle-aged women with choices usually have the intellectual and emotional capacity to enter the labor market. This capacity is reflected in their prior education and work experience coupled with the maturity and experience they have attained during the years of mothering, running a household, and volunteering. Fifth, middle-aged women have the capacity to enter the labor force because the social environment is increasingly supportive of women who are productive outside of their homes. This support emanates not only from their spouses, who are increasingly positively inclined to having an employed wife, but also from society in general.[27]

Women with choices also have the incentive to enter the labor force. Such incentives come from the rational assessment of options in middle age. Women have reevaluated their roles and their lives. They have thought long and hard about the satisfaction they derive from their families, as well as from the leisure, housework, and volunteering activities that filled their days during their second life phase, and they are inclined to try yet something else. They have a strong incentive to try to work for pay.

As a result of their capacities and incentives, middle-aged women with choices are free and able and inclined to start working. However, while most women with choices have such capacities and incentives, clearly not all of them choose to reconsider their options nor to alter their lives in middle age. Moreover, among those who do, there is variation with respect to timing. Therefore, two crucial questions in the discussion of the revisited employment choice are who and when?

Who are the women that, in middle age, want to pursue something new? They aren't merely the ones with the greatest financial capacity, since there are plenty of wealthy women who remain unmotivated to work throughout their lives. Nor are they the most capable ones, since there are plenty of women who are capable but opt to focus their capacities on activities such as hobbies and volunteering. Instead, the women who do choose to revisit their employment choice tend to possess a personality that drives them to change. Their psychological makeup predisposes them to take risks, to welcome novelty, to tolerate temporary insecurity, and to accept some unknown degree of turbulence in their lives. They have the creativity to allow their imagination to soar, the drive to pursue their goals, and the courage to invite change.

CHANGING SOCIAL CONDITION

The transformation of individual women is embedded in the social change that surrounds them. One could not occur without the other, and the other enables and reinforces the first. Indeed, social change promotes individual change, while individual change requires social change and in turn promotes further social change.

Several fundamental changes in social conditions and norms, discussed in detail throughout this book, have made women's entry into the labor force more acceptable in the 1990s irrespective of class background. First, two incomes are now necessary to achieve the standard of living that was achieved with one income in the 1960s. Women with choices whose wealth is borderline (or whose future wealth is questionable) may find this consideration relevant. Second, there is evidence that working mothers do not produce maladjusted children; indeed, it has been demonstrated that children of employed women are not at a disadvantage and some studies even show them to be at an advantage.[28] Third, it has become socially acceptable for middle- and upper-class women to work outside the home and earn money, contrary to the norm before the 1970s. Today even wealthy men feel compelled to create and make money, rather than merely spend it as former generations of the wealthy did.[29] Fourth, there is a consensus that women tend to feel good about themselves when they are employed in work of their choice. Women who like their work tend to be more fulfilled and content than those who do not. Finally, the nature of work and the workplace has changed so much that it can accommodate women of all dispositions: those who prefer to work at home as well as those who require flexibility in schedule and location.

All these social changes increase the choices and possibilities for middle-aged women. This breadth of options in midlife runs counter to the traditional view permeating the Judeo-Christian tradition according to which a woman's worth depended on her fecundity. Under that worldview, value is attached to motherhood and fertility so that once a woman becomes menopausal, she becomes obsolete. As a result, when women reached middle age, they were socially shunned and their choices became drastically limited. By the 1990s, the women's movement has contributed to giving women increased choices and the freedom to act in a wider variety of ways than they could a few decades ago. To the extent that middle-aged women are exercising their choices, pursuing their self-interest, and maximizing their utility, modern Western society seems to have cushioned personal gratification in acceptable terms.

Notes

1. In all hierarchical societies, people at birth do not all have the same opportunities. Louis Dumont, in his book on social organizations, *Homo Hierarchicus*, described this difference in choices and opportunities at birth (Louis Dumont, *Homo Heirarchicus*, London: Paladin, 1972). Clearly, a poor black baby in Chicago's ghetto or an Untouchable baby in an Indian village is not born with the same opportunities as newborns in a white professional family or an upper-caste Indian family. Relative parental advantage distinguishes babies at birth and thus predetermines numerous

characteristics of their lives, including the quantity of choices with which they embark on life.

2. Gerson describes choices taken by women: "neither chance, circumstances, nor individual personalities determined the paths these women took as they made decisions that shaped the direction of their lives. Their choices reflected instead an interaction between socially structured opportunities and constraints and active attempts to make sense of and respond to these structures." Kathleen Gerson, *Hard Choices, How Women Decide about Work, Career, and Motherhood*, Berkeley: University of California Press, 1985, pp. 192–193.

3. Not considering, for the moment, women who are receiving welfare payments and might be unmotivated to enter the labor force.

4. The *New York Times Magazine*, November 19, 1995.

5. Thomas J. Stanley and William D. Danko, *The Millionaire Next Door: The Surprising Secrets of America's Wealthy*, Atlanta: Longstreet Press, 1997, p. 9.

6. Gail Sheehy, *New Passages*, New York: Ballantine Books, 1995, p. 188.

7. The realistic cost of sustaining that expected standard of living is also relevant. This cost of living varies across the country—it is lower in the Southwest than in the Northeast, lower in rural areas than in urban centers.

8. Elizabeth Perle McKenna, *When Work Doesn't Work Anymore*, New York: Delacorte Press, 1997, pp. 140–141.

9. See study cited in the *Philadelphia Inquirer*, November 5, 1997.

10. The *New York Times Magazine*, November 19, 1995.

11. Susan A. Ostander, *Women of the Upper Class*, Philadelphia: Temple University Press, 1984, pp. 4–5.

12. Ostander, pp. 22–23.

13. For example, the upper class comprises 1% of the U.S. population but owns one-half of all corporate stock and one-fifth of the national wealth. E. Digby Baltzell, *Philadelphia Gentlemen: The Making of National Upper Class*, Glencoe, Ill.: Free Press, 1958, cited in Ostander, op. cit., p. 5.

14. G. William Dornhoff, *The Higher Circles*, New York: Random House, 1970.

15. Maryvonne Gognalons-Nicolet, "The Crossroads of Menopause: A Chance and a Risk for the Aging Process of Women," in Elizabeth Markson, ed., *Older Women*, Lexington, Mass.: Lexington Books, 1983, p. 40.

16. Kathleen Rowntree, *Coming Into Our Fullness*, Freedom, Calif.: Crossing Press, 1991.

17. Sheehy, p. 191.

18. Cited in Natasha Walters, *The New Feminism*, London: Little Brown, 1998, p. 101.

19. This was found in a study of women about themselves by Cleo Berkun, "Changing Appearance for Women in the Middle Years of Life: Trauma?' in Markson, op. cit.

20. See Ostander on upper-class women's views of their role pertaining to childrearing.

21. Fifteen percent of the 38 million baby-boomer women made the decision not to have children. They did so voluntarily, not because of infertility or because they did not have a spouse. They made the choice. See Jeanne Safer, *Beyond Motherhood: Choosing a Life Without Children*, New York: Pocket Books, 1996.

22. We also see a trend of women under 25 who are entering the labor force less rapidly than they did previously. This is not due to choice of domesticity, however, but rather to choice of longer education. See Bureau of Labor Statistics Report cited in *USA Today*, August 12, 1994.

23.   Robert Frost, "The Road Not Taken", Alexander W. Allison et al. eds., *The Norton Anthology of Poetry*, 3rd Ed., New York: W. W. Norton, 1983, p. 540.

24. Mainstream economists in the neoclassical tradition have viewed economic life as the result of rational choice made by free individuals who have pursued their own best self-interest. It follows then that the work vs. home decision is a rational choice on the part of informed women. (Radical political economists would put emphasis instead on the economic institutions and practices that affect women's decisions.)

25.   Opportunity cost can be quite high. A stay-at-home mom that gave up her partnership-track law practice that might have yielded a $750,000 annual salary is incurring an annual cost of that amount every year that she is staying at home and being "just a mom."

26.   Kathleen Gerson, in her book *Hard Choices*, a study of choices women make between staying home with their children and entering the labor force, offers an excellent overview of theories as to why women do what they do. She discusses the two general models that prevail. The structural coercion approach (associated with Hartmann and Rubin and Zaretsky) stresses the way in which male-controlled social institutions control women's options and thus coerce women's behavior (p. 25). The second approach, associated with Talcott Parsons, is the voluntarist approach, which focuses on socialization theories that explain how female personalities are created and how women, when they were children, internalized the motivations and the capacities that are considered appropriate for their gender role (pp. 29–37). Gerson added to these and said that there must be a theory that looks at people as they develop over time. What goals, motives, and circumstances shape them as they move through the various life stages, and how do the choices that they have made have an effect on what they do in the future. In other words, how do past choices affect future choices.

27.   This social acceptance of middle-aged women venturing outside the home has also been extended to even older women, namely, those 60-plus. Indeed, there is an abundance of writings that extoll the later years of life as challenging and exciting, including Betty Friedan's popular book, *The Fountain of Age*, New York: Simon and Schuster, 1993.

28. See the discussion in chapter 8.

29. The *New York Times Magazine*, November 19, 1995.

Chapter 2

Evolving Expectations of Women with Choices

Francesca Layten was out of breath when she arrived for the interview. She apologized profusely and explained that just as she was leaving home, the phone began to ring. Since she was in a hurry, she considered not picking it up. However, since she always has a gnawing worry about her children, she was drawn to respond. After some moments of ambivalence and indecision, she opted to indulge her fears. As she expected, it was her daughter calling from school. She had forgotten her physics term-paper at home and she begged her mother to bring it to school so that her senior grade wouldn't be affected. Of course, Francesca drove to school to deliver the paper. Of course, Francesca helped out her daughter. "It's the story of my life," she sighed. And so it was, as I learned by the end of the interview. Francesca had dedicated her life to her children. She was the epitome of a good mother: she spent time with her daughters, she loved, she listened, she taught, she guided. She was always available for them. She was able to be so available because, some 20 years ago, she had chosen to become a full-time mother. Now, 45 years old, Francesca recalls this decision with some regret and bitterness. She explained to me how, after graduating from college, she had worked for several years as an economist in a large corporation while simultaneously pursuing an MBA degree. Smart and energetic, she had lofty aspirations for a successful and satisfying career. She was a few credits away from completing her degree when she gave it all up in order to nurture a pregnancy that had become problematic. For almost two decades, she remained focused on nurturing and satisfying the needs of her family.

Using the physics term-paper as an example, Francesca describes the expectations that her family has of her. Her husband, traditional in his thinking about wife and home, had always been in favor of a stay-at-home mom who would raise children and provide a comfortable home life for them all. That was to be her job, while he would focus on supporting them. Francesca was expected to have the meals ready, the refrigerator stocked, the clothes laundered, the guests entertained, the furniture polished (whether she did this herself or hired someone else was never a concern of his). Moreover, she was expected to look nice, to lend him a supporting shoulder, and to travel with him. He wasn't pushy about those expectations, as long as she fulfilled them, of course!

The children, in Francesca's words, expect everything of her. She is to be there for them when they want her and to disappear when they don't want her. They expect her physical and emotional contribution at all times, ranging from clean school uniforms to advice about their dates. Francesca wonders whether her consistent availability has made them so expectant. She also wonders if other children are like them. "It's not that they don't appreciate me and what I do for them—they do . . . most of the time. They're usually really nice to me, they're loving and they recognize that if I were working, they wouldn't have what they have." But still, sometimes she wonders if it could all be a little different . . .

And different it became, but not as she expected. A few years ago, Francesca began noticing a change in what her husband, her children, and her friends expected her to be doing. Her husband started dropping hints like doesn't she ever want to do something else? Isn't she tempted to start working? Doesn't she miss the outside world? It was becoming clear—he wouldn't object if she became employed. What wasn't clear was why—was his law practice running into problems that he wanted to offset with Francesca's income? Despite his protests, she wasn't sure. At about the same time, her teenaged daughters started coming home with uncomfortable comments such as, "so-and-so's mother has a successful business!" (and by implication, you don't!). Also, "Judy's mother, the attorney, just tried that important case everyone is talking about" (in other words, what of importance have you done recently?). Her children began comparing her to mothers of classmates and in the comparison Francesca was losing out. It was no longer important to them that she be the chaperone on the class trip or the class mother because they no longer had chaperoned class trips or class mothers. Instead, other, new yardsticks for evaluating mothers began cropping up.

Francesca's girlfriends also seemed to be expecting her to broaden her range of daily activities. Numerous women who had volunteered with her over the years in civic, cultural, and educational associations were slipping away—they had started working or had gone back to school and were now starting to pressure Francesca into joining them in their new endeavors.

Francesca's family and friends had expectations of her that were changing and she wasn't sure how to react.

The Hindu god Shiva is often portrayed as having eight arms.[1] According to myth, he needs so many arms in order to accomplish his numerous duties and responsibilities. Alas, women in America have no such anatomical aid to assist them in satisfying the enormous demands on their time and energy. If they did, each one of those arms would perform one of the functions that fills the days of women. One arm might deal with childcare, the second with employment, the third with shopping, the fourth with cooking, the fifth with social engagements, the sixth with housecleaning, the seventh with laundry, and the eighth would pay bills. Moreover, some of those arms would have double duties in order to perform occasional tasks such as doctor's visits, auto servicing, children's extracurricular activities, carpools, and so forth. The number of duties requiring the attention of the average American woman often exceeds her capacity to fulfill them. In other words, the arms are too few for the expectations that women (as well as their family, friends, and society at large) have of themselves.

The overburdening of women has been true through history and is true across cultures. It is especially evident when an intergender comparison is made. For example, Rosalind Miles found that in prehistoric times, "women would be found doing five things where men did one." In modern tribal societies, she continues, males perform "one fifth of the work necessary for the group to survive, while the other four fifths is carried out entirely by women."[2] Not much has changed if we look at worldwide trends in the present era: a United Nations study recently found that when housework is accounted for, women across the world work twice as many hours as men.[3]

Are American women with choices less burdened in their daily responsibilities than American women in general? Two factors would seem to indicate that they are. First, because they are not in the labor force, they lack one major time-consuming and stress-producing daily activity. Second, by virtue of their wealth, women with choices eliminate many mundane chores from their daily lives, as these are often delegated to hired help. However, they do tend to participate intensively in two activities—childcare and volunteering. Full-time homemakers simply have more time and energy to spend with their children than working women do.[4] Moreover, they have more time and energy to be engaged in a variety of volunteer activities than women working full time in the labor force. While not all unemployed women make use of their capacity to be with their children and to volunteer, some do. Women with choices, given their education, their drive, their personalities, tend to be among those for whom childcare and volunteering, with all their concomitant stresses and strains, fill their days. Thus, while some duties are offset by others, it is not necessarily true that women with choices are on the whole less burdened than other women. The fact that they do not have to volunteer or to spend a lot of time with their children does not negate the fact that they nevertheless lead full lives, which they often perceive to be stressful. Just how overburdened they are was assessed by asking women with choices how they feel about their daily chores and responsibilities. The women in this study reported that the expectations they have of themselves, coupled with those that they perceive their family and friends to have of them, often makes them feel that they are stretched to the limit. When asked to describe their lives, 61% said they were too busy, 61% said they were stressed out, and 77% said that they had to juggle too many activities (by contrast, a survey of working women showed that 49% claimed to be stressed out).[5] Elise Troy, a 42-year-old mother, explained how she was just as busy as a full-time homemaker as she had been when she practiced law (only now "I no longer feel guilty all the time about the effect of my life choices on my family"). Elise's sentiments coincide with the results of a study on work and home conducted by Maxine Margolis, namely, that the chores of unemployed women expand to fill available time allotted to them.[6] In other words, full-time homemakers have more time to keep house, so they will spend more time keeping house. It follows that women who are not employed will fill their days with other responsibilities and chores and often feel as stressed out and overburdened as working women. Thus, women with choices, no less than women of other socioeconomic and educational backgrounds, perceive themselves to be overburdened by the demands they place on themselves.

Nuclear families, extended families, peers, and society in general have always had wide-ranging expectations of women. Those expectations contribute strongly to the outcome of women's choices. They are part of the package of exogenous drives that push women to alter their lives. Such exogenous drives (discussed in this chapter), together with the endogenous drives stemming from within (discussed in Chapters 3–5), motivate middle-aged women to alter the course of their lives. If exogenous and endogenous drives coincide, the process of exercising new choices in middle age is smoother and easier. When they fail to coincide, women are more conflicted, their choices are more limited, and the achievement of their goals is more questionable.

CHANGES IN ATTITUDE TOWARD MOTHERING AND EMPLOYMENT

Expectations are an integral part of prevailing social attitudes with respect to women's roles. Over time, the nature of American women's family and work lives has evolved in part as a result of the expectations that she and others have of her.[7] Most marked is the change in attitudes toward parenting and employment.

The child-centered household is a relatively recent phenomena in our culture, as pointed out by Kathleen Gerson in her study of women's home vs. career choices.[8] There is evidence that in the past, mother-child relationships were less emotional and less close than they are now, in part because women tended to have very little surplus time to devote to their children.[9] Over time, American women became increasingly oriented toward their children both in terms of the quantity and the quality of time they spend with them. This focus on parenting reached a peak in the post–World War II period, when social norms began to dictate that women should be engaged full time in childrearing in order to perfect their children. Parenting became a career for women and often required a negation of self as well as a selfless commitment to the family unit. At this time, women were defined solely with respect to their domestic skills, even though many actively participated in the economy (especially during World War II).[10] The expectation of women was very clear—the message received by women was to stay home with their children.

Since the 1960s, these expectations of women gradually began to change as a result of several factors. One of these, as mentioned in Chapter 1, is the evidence that children are not being harmed by their mothers employment.[11] While this evidence is not uniform across all women and all occupations, some trends are clear. The most important determinant of the effect on children of their mothers' labor force participation is how the mother feels about being employed. Barbara Heynes claims that if the mother is happy and satisfied, then she provides a better environment for the emotional and intellectual development of her children than a nonworking mother. If she is unhappy and hates working, her children will not respond well and are likely to be negatively affected by her experience (similarly, women who do not work yet are frustrated and hate being at home are not doing their children a great favor).[12] Moreover, it has been found that girls tend to benefit if their working mothers are in high-status jobs,[13] and that sons and daughters of working mothers tend to have more egalitarian sex role attitudes.[14] If mothers like their jobs, both sons and daughters will tend to be highly motivated and achievement-oriented because they have satisfied mothers that provide role models.

Expectations of women have also changed because women's work outside the home is no longer viewed as deviant behavior. While low-income women have always been employed, over the past few decades it has become acceptable for middle- and upper-income women to be so too. In 1937, 82% of the population disapproved of a married woman working if she had a husband capable of supporting her. In 1972, about 68% of Americans approved of married women working, and by 1982, 72% gave their approval.[15] Another study found that in one generation, 50% of all men changed their minds on the question of whether family life suffers if the mother works full time: 80% of men over 56 agreed with that statement, while only 30% of those under 25 agreed.[16] Still another study found that of the 1,000 men surveyed, only 36% said that they want a wife who stays home to care for the house and children. In an earlier poll, conducted in 1974, half of the men surveyed said they favored traditional marriages in which the husband has a career and the wife stays at home.[17] All this evidence of changing expectations is accompanied by studies indicating that wives' employment actually improves marital interaction in the opinion of both spouses.[18]

The changing expectations of women are reinforced by evidence that men are actually partaking more in those chores and activities that they previously shunned. Indeed, studies have shown that men are helping out with both childcare and household chores more than in the past. But not all men—only men in dual career households. Since nearly half of working women provide half or more of the households income,[19] it is understandable that some 45% of household chores are performed by men in dual career households.[20] Today, fathers are spending 66% as much time with children as mothers, up from 50% in 1981.[21] Harriet Presser studied working women and found that when wives become employed, one-third of the husbands do more housework and childcare in order to compensate, one-third do not change their habits, and one-third actually do less.[22] Also, Natasha Walters writes how in the 1980s, women tried to be superwomen, and now men are trying to do the same—to have it all—to have a career, kids, and good relationships.[23] Despite the evidence of increasing fatherly involvement, a debate about male-female household roles and equality continues. Indeed, some claim that even if fatherly involvement in the household has increased, it is rarely equitably shared with women. It is, in fact, far from equitable, according to Nancy Barrett, who found that although women engage in full-time paid work, they still do nearly all the unpaid work they used to do.[24]

The changes in attitude toward mothering and female employment are also evident in the lives of middle-aged women with choices. Women were asked to describe their perceptions of their husbands views on the home vs. work issue when they first got married compared to their current perceptions in order to assess if and how those views had changed. Women were also asked about their perceptions of the expectations their children, their extended families, and their peers had of them. Their responses are described below.

EXPECTATIONS OF WOMEN: THE NUCLEAR FAMILY

The expectations that most profoundly affect the attitudes and behavior of women come from their nuclear family, namely, their husbands and children. Parents, siblings, in-laws, and peers play a less significant role, not only with respect to the influence they have on women but also with respect to the demands that they place on them.

The evidence presented in this section indicates that overall, respondents perceive a transformation, over time, in the expectations their husbands and children have of them. The dominant response is that in the past, husbands preferred if their wives did not work but, for a variety of reasons, stayed in the home. Today, on the other hand, the majority is supportive of whatever the woman wants to do, although a large number would in fact prefer if their wives began working for pay. In other words, in the past a small minority of husbands favored female employment while today a large majority leans in that direction. This view was echoed by the older children, those who were old enough to hold opinions and to verbalize them, namely, the older teenagers.[25] In everyone's view, female employment was to complement the fulfillment of responsibilities at home, not substitute for it. In other words, the wife and mother was to perform the functions she already performs, plus more. These views are presented below, in the words of the respondents.

Husbands: Former Expectations

The women interviewed for this study left the workforce some ten to twenty years ago. In most cases, this choice was supported by their spouses. However, the nature and the degree of that support varied across marriages. A minority of husbands left the work vs. home decision entirely to their wives. They seemed to place more value on their wives' satisfaction than on their own preconceived views about what is appropriate female behavior ("My husband just wanted me to be happy" says Elise Troy, "I thought I would be happiest if I stayed at home with my children, so that's what I did!").

The majority of husbands had opinions early on in the marriage about the home vs. work issue, and they wanted (expected) their wives to hear and act upon them (the strength of their convictions and the way in which they tried to impose their views on their wives is not reliably measurable by this study). The most common opinion was the traditional view that a woman should stay at home for the following reasons: (1) so she could be available full time to their children, (2) so she could be available full time to her husband, and (3) so she would not earn an income. Rarely, husbands took a nontraditional approach and actually wanted them to work for pay. These are discussed in detail below.

Former Expectation: Be a Mom! Whose responsibility is the raising of children? When this question was posed across America in a general study, only 19% of men and women responded that raising children is the responsibility of the mother, whether she works or not.[26] In this study, all women thought that raising children was primarily their responsibility, and they all believed that their husbands agreed with this assessment. According to June Ellington, a 42-year-old mother of two daughters,

Years ago, when John and I were first married, his expectation was that I should be a full partner in the family, you know, with respect to income. We graduated from business school at the same time and we went after the same jobs. We were financial equals for the first two years, both earning more or less the same amount. Then I got pregnant and our views changed. We both decided that we wanted our children to have a full-time mother. I left my job and immediately the division of labor in our home became very clear and very different from what it was before. John became the breadwinner and I became the homemaker. We've basically split our roles in a very traditional way. I am expected to be at home to take care of the children and the house, to run the errands, to do the shopping, to do anything and everything that is necessary to make all of our lives easier. As long as I'm not working, that's what it's going to be like.

Jennifer Thomas is a stay-at-home mom who stopped working 12 years ago in order to raise her son and daughter. Her experience was similar to June's.

My husband didn't pressure me, I was the main reason why I stopped working. He wanted me to be a full-time mom all along but he wanted it to be my decision, not his. Although I used to work full time as an accountant, we lived off of Bill's salary and my income went entirely into savings. Our son was born and I continued working. I thought that we would never save anything if I didn't work. But then, after a year of leaving home at 7 in the morning and returning at 7 at night, I was beginning to feel really bad. During the week I only saw my baby while he slept, and I could only play with him on Saturdays and Sundays. The nanny would call me at work to tell me about his smiles and his gurgles. I learned of his crawling through someone else. Somehow, I made the decision to leave my job and after a few months I realized it wasn't nearly as hard a decision as I though it would be. We adjusted to the loss in income very quickly, and Bill's income soon rose to make up for it. Bill is glad I spent time with the kids. Even now that the kids are older, he still expects me to keep on top of the children, their education, and their social lives. He wants me to know the teachers and to be involved in their schools because he thinks that is the best for our kids in the long run.

Early on in their marriages, both June's and Jennifer's husbands expected their wives to be full-time mothers. They were thus supportive of their wives when they left the labor force.

Former Expectation: Be A Wife! In her study of upper-class women, Susan Ostander found that "wives speak of their responsibilities to make their husbands feel good, to protect them from personal and family problems, to make life comfortable for them, to be loving and attractive partners, and simply to be available in case the men want something."[27] A wife's function, then, is just to be there, to be available, to listen. Jesse Bernard coined a term, the stroking function, to describe how women give support to men: they help by rewarding them, agreeing with them, understanding them, and passively accepting what they do and say.[28] Similar views of their role were expressed by the women in this study. Second only to staying at home to be full-time mothers was the view that their husbands wanted them to always be available to cater to their needs. They wanted them always on call. They were supposed to have a nurturing and supportive role in the marriage. They were supposed to provide a sounding board where husbands can vent their frustrations and their anger in the home. It was deemed that women couldn't perform all these functions if they were employed outside the home and if they were focused on their full-time jobs; they wouldn't have the time or the energy or the inclination to provide the stroking function.

Ileana Diaz describes her husband's views on female employment, specifically hers. At 41, she is brimming with energy and enthusiasm about life, yet she has a husband who believes (and openly states) that her primary role is to cater to his needs. Her personality seems in such contradiction with her husband's expectations of her. Ileana recalls,

From the day we got married, Eduardo expected me to put him first! He was very clear about this. He wanted me to care for his basic needs or to administer someone else who will care for those needs. He thought I should be there for him when he needs me, where he needs me, at the time when he needs me. He's always expected that and I don't think it's going to change. Whenever I have worked in the past, my job became a problem between us because Eduardo sees his needs as coming before those of my work commitments. I point out to him that anyone who gets anywhere in life has to put their job first. And he agrees, but only when it comes to other people. Not to me—not to his wife.

Ileana's husband is not alone in his expectations. Maria Perez is also married to a man who believes that she should be at home, largely to be there for him and to do things with him. She did just that, for the past 18 of her 44 years. "My husband wants me at home to be there when he returns from work, to entertain his guests when necessary, and to accompany him on his trips. Also, he moves frequently for work, and I am expected to have only those ties that I can easily break when we relocate. He has absolutely no understanding of why I want to do anything other than what I've done in the past. In that sense, he's a typical Latin male." (Maria referred to the ethnic character of her husband, as did other women. In fact, every Hispanic respondent at some point during the interview said, "You see, my husband is Latin," as though that phrase explains it all.)

In addition to supporting, loving and spending time with them, some husbands also expected their wives to contribute in concrete ways to the husbands' careers. Although a variety of terms were used to describe this view, the concept of the "corporate wife" cropped up on several occasions. Corporate wives, according to the respondents, are expected to be involved directly in promoting their husbands' careers. The primary way in which they do this is by taking over all home-related duties and thus releasing their husbands to devote themselves to their careers. Second in importance is entertaining. According to Isabel Gutierrez, "I am expected to entertain in the home, to be a gracious hostess, and to throw memorable parties. It actually puts a lot of pressure on me and takes an enormous amount of work." Such expectations are not uncommon among men in certain business occupations. Indeed, Susan Ostander quotes a wife interviewed for her study of upper-class women: "There isn't a partner hired in the firm now where they don't look over the qualities of the wife. If my husband were to consider a new partner for the firm, he would make it his business to be entertained in their home to look over the wife."[29] Being a corporate wife, according to some respondents, also entails involvement in civic volunteer activities. A high profile in such activities can produce social linkage effects on their husbands' business, legal, political, or medical careers. Finally, some corporate wives think they are expected to look good and be presentable at all times (such a view has also been described in a study by Cleo Berkun, who found that some women feel it is necessary to look good in order to improve their husbands career).[30]

Former Expectation: Don't Earn! Money was a crucial factor in determining how some husbands felt about their wives' employment. The majority saw no financial need for their wives to work. If there was no need, the argument goes, then their wives might as well do whatever they want during the day (Melissa Donovan: "My husband always said that he'll support me so that I should just have fun doing whatever I want while our child is at school"). Alternatively, some adopted a stronger position: if there were no financial need for their wives to work, then why give the impression to their bosses and colleagues that they can't support their families (Helen Barkey: "For my husband, our family image is very important. If I had worked, his colleagues might have wondered why I work. None of their wives are employed").[31]

Former Expectation: Go Earn! Money also played a role in men's perceptions of their wives employment if they thought their household needed a second paycheck. Some husbands, albeit a minority, wanted their wives to work (read: earn) at least in the short run, until their own careers took off. Often these husbands resisted their wives inclination to leave their jobs and to become full-time homemakers because they worried about the ramifications of such a step on their lifestyles. They had no doubt that a major loss in income would require a long period of adjustment, and they were apprehensive about it. Julia Schuman described her husbands feelings about such an adjustment. Both she and her husband were attorneys, working in two major Miami firms. Before they had children, Julia earned more than her husband. When she left her law practice some 15 years ago, the loss of her income was so profound that her husband still talks about it. They have had to adjust to a lifestyle that was very different from what they had been accustomed to. Her husband had to give up a lot of luxuries that he didn't like giving up. Another respondent, Francesca Layten, had a similar experience: "I worked to help with the bills until Richard established his law practice. I got pregnant and thought that I would continue working through the pregnancy and just take a little time off when my child was born. Then I lost the baby. I was so depressed, I lost interest in my job and I just wanted to become pregnant again. I stopped working immediately. I said to Richard, 'please don't make me go back to work just because I'm not pregnant anymore.' He reluctantly agreed, but I continued to feel pressure from him to go back to work."

Husbands: Current Expectations

What now? What do husbands expect their middle-aged wives to be doing now? Skip to the present, some ten to twenty years after women made their original choice to become full-time homemakers. Just as women are reevaluating their lives and setting new goals, so too their husbands seem to be reevaluating their own views about the home vs. work issue. Husbands are reacting to their wives goals, whether they start a business, go back to school, or get a full time job, in one of three ways. A minority of men are taking a hands-off approach, leaving the decision entirely to their wives. Another minority view is discouraging and unsupportive of any change in their wives' lives. Finally, the majority of men have come to believe that it is time for their wives to do something new. These three views are illustrated below.

Current Expectation: Laissez-Faire. Some of the respondents described their husbands as virtually indifferent to their new aspirations. They believed their husbands would agree to whatever decision they made with respect to their future—work, no work, school, or status quo. The husband of Joanna Flex, who at 53 is bracing to search for a full-time job, exemplified this position. "Bob has no expectation of how I should or shouldn't spend my time now that our last child is about to leave home. Whatever I want is whatever I do. If I want to work, that's fine. If I don't want to work, that's also fine. He never interfered with my work choices and decisions. I can do whatever I choose to do."

Current Expectation: Status Quo. Only a minority of the husbands were opposed to their wives working, or going to school, or doing anything different from what they had been doing over the past decade or two. For these husbands, the "if it's not broken, why fix it?" attitude prevailed. While resistance and opposition to a woman's venture outside the home is often associated with working-class husbands, it nevertheless showed up even among wealthy and educated men.[32] Ileana Diaz expressed it clearly. Her husband has indicated to her that even if she were employed part time, with flexible hours, doing something she loves, while all household chores were taken care of by household help, he would *still* object to her working because "working is a state of mind." He expected his wife's state of mind would change in ways that he *a priori* knows he won't like.

While the negative attitude of Ileana's husband was general in nature, other husbands had specific concerns that molded their negative views about their wives' future employment. According to Melissa Donovan, a major concern for men is having to adjust to new schedules if their wives becomes employed. An employed wife becomes bound by a working schedule and loses the freedom and flexibility to adhere to her husband's schedule. Melissa says that middle-aged husbands who work all their lives with the expectation of leisurely payoffs when they attain seniority are unlikely to want a wife who works. She knows, her husband has told her so. By the age of 51, she has raised several children and has successfully packed all but one off to college. Although she has an ailing elderly mother, she is the organizer of her care rather than the main care provider. So, according to her husband, she is now completely free to do things with him. She explains:

My husband expects me to be with him to enjoy our life together. He has worked hard for many years so that we could do all those things we've always talked and dreamed of doing. He wants me to be free to travel with him, to play golf and tennis, you know, to do the fun things in life. He has achieved seniority at work so he can now slow down a little. Also, he is earning the income that enables him to take time off and to spend money on sports and activities. He feels that if I were working, I would have commitments and inflexibility at exactly the time when he is becoming less committed and more flexible. I used to work as an RN and that's what I'd like to do again. But it really did entail erratic and long hours, sometimes well into the night. He remembers that and is resisting it. He says I'll have no vacations, I'll be on a schedule, I'll be tired. Perhaps if I had some other job, with better, shorter, and easier hours, he might be less resistant.

Other concerns focused on the possible collapse of the household if the homemaker leaves the home. Husbands harbor a fear that order, maintenance, and timeliness in the home would suffer. Despite the array of hired helpers to prevent such an outcome, the questions of who will do the residual chores and who will oversee the hired help loom as potential issues. Brigitte Kelly, agreeing with this view, foresees major household disruptions. "If I went to work, there would be utter chaos here. We'd probably have a lot more fighting between my husband and myself over responsibilities and who's going to do what."

Last but not least is the concern among husbands that their wives' employment might change the preexisting division of power as well as the decision-making process within the family. On the basis of several studies, they are justified in harboring this fear. Susan Ostander found evidence of a positive relationship between income and decision-making power among upper-class men and women: Stephanie Coontz claimed that women who earn an income unequivocally participate more in the family decision-making process than women who don't; and Julia Lawlor described the sense of entitlement that comes with a wife's paycheck.[33] Among the women sampled for this study, a minority raised the issue of power, but only *a posteriori*. In other words, only those women who had just recently begun working said that their husbands were concerned with the issue, while none of the women who were yet to leave the home thought it would be an issue.

Clearly the respondents who raised the issue are the ones who had experienced the effects of earning. These women claim there is unequivocally a difference in the family decision-making process before and after a woman starts bringing home a paycheck. While their paychecks are neither significant in the overall family budget nor their jobs overly prestigious, the distribution of power in the household has changed. Martha Ross, who started working in community organization a few months ago, said, "Oh yes, there is a difference in the division of power in my household. The change is gradual and it is subtle, but since I began working, or rather since I began earning, everyone listens to me in a different way. That includes my husband, my children, my girlfriends, even my housekeeper. It's so stupid—I'm the same person I was before and I think in the same way I thought before. But now it's as though what I think and say counts more. It's as though decision making is weighted differently now." Martha's sentiments are shared by other newly employed women, all of whom claimed that their husbands listened to them more carefully and took their opinions more seriously after they became employed. They all perceived they acquired more power in the home; they all felt more respected.

Current Expectation: Support-Pressure. A surprisingly large number of women believed their husbands wanted them to change their lives by altering their principal daily activity. In fact, some 45% of married women were told by their spouses that they should work for pay. Their motivations fall into the following three categories: be fulfilled, be a trophy wife, and go earn.

Some husbands genuinely want their wives to benefit from being fulfilled in a new way that is unrelated to their role as mother or wife. Roberta Martin said that her husband began suggesting that she 'go out and do something'—something for herself that will make her feel good. Roberta has only one more child at home, the other having left over three years ago. She turned 46 years old recently and on her birthday she pulled out her dusty resume to review it with her husband. "There isn't that much for me to do in the home anymore and my husband is concerned with what I'll do with myself," she explained. "He thinks I'd be so much happier and so much more fulfilled if I start working."

Other husbands seem to want their wives to become a new source of pride for them. They want to be able to show them off, they want to brag to their friends about the new, creative, prestigious activities their wives are involved in. Quite suddenly, having an interesting, successful wife has become of value, and stay-at-home wives are taking note of this new sentiment. Brigitte Kelly has clearly recognized such a transformation in her husband's views. At 42, having raised two children, kept an immaculate home, and participated in the community in a variety of ways, she is now hearing new messages from her husband of 17 years. "I truly haven't figured out why my husband wants me to go back to work so much. I'm beginning to think he wants a new kind of trophy wife. He's always wanted a trophy wife. But his definition of trophy seems to have changed over the last ten years. He's always had very high expectations of me, of being able to do many things. Now he just wants me to take it a step further."

Martha Ross had a similar experience with her husband of 26 years. She was a particularly active volunteer with leadership roles in numerous important civic and educational organizations. One of her children has already left home and at 47, she finds herself pressured by her husband to begin working for pay. "Julius is downright pressuring me to work. He doesn't value the volunteering I've done for years because it doesn't pay me. He's very interested in the bottom line, not because of the money (he makes enough for our needs and anyway, I have money from my parents). Rather, he sees the paycheck as an affirmation of one's worth. He thinks I'm wasting myself, he keeps saying that I'm too intelligent to waste my brain. He thinks that I could be the president of a corporation and that I'm not living up to my potential." Martha suspects her husband would derive pleasure from showing off about a wife who had become a "somebody."

While other women agreed with Brigitte and Martha about the pride component in their husbands' new expectations, a few also expressed skepticism. They believed that a huge difference exists between theory and practice, and that in practice, pride would take second place to general comfort. Francesca Layten described her husband's views with the insight of a wife of 24 years. "If I began working now, I know Richard would be proud of me. But for how long? When he came home to an empty house or no dinner, or when I couldn't go on vacation with him because of my work commitments, he might have second thoughts. He may decide he'd rather have a wife who he wasn't so proud of but who at least was there for him."

Other husbands merely want their wives to earn an income and seemed uninterested in questions of her fulfillment or the prestige associated with a successful wife. Jenny Checkmon just recently went back to work, after years of relentless pressure from her husband. "Joe wanted me to get a job. It had nothing to do with the satisfaction that I might derive from working but rather it had everything to do with my paycheck. He had just changed jobs, he went out on his own, and he was very nervous about this ability to keep providing for the family in the way he did before. Plus, we had two children just about to go to college and our expenses were on the rise. I wasn't so thrilled with the idea of working, yet I still wanted a few more years at home. But then he convinced me that the time had come." Incidentally, husbands who want their wives to contribute to the household finances implicitly set a condition, namely, that their wives don't earn more than they do. Several respondents felt that as long as the men remain the principal breadwinners in the household, they welcomed a second paycheck.

Children: Current Expectations

When middle-aged women were asked what their children expected them to do and to be, virtually all responded, wryly, "Everything!" It seemed so obvious. Mothers are simply expected to "be there" for their children at all times. They are expected to satisfy all their children's needs, to provide emotional support, and to cater to their physical demands. This translates into providing a broad range of goods and services such as clean clothing, warm meals, pocket money, chauffeur services, as well as a sympathetic ear to listen to them, a shoulder for them to cry on, a comfortable environment to receive their friends in, and so forth. They are expected to cater to their children's call of "Figaro here, Figaro there!" Francesca Layten's perceptive analysis of her children's expectations follows: "I am a personal slave to my children. I'm supposed to pick up their clothes, feed them, and just generally be there. My kids want me at home when they get home. And that's OK. I support that, I want to be there. You see, I was a latch-key kid when I was growing up. I knew at the time, as I believe now, that the whole idea of quality/quantity time with your kids is BS. Quality time does not make up for quantity. My kids wanted quantity and I wanted to provide it. I'll do everything for them. But believe me, as soon as I feel they no longer need me, I'm outta here [and in the labor force]!"

Whether children's needs are emotional, physical, or both, the expectations children have of their mothers change as rapidly and thoroughly as they themselves do. Young children, from their limited and sheltered perspectives, believe that whatever exists in their own households is normal and is uniform across their peer group. If their mother is at home, that is normal; if she works, that too is normal. The unquestioning acceptance of their particular circumstances is due to their lack of exposure to variety. As they grow, they begin to see differences and they begin to compare. In their preteen years, children with working moms perceive themselves to be at a disadvantage because the stay-at-home moms are visible around their school as volunteers and carpool drivers. Their perception is conveyed to their working mothers, reinforcing the guilt and pressure they already harbor. By the time children reach high school, their views of their mothers undergo a transformation. They no longer cherish their proximity, and they are uncomfortable with their public presence on the school campus. They tend to be more impressed by the professional mother who has a glamorous job and is earning a lot of money, the one that their peers admire. The working mom becomes the role model for the teenagers. It is the stay-at-home mom who then begins to feel inadequate and unappreciated. Numerous respondents have heard the following phrases from their adolescents: "Mom, get a life!", "Mom, do something with yourself," "Mom, how come X's mother is a Y and you don't do anything?"[34] When Abby Williams told her children she wanted to start working, they responded, "Finally!" Abby suspected their response was rooted in ignorance about her work possibilities. "My children are thrilled that I'm going back to work. But they're thrilled because they have an unrealistic idea about it—they think that I'm going to be a Bill Gates!"

Such a lack of realism about mothers work extends also to the ramifications of work, any work, on mother-child relationships. Respondents describe how their older children think nothing at home will change if the mom becomes a Bill Gates—in other words, she will continue to be there for them. And why not, after all it is so easy to be a mom and perform mothering duties! Children underestimate the work and energy involved in raising children. They overvalue the professional fantasy while undervaluing their mothers' contribution to the home. While they expect more of their mothers, teenagers resist giving up the benefits of a full-time mom. Francesca described this view: "Just like my husband, my daughters would be thrilled if I got an exciting job and earned loads of money. But you see, none of them want to be inconvenienced. In other words, 'mom, after your job, come home and do the laundry please, I don't have a clean blouse!'" Another respondent, a 49-year-old mother of three heard a similar message from her older children. They at once wanted her to have an important career and at the same time they wanted her to be available whenever they needed her. Denise Bentley recalls, "Just a few days ago, my daughter told me, for the millionth time this year, to get myself a life (I'm not sure what that phrase means to her, but I think it has something to do with a life other than the one I have now. I think she wants me to have an important job, to do something glamorous or to make a lot of money). Then, mid-afternoon, she asked me to go to a store and run an errand for her. I said I couldn't, that I was working on trying to get myself a life. And she responded, completely seriously, 'mom, can't you put off getting a life by one day?' There it is! That's what my kids think—have an exciting life but always be there for me!"

EXPECTATIONS OF WOMEN: THE WIDER SOCIAL CIRCLE

Peers and Female Friends

A divergence in the ideology of mothering has developed in the 1970s and persisted into the 1990s, creating severe cleavages between women. It is expressed in the division between stay-at-home moms and mothers in the workforce and is often sharp and unfriendly. On one side of the divide, some women contend that full time mothering, at least until children are in school, is the only decent behavior and anything less than that is both irresponsible and reprehensible. On the other side, some women believe that by working they provide their children with role models, they contribute to the household's standard of living, and they feel good about themselves. Each group perceives the necessity to defend its choice, each group feels that it is necessary to justify its condition. Members of each side have a strong sense of the importance of what they do, of the superiority of their own choice, and by implication of the undesirability of the path not chosen. It has become within the interest of members on either side of this great divide to spread the word about the superiority of their position. There is a sense of sisterhood and solidarity among women within each group; it is lacking among groups. Disrespect and disdain for members of the other group is rarely disguised. Katherine Wyse Goldman, in her book on mothers, has called this phenomenon the "mommy wars."[35] She claims that it is everywhere, from the park playgrounds to the corporate boardrooms. Ann Landers writes about it, "You wouldn't believe the mean-spirited letters I receive from women lambasting their sisters [who choose to stay at home with their children]." She says, "Women, give sisters a break."[36]

Women are undoubtedly influenced and molded by the attitudes of their female friends. Given the great divide between stay-at-home moms and labor force moms, breaking out of any one side is extremely difficult. The pressure to conform, once inside one of the tracks, is quite strong. When a woman tries to break out of a track in order to embark upon another, she is viewed both as a traitor and a newcomer. There is a sense of mistrust and competition if a woman begins to consider breaking ranks. It is a very lonely route to take.

Whether friends support a woman's venture into the workplace or not in part depends on whether they are themselves working. Those who are working are usually enthusiastic to embrace a newcomer to the workforce. "Its about time!" was how one respondent described her employed friends' reactions. Some homemakers, however, resent the so-called encouragement of their working friends. Francesca Layten describes the lack of understanding she encounters among friends and acquaintances. "I'm under so much pressure from my employed friends to start working. It's really hard to be a housewife in the '80s and '90s. People say, 'What, you're at home? Are you one of those women who watch soap operas?' I am made to feel like a lesser individual, a lesser human being, just because I'm not employed."

Unemployed friends react in a variety of ways when a homemaker expresses a desire to start working. While a few women thought their unemployed peers would support them in their quest for work, the majority were apprehensive about their friend's reactions. Jennifer Thomas, for example, didn't look forward to the changes she expects will occur in her relationships with her women friends. "I think some of my girlfriends would be terribly disappointed if I went back to work. All of a sudden, I wouldn't have time to do things with them. They couldn't call me at the spur of the moment and say, let's do this or let's go there. It would certainly change the nature of our relationship." June Ellington recalls how she felt when some of her friends crossed the divide and foresees the same feelings among her peers when she starts working. "I think homemakers feel even more isolated when they see their friends going back to work. It's as though they were deserting you in some way, and you know your relationship will be different. You're not going to see them as often and you're threatened by the change. Also, they're doing something and you're not. And that doesn't feel so great." Then, June continues, "If I went to work, I'd probably lose my friends who don't work. And I don't expect to make many new ones in my workplace because everyone is so busy and rushing home to their families after work. So when I start working, I'll simply have less friends. But that's OK. It's a price I'm willing to pay at this point in my life."

Ruth Schneider speaks of her experience when she recently crossed over and became a working woman. She spoke of her friends' reaction with some bitterness, since she was expecting them to be exhilarated and thrilled for her when she managed to successfully start a business. Instead, she got a cold shoulder from them. "I recently opened a store and it's doing very well! I'm very busy, happy, and financially successful. All of that has provoked funny feelings in some of my friends. Some of them are simply envious. Even though I can understand that feeling, it also hurts me a little. I know that they too would like to have something in their lives apart from their children. And I know they care for me, yet it's hard for them to see it all happening so well and so quickly for me."

Unlike Ruth, Tory Cohen expects her friends to have unfriendly responses when she starts working. At 42, she is considering doing what none of her friends have done, namely, venturing into paid employment. "My peer group is the hardest to deal with. I don't know if it's that they don't understand why I want to work or whether they're just slightly envious. I find that generally women tend to be envious of other women who appear to be able to do it all."

However, making new choices in middle age need not necessarily imply breaking ranks with one's peers. Many find that they are not alone in their desire to break out of their role as stay-at-home moms, and that in fact large numbers of their cohorts are exploring the same possibilities they are. When asked how many of their five closest women friends were presently employed, 35% of the respondents said three or more of their friends were working, while 26% said that they had no employed women friends.

Extended Family Members

Parental influence in a woman's formulation of goals and choices has been amply explored in the literature. The nature of the division of labor in the household in which they grew up, as well as the expectations their parents had of them, is a crucial component of the parental influence on women's life choices. Mothers especially have been found to play an important role in determining women's work vs. home choices—specifically, what their mothers did, how they felt about what they did, and what they encouraged their daughters to do.[37] Yet, while women are undoubtedly influenced by their mothers, they don't blindly follow all their advice.

Several women in this study are very cognizant of their mother's influence. Robin Bifflow, at age 47, still recalls her mother's experience and how it molded her present views. "My mother didn't work during my early childhood. I don't think it ever occurred to her. You see, both of my parents just assumed that my father would support her. Then, he suddenly died and she had to go to work to support us children. Since she had no education and no training, she had a very hard time of it. When we were growing up, she repeatedly told my sisters and me never to be without a job. She is now deceased, but I know she'd be very unhappy if she knew that I'm not working. I'm going to start working because I really don't want what happened to her to happen to me."

Jennifer Thomas also learned from her mother's example and continued, throughout her adult life, to wish she could emulate her. She thought her mother had the perfect combination of work and home. "My mom worked for my dad—she was the business manager in his orthodontist practice. That's very different from working for someone else. She and my dad agreed that the kids came first and if one of the children was sick or had a school activity, there was no question of her being able to take time off. I think my mother had the best of both worlds. She thought so too and always urged me to try to find a similar solution. Of course, since Bill isn't in private practice, it's not an option for me." Despite her parents' positive assessment of their own work situations, Jennifer goes on to describe her father's negative view of her own upcoming employment. "My dad will be very upset when I start working. He thinks that if it's at all financially possible, I should be there for my kids and my husband. Over the years, he's made numerous comments about it so I guess you can call that fatherly pressure not to work." Jennifer's mind is made up, despite her father's efforts to dissuade her from entering the labor force.

Parental views of their daughters work vs. home choices can be sufficiently strong to translate into concrete aids or hindrances. Ann Bowden's mother, for example, was so supportive of her daughter's desire to get out of the house that when Ann embarked upon a graduate program, in her forties, her mother took over some of her household responsibilities. In order to free Ann up so she could attend evening classes, her mom cooked dinners and brought them to Ann's family. Another respondent, Rebecca Miller recalls how her father was crucial in her law school experience. Not only did he provide financial assistance but he supported her whenever her commitment wavered.

What about parents-in-law? Are they largely supportive or obstructionist in a woman's search for change? While the majority of respondents found them to be lukewarm and noncommittal, offering neither excessive advice nor support, some had opinionated mothers-in-law that attempted to dissuade women from their goals. Ruth Schneider, for example, has a vociferous mother-in-law who didn't hide her feelings about her daughter-in-law's new job. "My mom always worked, so she really supported me when I went back to work. However, my mother-in-law is a different matter. She never worked so she's very upset that I'm working. She argues that her son can support me so I don't need to earn money. She can't understand that money isn't the reason why I'm working. I love what I do and I feel good about doing it. She also thinks the children are suffering, although my husband and I tell her that they're not (my husband has started spending more time with them and he fills in for me). . . . I really resent her attitude and she'll just have to get used to [my working]!" June Ellington's mother-in-law was also very uneasy about her decision to start working. "She was worried about the effect it will have on my children. Since she suspected that I wanted to work because John's income wasn't sufficient for us, she offered to pay for private school for our children, just so that I'd stay at home. So, I'd say no, she doesn't support my desire to work." Christina Garcia's mother-in-law also has strong views on women's employment. "In theory, my mother-in-law supports me," Christina says, "but anytime I mention work, she immediately asks 'how will you handle Tomaso?' She's a lot more interested in her son's well-being than she is in my needs and she certainly lets me know it."

The expectations extended family members have of women are in part determined by their own expected future needs. In other words, do they expect her to provide care in their sickness and old age? Are they counting on her time and her attention? If so, they may be threatened by the change of life she is contemplating. One of the respondents, Amanda Adams has siblings who protested her decision to become employed because they counted on her to provide elder care for their parents. Since Amanda's elderly parents happen to live near her, all her (employed) siblings assumed that she'd be the one to care for them when they come to need it. Full-time employment is incompatible with such care as it would decrease the time, the flexibility and the energy left to devote to them. As a result, Amanda's siblings are putting pressure on her to reconsider her decision.

While the views of extended family members might have been important when women made their original home vs. work decision, they are less relevant in their current choices. Middle-aged women have had decades of independent living during which to mold their own views and make up their own minds. While they believed their new choices will ultimately be supported, none seemed to be overly concerned if they weren't. As Kathleen Gerson pointed out in her own study of women's choices, parental attitudes and expectations are inadequate in explaining women's behavior on their own. Indeed, women are not uniformly motivated to comply with their parents' expectations, and usually their messages are reinterpreted and reassessed in adulthood.[38]

CHANGING EXPECTATIONS AND OTHER PUSHES OUTSIDE THE HOME

American women are undergoing a fundamental transformation with respect to their aspirations. This phenomenon is evident across age groups, income categories, and geographical zones. A focus on advantaged middle-aged women indicates that the sources of their transformation lie in a series of pushes and pulls. Women are simultaneously pushed out of their former lives and they are pulled into new ones. While the principal push comes from the changing expectations described above, several other pushes are also relevant in the formulation of other goals. These are described below (while pulls are described in Chapter 3).

Grown Children

According to an old Jewish anecdote, a rabbi, a Catholic priest, and a Protestant minister are embroiled in a discussion about when life begins. The Catholic priest claims it begins at the time of conception while the Protestant minister disagrees vehemently and argues that life begins when the baby's heart starts beating. The rabbi wisely shakes his head throughout this discussion. When pressed for his opinion, he says, "It's very simple. Life begins when the children move out of the house!" For American mothers in the 1990s, a new life emanates from the emotional and physical departure of children. In most cases, the transformation of their mothering role from a full-time occupation to a part-time observant constitutes a push out of the home (indeed, a poll of members of FEMALE [Formerly Employed Mothers at the Leading Edge] indicated that 97% of polled women planned on going back to work after their children grew a little.)[39] Middle-aged mothers have outlived the motivation behind their original decision not to participate in the labor force. Although the decrease in childrearing demands sets in gradually and varies with each mother-child relationship, there are some demarcations that are universally shared. The most obvious is when the child moves out of the home. Less dramatic is the move into high school, the attainment of a driving license, the first summer job, or the first trip without parents. As the children's focus becomes oriented toward peers and as activities outside the home begin to attract their attention, the bonds that link them to their mothers weaken. These mothers are then left with both a void and a freedom that they hadn't experienced for years. While some women are terrified of this void, others look forward to it as an opportunity to be filled with heretofore suppressed interests. Whether women welcome the void or not, it is unavoidable. But just as nature abhors a vacuum, so too voids do not remain empty for long—women are pushed toward filling them.

The children move out (or at least grow up) and the contours of future possibilities start taking shape in the minds of the middle-aged respondents in this study. Women in this study spoke of the void that they need to fill. Melissa: "I've always had the need to be productive. While the children needed me, I ran the household and 'produced' for them. Now that the last [child] is about to leave, I want to find something new to produce."

Women are apprehensive about the void they expect will permeate their lives when their children depart. The concomitant fear of that void pushes them into the outside world in search of something to fill it. Joanna says: "One of my daughters has left for college and the other is going next year. I think the new period in my life will require so much adjustment. I'm scared and I don't know what to do with myself. If I could, I would remain a full-time mother all my life but since I can't, I have to find something else to do."

Wealth

Wealth also pushes women toward new aspirations in two different ways, depending on whether they think they have enough of it or not. Those who deem they are financially comfortable feel they are liberated from having to work in order to survive. As a result, they feel they have the freedom to do a whole range of other things. That freedom pushes them to new aspirations while simultaneously enabling them to be choosy in terms of which aspirations they pursue. Judith Bardwick, in her study of women's choices, quotes wealthy women as saying, "affluence provides us with freedom of choice (and the burden of finding new goals)."[40] Also, the status they enjoy as upper-income women, often married to professional men who are usually (financial) leaders in their communities, reinforces the confidence they derive from their freedom of choice. Together, the freedom and the confidence associated with wealth empower middle-aged women with choices and push them to new aspirations by instilling them with the belief that they can indeed change their lives.

Alternatively, some women with choices feel that they don't have enough money. The perception that their household wealth is insufficient or that financial problems are on the horizon (which will in turn affect their future supply of money) pushes women to new aspirations. Some feel the squeeze of the economy as their husbands' jobs became less secure or as new jobs don't turn out as remunerative as expected. In order to take the slack off their husbands, some women become motivated to work for pay. While none of the respondents thought they could entirely offset the (actual or potential) loss of their husband's income, they certainly felt that their contribution would make a difference to the household.[41] It was a change in her family's financial condition that forced Jenny Checkmon, at 48, to reevaluate her contribution. "My husband changed jobs and soon after his income dropped, I just needed to get a job. Period." Other women were pushed into considering employment because of concerns about future macroeconomic performance that might alter their personal finances. June describes such concerns: "My husband's business is very dependent on his consumers and their income. In the last couple of years, his income has varied wildly because their income has varied. As a result, we sometimes have a large cash in-flow and at other times we have to tighten our belts, quite suddenly. He'd like me to work in order to even out some of these fluctuations." Alternatively, women are worried about their future financial picture if their husbands become sick, incapacitated, or if they die. Francesca Layten expressed such fears very openly and cited them as the reason she is contemplating joining the labor force. "My father died suddenly and left my middle-aged mother to support herself without a job or a career. I really don't want that to happen to me. Although my husband has no pressing health problem at this time, he's at an age when anything can happen. I want to be prepared. I don't want my kids to go through what I went through when my mother had to struggle."

Others yet are worried about their financial future if their marriage fails. One woman in particular had concerns about marital disharmony and explained that she wanted to be financially prepared in case she becomes divorced (Robin: "I don't think my marriage is going to last after the children leave home. My husband and I have so many problems that we try to cover up in order to provide a decent home to our children. When they leave, we won't be motivated to keep it all together. So of course I worry about my financial future. I want to be prepared for being on my own. The only way I know how to do that is to get a job, right now"). Some divorced women found themselves with insufficient funds to sustain the standard of living they had while married and so were pushed to new aspirations (Abby Williams: "I never had to think about money before my husband and I divorced. It was all such a shock—I still haven't gotten used to being divorced, let alone not having as much money as I did before").

Boredom

Some middle-aged stay-at-home moms are bored. They have done the same things year after year. They have spent most of their time with children and the mothers of other children, repeatedly discussing child-related issues. Boredom with their daily chores, their routines, and their lives in general may provide the push that induces women to reevaluate their choices and formulate new goals. June Ellington identified boredom as the principal push and the most compelling reason for her attempts to venture outside the home. She is a full-time mother with an MBA degree. Overall boredom with all aspects of her life percolated for years until it became explosive and gave an urgency to her thoughts about employment. She says: "While I was raising my young children, I operated on a basic level of boredom all the time. I was either running around or doing errands or making dinner or giving the kids orders or simply being a chaperon. It was all mindless stuff. I want to use my brain again. I want to be a thinking person again. I've had it with this full-time mothering stuff!"

Boredom does not only result from extensive and exclusive contact with children. It can also result from the loss of a spouse and the concomitant emptiness that permeates those left behind. Isabel Gutierrez recounts: "When my husband left, I didn't know what to do with myself. I knew I had to get out of the house. I felt I had to change my daily routine. Part of this feeling was because of boredom and part was because I knew that my ex-husband didn't sit around and mope for me all day. You see, he got out and got a new life (and a new wife!) I want to do the same."

Education

Education pushes women into living out their fantasies and aspirations. Highly educated women are by definition more open to new ideas and more prone to taking risks and breaking with the past. Education also makes women feel they have the capacity to do whatever they set out to do. According to Francesca: "You know, the fact that I have a master's degree means something to me, despite the fact that I haven't worked for about 20 years. It makes me feel that I have accomplished something in the past and if I set my mind to it, that I could do it again. Oh sure, it would be harder now. I'm probably not as quick at learning as I was before. But still, the fact that I did it once makes me feel that if I wanted to, I could do it again."

Health

Good health is yet another push for middle-aged women. According to Blau and Ferber, healthy women feel that they have both the energy and the physical potential to pursue new aspirations.[42] American women in the 1990s are enjoying better health than their corresponding age group did in any other historical period. While this health improvement occurred across all income and age categories, it is especially pronounced among high-income populations whose members pay more attention to their health and well-being—indeed, they have information about health issues and take the time to eat correctly, exercise more, smoke less, and generally pay more attention to their lifestyle. According to Joanna: "I feel fine at 53. Oh sure, I have some aches and pains, but I'm still around, am I not? So why not go for it? I'm healthy now, I may not be in ten years. I want to do whatever I can now, whatever my body will still let me do."

THE TRANSFORMATION OF EXPECTATIONS INTO PRESSURES

Erma Bombeck, an astute commentator on modern society, described the demands on mothers by saying that it was as if they had to climb the Pyramids in heels every day carrying a bucket of ice to the top before it melts.[43] Indeed, in the 1990s, the expectations of women at large are enormous, contradictory, and in constant flux. They are so also for women with choices. Indeed, the majority of these women are perceiving new pressures from their families and friends to "do something with their lives." The pressure is the strongest from some spouses and older children. While pressure from husbands does occur in households where financial security is or may be threatened, it seems to predominate in families in which the financial conditions remain unchanged. In those cases, neither the woman's prior education, nor her prior career, nor any other family variable seemed to be relevant in explaining her spouse's pressure.

Clearly, middle-aged women who feel the pressures to do something new with their lives will need several more arms in order to satisfy the new expectations that their families have of them. These women will wish for the arms of god Shiva to enable them to function.

Notes

1. Shiva is usually shown to have four arms. However, some manifestations of him show him with six, eight, and sometimes sixteen arms. Other Hindu gods, such as the Great Goddess Devi (or Durga) had to, according to myth, have eight arms because it was the only way that she would be able to defeat invincible armies. See Stella Kramrisch, *Manifestations of Shiva*, Philadelphia: Philadelphia Museum of Art, 1981.

2. Rosalind Miles, *The Women's History of the World*, London: Paladin Grafton Books, 1988, pp. 152 and 22.

3. Report of the World Conference for the United Nations Decade for Women, Copenhagen 1980, A/Conf 94/35, cited in Naomi Wolf, *The Beauty Myth*, New York: Anchor Books, 1991, p. 23.

4. There are plenty of full-time homemakers who are overburdened with chores that they cannot devote time to their children. However, they are not the ones who chose to leave the labor force in order to raise children. There is some discrepancy surrounding this issue. There are studies that indicate that working mothers spend as much time in involvement at their children's school as nonworking moms do. See, for example, "Running in Place: How American Families Are Faring in a Changing Economy and an Individualistic Society" a study by Child Trends Inc., Washington (cited in the *New York Times*, September 5, 1994).

5. A recent Gallup survey of 800 working adults showed that among women earning over $75,000, 49% were stressed out (as compared to 31% of the men in that income

category). As income decreases, the proportion of women claiming stress decreases. See the *Miami Herald*, September 7, 1998.

6. According to this view, much of housework is make-work. See, for example, Maxine Margolis "In Hartford, Hannibal, and (New) Hampshire, Heloise Is Hardly Helpful" *MS* 4, no. 12, June 1972, pp. 28–32.

7. It has also changed as a result of the changing economic conditions of Americans. While this issue is discussed in detail in Chapter 6, suffice it to say here that in the 1990s, two incomes are necessary for a household to maintain the standard of living it enjoyed in the 1960s with one income. Moreover, in order to maintain their wages, males and females alike are having to work longer hours.

8. Kathleen Gerson, *Hard Choices: How Women Decide about Work, Career, and Motherhood*, Berkeley: University of California Press, 1985, pp. 4–5.

9. Juliet Schor, *The Overworked American*, New York: Basic Books, 1992, pp. 92–93.

10. Women's participation in the economy during World War II was the result of economic trends in the labor market that resulted in fundamental changes in the labor supply and demand. Men had left the labor force in order to fight the war (the supply of labor decreased), while at the same time economic activity increased in order to satisfy war needs (so the labor demand increased). As a result, the wage increased and women were drawn into the labor force by that increased wage. In order to enable their participation, the government sponsored daycare centers to accommodate their children and free up their days. These centers were subsequently closed to pressure women to exit the labor force and vacate jobs for the men returning from war.

11. Cheryl D. Hayes and Sheila B. Kamerman, eds., *Children of Working Parents: Experiences and Outcomes*, Washington, D.C.: National Academy Press, 1981.

12. For this perspective, see the research by Barbara Heynes, "The Influence of Parents' Work on Children's School Achievement," in Sheila Kamerman and Cheryl Hayes, eds., *Families that Work: Children in a Changing World*, Washington, D.C.: National Academy Press, 1982. Also, Lois Hoffman, "Effects of Maternal Employment on the Child: A Review of the Research," *Developmental Psychology* 10, pp. 204–228.

13. Suzanne M. Bianchi and Daphne Spain, *American Women: Three Decades of Change*, Washington, D.C.: U.S. Dept. of Commerce, Bureau of the Census, 1983, p. 237.

14. Francine D. Blau and Marianne A. Ferber, *The Economics of Women, Men and Work*, 2nd. Ed., Englewood Cliffs, N.J.: Prentice-Hall, 1992, p. 276.

15. Bianchi and Spain, p. 238, cite research by Valeria K. Oppensheimer, *The Female Labor Force in the United States*, Westport, Conn., Greenwood Press, 1970) and unpublished 1982 data from the National Opinion Research Center.

16. Natasha Walters, *The New Feminism*, London: Little Brown, 1998, p. 161.

17. Walters., p. 18.

18. Ida Harper Simpson and Paula England, "Conjugal Work Roles and Marital Solidarity," *Journal of Family Issues* 2, June 1981, pp. 180–204.

19. Poll by Families and Work Institute, 1995, cited in the *Wall Street Journal*, February 21, 1996.

20. This study was conducted by Rosalind Barnett of Radcliffe College and cited in the *Wall Street Journal*, February 21, 1996.

21. This study by Joseph Pleck, University of Illinois, was cited in the *Wall Street Journal*, February 21, 1996.

22. Harriet Presser, "Female Employment and the Division of Labor within the Home: A Longitudinal Perspective," paper presented at the Population Association of

America, St. Louis, 1977, cited in Arlie Russel Hochschild, *The Time Bind*, New York: Metropolitan Books, 1997, p. 184.

23. Walters, p. 153.

24. Nancy Barrett, "Obstacles to Economic Parity for Women," *The American Economic Review*, 72, May 1982, pp. 160–165. As part of the debate on male/female roles, a recent study by the Families and Work Institute showed that men now spend as much time caring for children as mothers do (however, that study in turn was criticized because the responses were said to be unreliable since they were based on self-assessment by fathers—a method that is notoriously inaccurate. See the *New York Times*, April 16, 1998). Natasha Walters has entered the debate claiming that the gap between men's and women's household chores is quickly closing and may equalize in a decade or so (Walters, op. cit., p. 162).

25. In this way, this study differs from that conducted by the Whirlpool Foundation which found that out of 15 possible characteristics of the "ideal mother," having an important job was ranked fourteenth (cited in the *New York Times Magazine*, November 15, 1998, p. 84). It is possible that this difference arose because the latter study included children as young as six years, while in my study, sentiments in favor of mothers employment were expressed by older teenagers.

26. Louis Harris and Associates, *Families at Work, Strengths and Strains, General Mills American Family Report, 1980–81*, Minneapolis: General Mills, 1981.

27. Susan A. Ostander, *Women of the Upper Class*, Philadelphia: Temple University Press, 1984, p. 41.

28. Jesse Bernard, *The Future of Marriage*, New York: Bantam 1972.

29. Ostander, p. 45.

30. Cleo S. Berkun, "Changing Appearance for Women in the Middle Years of Life: Trauma?" in Elizabeth Markson, ed., *Older Women*, Lexington, Mass.: Lexington Books, 1983, p. 21.

31. None of the women seemed to think that their husbands would be concerned about their salaries if they went to work. Yet, there is evidence that men whose wives are employed earn less than those whose wives stay at home. This phenomenon come to be called the Daddy Penalty. These findings come from a study of 231 men in which those with traditional wives earned 25% more than those in dual career families. The study was conducted by Freida Reitman of Pace University and Joy Schneer Rider University (and cited in the *New York Times*, October 12, 1994). Why does this occur? Some say it's because sole breadwinners will work longer hours and harder because they alone are responsible for the family income. Alternatively, there may be corporate prejudice.

32. Such opposition was also found by Lillian Breslow Rubin, who presented evidence of negative attitudes of working-class husbands toward their wives working outside the home. At the same time, she found that is less so if the woman works for choice and has flexible hours. Lillian Breslow Rubin, *Worlds of Pain*, New York: Basic Books, 1976, p. 176 (cited in Blau, p. 273).

33. Ostander, chapter 3; Stephanie Coontz, *The Way We Really Are: Coming to Terms with America's Changing Families*, Basic Books, 1992; Julia Lawlor, "The New Breadwinner," *Working Mother*, June 1997, p. 13.

34. Many of the women in this study identified with the mothers described in Anthony Wolf's book on adolescents called *Get Out of My Life But First Could You Take Me and Cheryl to the Mall*, New York: Noonday Press, 1992.

35. Katherine Wyse Goldman, *If You Can Raise Kids, You Can Get a Good Job*, New York: HarperCollins 1996, p. 116.

36. Quoted in Shirley Burggraf, *The Feminine Economy and Economic Man*, Reading Mass.: Addison-Wesley, 1998, p. 77.

37. What the mother did is no indicator of what she advises her daughter to do. Indeed, mothers can have expectations for their daughters that gear them for a life no different from their own, be it in the labor force or in domesticity. Alternatively, mothers urge their daughters not to do what they did.

38. Gerson, p. 54.

39. The average age of the members was 33. Goldman, p. 17.

40. Bardwick, p. 57. Parentheses mine.

41. As such, these feelings coincide with the general trend across the United States according to which it now takes two incomes to retain the standard of living of one income some 20 years ago. There has been a decline in the standard of living as a result of the inability of one paycheck to sustain the same purchasing power as it did in the 1950s. Gerson, p. 207.

42. Blau and Ferber, p. 269.

43. Quoted in Burggraf, p. 45.

Part II

INCENTIVES

Chapter 3

The Transformation of Aspirations

Laura Carleson leaned forward and looked at me straight in the eyes. She didn't avert her glance for what seemed like an eternity. She slowly enunciated every word she uttered in a husky whisper, emphasizing each syllable so as to reflect the enormity of her underlying emotions, "I-desperately-want-to-do-something-new-but-I-don't-know-what!"

Yes, Laura was aspiring to change her life. As many of her peers in their forties and fifties, she wanted another chance and she wanted a new beginning. She wanted to do something she had not previously done. She was in perfect health, she looked younger than her 49 years, she could sustain a challenging tennis match as well as anyone else at her club. In short, she had the physical requirements to undertake a major reformation. Moreover, she was insatiably curious about the world around her, she was devouring fiction and nonfiction at a rate that pleased the local bookseller immensely, and she prepared proposals and wrote reports for the civic organization where she volunteered. She certainly didn't lack the intellectual requirements to try something new.

However, by her own admission, she wasn't sure if she had the emotional requirements to take on a major reorientation. She was still hurting and reeling from an involuntary life change imposed on her by her husband of 23 years. One day last year, he came home and shattered her world: with no advance warning, he announced that he was moving out because he had fallen in love with another woman! Laura only learned the full impact of those dozen words slowly, over the next year. Everything she had done for the past two decades now seemed futile. Everything she had cherished now seemed worthless. She began to regret her past choices, her past decisions, her entire former life.

Despite what happened to her, Laura didn't want to dwell on her past—she wanted to focus instead on her future. She described how she wanted to do anything and everything that would be different from what she did before: she wanted to spend most of her days outside the home, she wanted to earn money, she wanted to feel fulfilled by something that she did for herself, only for herself. She wanted to create (outside the home), she wanted to channel her energy into something (outside the home), she wanted to love what she does (outside the home). Laura recognizes that despite her pain, she is very lucky in one major respect that distinguishes her from most other divorced women: she has sufficient wealth that she is not compelled to work right away, doing any job, just to survive. She can take the time to heal, regain her confidence, and reequilibrate her emotions before she faces the outside world.

Her biggest frustration comes from not knowing just how facing the outside world is supposed to happen. Should she go back to school? She loves to learn, but to learn what? There are so many things she's interested in—literature, law, biology. But then, what would she do with that education? Be a teacher, be an attorney? Start from scratch, at her age? Or should she go back to what she was doing before? With her liberal arts degree, she hadn't really had a career, but rather had drifted from job to job, trying all sorts of work. She didn't really enjoy any of them and was happy to give up working when she married (her husband had assumed she wouldn't work, he expected her to become a corporate wife, which she duly did). So it really makes no sense to go back to any of her old jobs, right? She is unsure. She wavers. Maybe there are advantages to going back to what she has experience in. But then, prospective employers probably wouldn't be interested in experience that's a quarter of a century old, right? What about starting her own business? She used to work in the business world so she has some sense of it. Plus, many of her friends are part of that world so she could turn to them for advice and networking. But then, what kind of business should it be? Something that will make money or something that she loves?. . . . The possibilities make her head spin. They also seem unattainable. The desire and drive is there, but Laura is all over the place with her aspirations. She seems unable to channel those aspirations into a clear, ultimate goal.

The singer Marianne Faithful expressed feelings shared by numerous women in her cohort, feelings of sorrow and bitterness when they recognize that a dream they dreamed will never become reality.[1] But bitterness does not have to be the dominant sentiment when age narrows the range of possible dreams. For the contemporary American woman, middle-age can also be a time for formulating other new dreams, setting new goals, and aspiring to new heights. It can be a time for grabbing that second chance. It can be a time for fundamental changes in their lives. Just how fundamental? The mere existence of a travel agency that specializes in one-way tickets to accommodate people who want to go away and never come back indicates a demand for drastic lifechanges.[2] Moreover, the *International Herald Tribune* carried a classified ad placed by a middle-aged Parisian woman who yearned for a major, albeit temporary, change.[3] She was seeking to trade places, for three months only, with another woman whose lifestyle was completely different from her own. In the exchange, she was offering a good-looking and successful professional husband, two well-behaved children, household help, a luxurious apartment in Paris, and a vacation home in the Parisian countryside. This was not a hoax; it was a real plea, a plea for help, the kind that Hollywood has capitalized on. Indeed, efforts by advantaged (but unfulfilled) middle-aged women to give new meaning to their lives by changing their lifestyles have been glorified by the screen: witness films such as *Belle de Jour* and *Montenegro*, both featuring the wealthy, unemployed wives of physicians who gladly trade their enviable comfort and tranquillity for temporary squalor and decrepidness.

While only a tiny minority of women feel compelled to seek such reorientations and to go to such drastic lengths in order to inject meaning and fulfillment into their lives, many do feel the urge to seek change. This change is most often incremental, gradual, and nonthreatening in nature. While there is much variation in the thresholds of women and in the boundaries of what they define as threatening and gradual, most share the goal of a personal transformation and a change in how they spend their days. They have aspirations, novel aspirations. They aspire for a new beginning. They seek a transition from their old lives and they welcome the challenges and ramifications associated with such a transition.

MOVING BEYOND THEIR ORIGINAL CHOICE

In her study of women's roles, Judith Bardwick identified existential anchors that she described as "the commitments and responsibilities that give life direction and meaning."[4] In traditional societies, younger women relied on the guidance provided by older women with respect to the way in which they should live their lives. In societies undergoing rapid change, such as that of modern America, women choose not to rely on the way life was in the past to give them direction in the future. Today, women find their own existential anchor, and they can, if they choose and if their conditions permit, change that anchor as their circumstances change. They can move on. They can entertain notions of change. While their principal anchor may still be in their families, they may also develop others.

Middle-aged women acknowledge that there are few valued role models for their generation of women, yet they are aware that the baby-boom generation is creating them. Baby boomers have made being 50 attractive and hopeful. That generation has turned the focus on being middle-aged and has made it popular. In the process, it has enlarged the scope of aspirations that can be aspired to. One of these is personal gratification. In the past, if a middle-aged woman sought to realize her individuality, she was diagnosed as suffering from neuroses. Today, it is acceptable for women to want, to aspire, to set goals, and to dream, in midlife and beyond. According to Susan Pevear, a financial adviser who helps women plan their financial futures, "unlike previous generations, baby boomer women are looking forward to the second half of their lives as a time to concentrate on *their own* needs."[5]

This excitement about future possibilities translates into fantasies about future realities. Fantasy, the first step in moving beyond their original choices, is focused on two distinct time periods: the short run and the long run, in other words, the immediate or near future and the one that is a long way away. The near future, approximately two decades in length, is a time when women complete the task of raising children and they still have one or two decades ahead of them before their spouses retire. It is a time when they can still engage in productive and creative activities: indeed, while men in their fifties are often worn out, women in their fifties are raring to go. Many view the upcoming years, before illness and old age set in, as potentially the best of their lives. The long run is the future that begins some two decades hence. At that time, the husbands retire and a period of togetherness sets in. Many women fantasize about travel, serenity, and leisure activities shared with their partners. While the distant future is more nebulous and less pressing, it is the immediate future that fills women's minds. Middle-aged women have an acute sense of "if not now, then never" and thus the near future is the Now. Women with choices aspire to fill their near future with activities of interest to them.

Moving beyond their original work vs. home choice does not imply a rejection of that choice and its concomitant lifestyle, nor does it imply regrets about it. Rather, it does imply that women's personal conditions have changed and that they are ready for new alternatives.

When moving beyond their original choice, middle-aged women wonder how many new choices they can realistically expect to have. Women in this study were asked to ponder their backgrounds and conditions and then to make realistic assessments of their possibilities for change. Specifically, they were asked to ponder the breadth and depth of the choices that they, as women in their forties and fifties, think they have. Respondents were asked to compare themselves to the overall female population and to answer the question, Who do you think has more choices than you? A small minority of women said that no other group of women had more choices than they. They recognized the advantages they had with respect to wealth, well-positioned spouses, and generally comfortable lives, and felt that the benefits of those offset any costs they might encounter. Melissa Donovan stated this view clearly, "Oh sure, there are lots of things wrong with me and lots of things that I don't have. However, I have enough money and that makes me feel like I have choices. I might not actually have them, but I feel like I do." Martha Ross also recognized the subjective aspect of her feelings about choices: "I feel like I have more choices than most women because wealth gives me more choices. It's the one factor, more than anything else, that allows women to do what they want, since they have no pressing needs."

By contrast, most women found some fault with themselves and expressed it as the reason why others might have more choices than they. Their perceived shortcomings fell into one of the following categories: qualifications, age, and family attachments. One-half of the respondents said that women who were more qualified than they had more choices in middle age. Some of them focused on the amount of formal education that they had (Robin Bifflow: "I wish I had gone to graduate school. If I had, I would be able to do so much more now"). Others focused on how redundant their skills had become and how out-of-date their training really was (Melissa Donovan: "Those women who kept their skills up-to-date or who recently acquired new ones have more choices than I"). Computer literacy was seen as the most important factor in distinguishing between middle-aged women, with those proficient in new technologies having a marked advantage over those without (Joanna Flex: "If I had some knowledge of the computer, I'd certainly be facing more possibilities now").

Age was the second most often cited reason why some women had more choices. Younger women were identified as having more options and a wider range of possibilities (Brigitte Kelly: "Well, clearly a young woman with less baggage has a wider array of choices"). Age is relevant both in terms of how women feel about themselves (and therefore the image that they project) as well as how they are perceived by society at large (and, in particular, by prospective employers). Ileana Diaz says, "My time on earth is getting shorter and I am acutely aware of this. It affects the way I think about myself, my future and my options." June Ellington focused on how others perceive her age: "I feel fine about my age but I think that employers will think I'm too old."

There were also some miscellaneous reasons why women perceived others to have more choices than they. One married respondent said that women who were unattached had more choices (yet no single woman in the sample said she had more choices than others because she was single). One single woman said that she would have more choices if she were married, while a mother said she would have more choices if she had no children. Another said that if her husband were home more to occasionally relieve her from childcare duties, she would have more choices than she currently does. Finally, one woman spoke of money as a deterrent in her choices. She said that having a lot of money is a problem because it gives a woman so many choices that they are all ultimately useless: "Having as many choices as I do is a drawback because you can do what you like so you end up doing nothing. You explore one direction one day and another the next. And so I find that I compare myself to women who have less choices, and I almost think they are better off. They have had to focus more, so they have achieved more." (Then, as an afterthought, she added, "But still, I'd rather have more choices than less.")

WHAT WOMEN WANT

When women are pushed out of their old lives and pulled into new worlds, what exactly do their new aspirations entail? Phrases such as "I want something new in my life" and "I want more in my life" are repeated over and over again by the participants in this study. Most women have difficulty conceptualizing exactly what they want—they have nebulous ideas, they lack useful information pertaining to opportunities, their thoughts are often dominated by emotions. Often they can not define exactly what they want so they describe their aspirations by negation, namely, by describing what they don't want ("I don't want to work full-time"; "I don't want to stay at home for the rest of my life"; "I don't want to give up traveling with my husband"). Alternatively, women describe what it is that they would like to change ("I want to become financially independent of my husband"; "I want to do something more exciting"). When asked to fantasize about their future, many women lack concrete visions beyond the known parameters within which they currently operate (home, spouse, children).

However, slightly over one-third of the women (36% of the respondents) are directed in their desires and envision their goals with lucidity. To the extent that they made mistakes in their past, they want to rectify them. To the extent that they are reasonably content with their prior choices, they want to build on them. Even those who profess complete satisfaction with their past lives yearn for the opportunity to experiment and to taste diversity.

Middle-aged women were asked what they aspire to. The question was not intended to elicit a specific answer, such as "I aspire to become a nurse." Instead it was a solicitation of a description of the end rather than the means to achieving that end. Picking a profession, becoming a nurse, and studying law are all means of reaching an end. What are the ends, what are the final goals, what are the ultimate aspirations? The end is not becoming an attorney: the end is having the personal fulfillment, living out the dream, and earning the income that results from becoming an attorney. Women spoke extensively of personal fulfillment, financial independence, and the desire to expand their social circle. Their aspirations are discussed below, in the order in which they were most frequently ranked by the respondents.

Personal Fulfillment

The possibility of personal fulfillment was cited by 77% of the respondents as a reason to change their lives. It is an aspiration shared by women who derived immense satisfaction from motherhood as well as by those who perceived its benefits to have been grossly exaggerated. For all of them, the gratification derived from the daily drudgery of repetitive activities yielded some satisfaction, albeit insufficient personal fulfillment. The quest for fulfillment that women feel in middle age is, in their view, legitimate and entirely justified. Women are now asking themselves how they feel, they are asking "What's in it for me?" They are examining carefully what they have been doing and questioning whether they are happy. Most have assessed that they have done their share for their families and that its time to change their focus. Joanna Flex says: "I want to do something that will fill my heart and soul. I want to spend the next two decades of my life being satisfied and happy. I have been satisfied with my children, don't get me wrong, but I keep thinking that there must be more to life, for me personally. I am more than just a mother, so I want to be fulfilled in more ways than just by motherhood."

In their search for self-fulfillment, some women want to explore an interest or satisfy a longing or a drive. In so doing, they hope to discover a new satisfaction, one that is deeper and broader than what they have thus far experienced. June says of her long overlooked interests, "I have so many interests that I've neglected because I wanted to be the perfect mother and wife, always available for my children and my husband. I used to want to do everything for them, but now I feel differently. Now I want to do everything for me."

The pursuit of fulfillment motivates women to be all that they can be. Although this phrase has been trivialized by endless commercials, it nevertheless captures the essence of what many middle-aged women are feeling. They are ready to be challenged in ways that they haven't been for a while, and in responding to those challenges they expect to awaken sensations long dormant. Jennifer expresses such desires: "I haven't been challenged for so long, challenged in an exciting way, challenged intellectually. I'm challenged every day by trying to be in all places at the same time. But that's not the kind of challenge that I'm talking about. I want the sort of challenge that will test more than my abilities to go to the supermarket and chauffeur my children and cook dinner, all simultaneously."

Expanded Intellectual Horizons

Some women felt they had been intellectually dormant for a significant portion of their adult lives, namely, when they devoted themselves to homemaking. During the interview, they reminisced about their past, about a time when they were stimulated and excited by ideas and events. June didn't mince words when explaining this sentiment: "I sometimes think that I'm brain dead! My husband comes home and doesn't really talk, he's all talked out. My girlfriends only talk to me about their kids. I can read only so much on my own. I belong to a book club, but it only meets once a month. It's just not enough intellectual stimulation for me."

Francesca describes how she feels about her intellectual capabilities, given the way in which she has spent her days over the past decade.

My husband comes home from work and I feel that I have nothing intelligent to say to him. I can tell him about what the children did and what I did at their school. I can try to explain to him how hectic my day was. But sometimes I feel like, "so what?" Why even bother telling him this trivial stuff? I remember when we were graduate students, we used to talk about so many things. We'd stay up talking for hours and hours. Oh, I know that now my husband comes home tired and that we have so little time together. But you know, that's only part of the problem. The truth is that I don't feel I have as much to contribute [to our conversations] as I once did. And what's worse, I think my husband would agree.

Clearly, women yearn to learn more, to understand more, and to think more. Irrespective of their former intellectual endeavors, these middle-aged women hoped to expand their horizons and to push themselves to the limits of their intellectual and creative abilities. Among the sampled women, 90% expressed a desire to feel more intellectually stimulated.

Purpose

Middle-aged women yearn to have a new reason to get up in the morning and to face another day. They want to give their lives a new purpose. It's not that they didn't have one in their role as full-time homemakers—they did. Their purpose was to provide their children with the richest emotional and intellectual environment they could, to be a supportive and loving partner for their husbands, and to manage the functioning of their households. Many also found purpose in volunteering and doing a service for the community. But, says Nancy Goldstein, "Now I want a new purpose. It's not that I don't have a purpose—I do—my main purpose is and will always be my children. But I also want a new purpose that has to do with me only. Why shouldn't I have more than one purpose?" Seventy-seven percent of the respondents agreed with Nancy's quest.

While the motivation to search for a new purpose usually develops gradually, it can also be induced by a sudden event such as the departure of children from home, divorce, or the death of a spouse. Joanna explains how she expects to feel that a rug is pulled out from under her when her last child leaves: "I'm really scared about my life when Sami leaves for college. I don't know what I'll do with myself. Not only will I not have her to care for, but I'll also lose her school as a focus for my [volunteering] activities. In order to prepare for the loss and to ease the transition to the future, I've been gradually pulling back from her school. I need to find a new purpose to replace the old. But it's hard. My children, their sports, and their schools were my purpose for so long that I can't imagine living in any other way."

Sarah, Alexandra, and Laura all involuntarily lost their primary purpose when their marriages broke up. While in two of those cases children continued to provide a reason to get up in the morning, it was a valid reason only in the short run. In the long run it proved insufficient. All three divorced women sought new meaningful activities to focus their lives around. One went to graduate school, another began working, and the third is still groping for answers. According to Laura,

When my husband was living at home, I had a clear, daily purpose. I catered to his needs, I took care of the home, and I looked forward to our evenings together after his work. I always hurried home in the late afternoons to make sure that I'd have a nice dinner ready and that I and the house were tidied up before he walked in. I liked to do all that. I liked to have drinks with my husband in the evening and to cook dinner for him and to be responsible for his clothes and his social arrangements. After he left, I had no one to care for, no one to do things for. It was horrible. I felt so empty and I didn't know what to do with myself.

Financial Independence

Currently one-fourth of working women in America earn more than their husbands.[6] While becoming the principal breadwinner is not an aspiration of women with choices, some 60% of the respondents indicated that they did aspire to some financial independence from their husbands. It may seem ironic that women from wealthy households should be concerned with financial issues. However, for the most part, it was not the absolute quantity of money they hoped to increase but rather the source of that money that they yearned to change. Women wanted their own income! They wanted to earn money themselves! They wanted to feel that they were contributing participants in the household finances.

While financial independence is attractive to many women, its appeal is strongest among those who have earned in the past and who have been satisfied with those earnings. They remember clearly what it was like to bring home a paycheck, especially one that they felt good about. Brigitte, for example, misses the hefty salary she once earned. She misses both the money and the feelings associated with earning it: "I dislike not having my own personal income. My husband provides for me and the kids just fine, but that's his money, not money I earned. I want to earn my own paycheck." Ruth Schneider concurs: "I don't like being 100% dependent on my husband. He never made me feel bad about it, but I always felt that I wasn't a contributing person, financially speaking. That was very frustrating for me." According to Ileana, "I have never considered money to be important. It has never guided any of my life choices. However, if I had to do it over again, perhaps I would have been wiser about [money matters] because I think that as you get older, you begin to appreciate your own financial stability. Not that I don't have stability with my husband, but I don't have it in terms of myself. I don't suffer from it in any way other than psychologically." Finally, Christina Garcia was determined not only to reverse her own financial dependence but also to convey the importance of such independence to her growing daughter: "From the moment I married, I never had to worry about money. My husband was older than I, and at a very young age I was living a life that people my age usually can't afford. Although I had everything money could buy, I was always unhappy because I was not earning any money myself. Now I'm constantly telling my daughter that she must get a good education and work and that no matter how rich her husband is, she should always earn some money of her own!"

A smaller number of women were not concerned with who earned the additional income, they simply aspired to having more of it. They were motivated to supplement the family income in order to increase their household's consumptive and savings possibilities. Those with several children in college were especially concerned with augmenting the family income.

Respect and Status

Some middle-aged women with choices yearn for a new kind of respect, one that is associated with their personal accomplishments outside the realm of home and children. While most respondents already enjoy community respect and status indirectly through their family's socioeconomic position, some 50% reported a yearning to be respected for their own merits and accomplishments. According to Rebecca Miller: "I know I have a lot of status in Miami, but the source of that status is mostly through my husband. When I worked, I used to have respect and status on the basis of what I did. That's something I'd like to have again one day."

It's no wonder that Rebecca feels this way. Americans largely base respect and self-esteem on what one does for a living. Indeed, the opening sentence of cocktail party small talk is often ". . . and what do you do?" Elizabeth Perle McKenna, in her study of women and work, said that we now get our identities from business cards, while economist Juliet Schor claims that we have become walking resumes.[7] It is a fact that in modern American society, women with careers are perceived differently from those without. A woman with a career commands more respect, her word is heeded, she conveys the impression of strength and control. A full-time homemaker, even if she is a professional who left the workforce out of choice, often answers automatically, "I'm just a housewife" when asked questions about what she does. Women outside the workforce feel that they are not taken as seriously as women who work. They often feel that they are nobodies and as such do not receive the recognition and respect that they would (or did) if they were employed. Women in this study shared many of these views. June Ellington, despite her MBA degree and years of experience in corporate marketing, explained how she sometimes forgets the overall importance of her homemaking activities and is overcome by a lack of self-respect, especially in the presence of career women: "I think that I will respect myself more when I become employed. I know that what I'm doing now is important. I stopped working so that I could be doing it. But I also know that being a homemaker entails a lot of unimportant things such as folding of laundry, driving around and other meaningless tasks that I don't respect myself for doing. . . . I think that I'll just like myself better when I begin working."

In addition to self-respect, women want to increase the respect that they elicit from their husbands and children. Such respect will lead to greater appreciation and better treatment, they hope. Francesca expressed this sentiment succinctly: "My husband and my children would treat me differently if I were employed, I'm sure of it. If I earned a paycheck and if I were 'out in the world' more, they'd think that I was more important and they'd probably value me more." Christina Garcia's husband shows no respect for how she spends her time. This manifests itself in his lack of appreciation for her commitments and the value they hold for her. For example, by coincidence he often asks her to run his errands on days when she has prior engagements. When she protests, he expects her to break her commitments. "Even if I'm chairing a meeting, he says I just shouldn't show up so that I can do whatever he wants me to do at that time. He tells me that I can stand people up because I'm 'just a volunteer.' He doesn't value my volunteering efforts, or anything else that I do. He would only respect me and my time if I were earning a paycheck. Then I guess he'd stop expecting me to drop everything in order to run his errands."

Are all these women correct in thinking that they'd be more respected if they went back to work? Martha thinks so. After just a few months at her new job (following some fifteen years of full-time mothering), she is astonished at the effect a paycheck had on people's perception of her: "The most amazing thing happened when I went back to work. People all around me began to treat me differently—they now act more respectful and more adoring. I'm not a new person, I'm the same person who drove carpools and worked on school projects. Except that now I get a paycheck."

An Expanded Social Circle

The homogenization of the mommy circuit within the suburban lifestyle stifled some women to the point of suffocation. As a result, they aspire to break out of the social circles that are filled with people identical to themselves. They view getting out of the house as an opportunity to invigorate their social lives and instill them with new blood and energy. They want to meet interesting people and to be exposed to a larger variety of individuals across a larger number of professions. They want to open up new worlds of social stimulation thus far closed to many of them, despite their advantaged position within society. Gloria Curran says, "I believe there is a whole new world out there, filled with exciting people and places. My life so far has been limited to women who are very much like myself, who are raising children and driving to and from school events and kid's activities. Not that I don't like these women—I do, they are my best friends. But I'm also curious about other people. Other kinds of people. There must be different people out there, people who talk about things other than the soccer game and the science teacher. Even the friends we socialize with on the weekends are just like us."

Women who have been divorced or widowed find themselves drawn to new social circles for several reasons. There is a natural attraction to other single women, not only because they share experiences but also because socializing only with couples tends to accentuate one's one-ness, especially in the initial stages of divorce or widowhood. Moreover, single women who are receptive to the possibility of a new relationship are driven to expand their social circles so as to increase their chances of meeting eligible men (Laura: "I've got to get out of the house. I'd like to meet a man some day and he certainly isn't going to come knocking at my door").

Insurance

Women were asked whether their desire to change their lives had something to do with a need for insurance in case their lives became involuntarily altered in the future. It was an open-ended question in which the key term, insurance, could be interpreted in several ways. Indeed, the responses were varied. Some women focused on insurance in the event of a marital breakup, others focused on the possibility of a husband's illness, and still others focused on possible future changes in their spouses' earning power. Whatever their focus, the underlying concern was that their stable and comfortable lives may change in unforeseeable ways. They harbored fears that what looks stable may in fact be unstable, and they expressed apprehension because there was no assurance that their present comfort would continue forever. As a result, the interviewed women aspire to some form of insurance to protect them against unforeseen circumstances. Helen Barkey, for example, keeps her nursing license active by regularly attaining her continuing education units, even though she has no intention of ever working as a nurse again ("unless something terrible happens"). Elise Troy, out of the workforce for nine years, never misses updating her attorney's license. While she does plan on returning to her law practice as soon as her children leave home, if an emergency arose she would do so sooner. Both Helen and Elise thought they were being very careful by leaving their options open because "you never know. . . ."

While Helen and Elise sought insurance against emergencies in general, others specifically mentioned marital issues. It's not surprising that even women in good marriages sometimes wonder about their marital future. Across the United States, there has been a universal decline in marriage stability, as people divorce and separate at all-time high rates. (It is estimated that among marriages that began in 1950, 30% have ended or will end in divorce, whereas that percentage rises to 50% for marriages that began in 1970.)[8] Marriage is no longer associated with permanence and women have responded to this reality by contingency planning. Talking candidly about her apprehensions about the future, June said: "Oh sure, my marriage is OK now, but I don't know what will happen in the future. You never know with husbands and marriage. Not that I'm really worried, but I have thought about it. What middle-aged woman hasn't? And when I think about it, I feel that I better have a life of my own and a job of my own in case a breakup does happen." June, as other women in this study, views employment as an insurance policy in case a husband walks out.

Women also worry about the change in their lifestyle that would occur if their marriage fails since there is ample evidence that divorce entails a decrease in living standards of most homemakers. In the words of Isabel Gutierrez, a recently divorced woman: "If I had a career and if I was earning, I wouldn't feel so lost now, now that my husband left. I have had to adjust to living with much less money than I had before. And, you know, with no advance warning. He just left me for another woman, a successful woman with a career. And yet, when we were married, he wanted me to stay home and raise his kids. I don't regret what I did, but I sure feel like I should have taken out some kind of insurance against this. It sounds funny, but why not? We have life insurance, automobile insurance, and health insurance, why not have divorce insurance so women like me don't get into trouble."

Women also wanted to enter the labor force as insurance against the consequences of illnesses that might afflict their husbands. Most spouses of the participants were professional high-income men who work exceedingly long hours, assume enormous amounts of responsibility in their workplace, and suffer stresses and strains in a heavily competitive professional labor market. Given those work conditions, women are understandably concerned for their husbands' health. A few said bluntly that they worried their husbands would drop dead from a heart attack! Roberta's husband, for example, is a 49-year-old partner in a major law firm. His job is very demanding, causes him a lot of stress, and absorbs most of his waking hours. Roberta laments: "I'm worried about my husband's health. He works so hard and has so many pressures both at work as well as at home, you know, trying to provide for us and to sustain the lifestyle that we have. Several men we know, all our age, have recently gotten sick. One just had a heart attack. And its all because of the stresses of their lives. So I worry about him. I worry that he too may become debilitated and not be able to work. That's one of the reasons why I'd like to get out of the house and start working. I don't want to be caught off guard if something happens to him." Another participant, Anna Moore is also concerned with the possibility of her professional husband's premature death although she doesn't focus on financial consequences. Rather, she says, "If my husband dies before me, I want to be working because of the psychological benefit that my job would provide me at that time." In other words, she views work as an insurance against future emotional pain.

Other women worry about the future earning potential of their husbands. Whether they are professionals in private practice or employees in companies, they are all subject to the fluctuations of the business cycle. Francesca, the wife of an attorney in private practice, spoke of her fear: "My husband makes enough for us to live comfortably, however that can change at any moment. His income depends on his clients, and we have no control over them. So I want to know that I'm financially independent and that I can rely on my own earnings. In that way, I'd also be taking some of the pressure off my husband."

Despite family investments that could provide for their needs in an emergency, a minority of women thought there is ample room for concern about their future stock of money. Elise reports that she worries a lot about the volatility of her wealth. She regularly follows the fluctuations of the stock market and carefully observes the overall health of the economy because of their effect on her household's consumption and stock of assets. She defends her concern with the economy: "We're wealthy on paper, but so much of that wealth is in the form of stocks that we can't sell at a moment's notice. And anyway, there's so much insecurity nowadays with investments. It's just so scary. Maybe homemakers like myself should go to work to ensure against a stock market crash."

Structure

A small portion of the sampled women aspired to introduce structure and organization to their days (and by extension, their lives). They yearned for a prefabricated framework for their day, one they could just slip into. They wanted to have someplace to go to, with regularity. Joanna thinks: "If I had to go somewhere and do something every day, I think I would actually get more done. I would learn to be more efficient. Whenever I had a lot to do at once, like out-of-town guests and children's parties and volunteering projects all converging at once, then I was more efficient in everything I did. I'd like some kind of structure in my life. I'd like consistency also, if you know what I mean."

Control

If women define their identities by their husbands', they often feel a lack of control if their lives fail to turn out as they expected. Control over events that directly affect them is out of their hands, often producing frustration. The desire to alter the perception that they weren't controlling their destiny was cited by some women under study. According to Robin: "I sometimes feel that most of the things that happen in my life happen not because of me but despite me. I feel that I have little control over what goes on in my life. When the kids were young, I had some control over their lives. Now they don't really consider me in their decisions. My relationship with my husband is not great so he doesn't really consider my opinions or feelings. The household sort of functions by itself, as if it had some internal momentum of its own. I'd like to feel more in control of my life; right now it's just sort of happening to me."

ASPIRATIONS AS PULLS OUT OF THE HOME

Clearly, women's personal and financial aspirations are pulls that lure women to formulate and pursue new goals. Both types of pulls entice, seduce, and titillate women out of their current lifestyles. Both challenge them to explore new avenues. As the pushes discussed in Chapter 2 are multidimensional and complex, so too are the pulls. Personal pulls affect women's psyches and their sense of self. Women are pulled by the possibility of enhancing the personal gratification they derive from their daily activities. The idea of doing something different and possibly more exciting or important than what they have heretofore done is a strong draw. While personal pulls are directed at women's emotional and intellectual sensibilities, financial pulls are directed at their pocketbooks. Despite their family wealth and financial advantage, some women with choices are attracted by the prospect of increased household income. Alternatively, they are drawn by the possibility of earning their own income.

The interplay of push and pull factors form the package of incentives that influence middle-aged women and propel them to consider new alternatives. Clearly, not all women are attracted by the possibility for change nor is the attraction, when it exists, of equal intensity. Pushes and pulls occur at different times and affect women in different ways. Women's susceptibility to these forces waxes and wanes with changes in their life conditions and circumstances. Yet, if the pushes and pulls overwhelm a woman at an appropriate time in her life, she may be ready to take off. If she is ready, it implies that the combination of pushes and pulls generated sufficient internal momentum to make change possible and likely. Alternatively, a single event such as a divorce, sudden financial distress, or an unexpected opportunity may occur which, when bolstered by festering pushes and pulls, is responsible for inducing change.

HOW WOMEN PLAN TO REALIZE THEIR ASPIRATIONS

In the minds of middle-aged women with choices, undoubtedly the way to achieve most of the aspirations they have is to enter the workforce.[9] While many middle-aged women do not have clear ideas about what the labor force entails and while there is confusion as to their realistic possibilities, two concrete views have emerged. First, working for pay is seen as the single most direct way to realize the largest number of aspirations. It is seen as the avenue to self-fulfillment, it is viewed as the way to simultaneously become more financially independent and to have insurance in case of unforeseen events. It is believed that employment provides the opportunity for both self-actualization as well as the development of one's creative and intellectual potential.

Second, while middle-aged women are drawn to the workforce, they do not aspire to a high-stress, time-consuming, and all-encompassing career. While their views on this issue are discussed at length in Chapter 11, suffice it to say that many women with choices know what it means to be a superwoman and to combine a high-level career with child raising and household management. Despite her successes and achievements, the superwoman is perceived to be suffering from perpetual and unrelenting anxiety, guilt, stress, and exhaustion. While the female achiever has become the female myth of our society, middle-aged women who are contemplating entering the labor force have rejected this image as a focus of their aspirations. They, like the women surveyed by *Good Housekeeping*, view the concept of the superwoman as being history.[10] Nancy Goldstein, a stay-at-home mom who had been a superwoman for eight years when she worked in marketing, was clear about her current views on employment. "I know that I don't want my job to consume me. I remember how it was when I worked in the past. I was always torn. When I was at home, I wanted to be at work. When I was at work, I wanted to be at home. I want my future job to be an enriching part of my life, I don't want it to be my whole life like it was before." Another participant, Julia Schuman had worked as a litigation attorney. She remembers the strains and the stresses, and she wants no part of that, ever again. While she does plan on practicing law in the future, she also plans on steering away from litigation and instead veering towards mediation as a less stressful option in the law profession.

Paradoxically, middle-aged women with choices are more realistic about their future and potential and at the same time romanticize about the myth of working. They are more realistic because they have access to mounds of evidence about how working is not all the liberating ecstasy that women thought it may be some 20 years ago. Those who were previously employed also know this from their own experience. At the same time, there is the myth of the independent and self-fulfilled woman that is difficult to resist. There are romantic notions about how the right job could bring out the best in them. The tedium of the daily drudgery of most jobs is often overlooked, as is the sweat of the discipline needed to begin, pursue and complete the numerous tasks that form the backbone of any job. In other words, in the fantasy, the benefits are exaggerated and the costs are minimized.

Yet, middle-aged women with choices, more than other members of the female population, may have a better chance at actually deriving bigger benefits and incurring lower costs of work than most women (this is discussed in Chapter 11). While middle-aged working women largely look forward to retirement in order to find peace and to do all those things they never had time to do before, nonworking women with choices are also aspiring to do what they haven't done in a long time, namely, to work for pay. But they aspire to do it in a unique way. They don't want just any job. As discussed in Chapter 10, women with choices go for that which is apt to maximize their satisfaction. They want to do what they love and they want to love what they do.

CONCLUSIONS

Several tentative relationships can be described on the basis of the evidence provided by the respondents.[11] First, there seems to be no correlation between the quality of a woman's marriage and her aspirations to do something new. When a marriage is good, it follows that a husband will support his wife in her choices. Such support will stimulate her aspirations. Indeed, women who had aspirations to enter the workforce or go back to school reported that their marriages were good and that they expected their husbands would support them in their choices. However, women who reported to have bad marriages (and were either divorced or still married) also had strong aspirations to change their lives. Therefore, the quality of the marriage did not determine women's aspirations. It is also noted that there was no link between the quality of marriage and the husband's support among three of the Hispanic respondents. Although these women described their marriages as good, they simultaneously regretted that their husbands neither understand nor supported their aspirations.

Second, there seems to be no correlation between the quantity of education women attained in their youth and their aspirations in middle age. While women with post-graduate degrees are possibly more aware of their ability to achieve what they set out to achieve, there are also highly focused and motivated women with no professional degrees who have aspirations to work or study. A post-graduate degree only seems to affect women's goals for the future insofar as the women who have them tend to have clearer ideas about their future goals (possibly because they plan on staying within their professions).

Finally, there seems to be no correlation between the length of women's previous work and their current aspirations. In other words, those who had long careers prior to their hiatus were no more likely to have strong aspirations to work in middle age than those who frequently zigzaged in and out of the labor force. For every woman who had a satisfying previous career and who yearns to relive its benefits there is a woman who had neither a meaningful nor long work life and therefore wants to experience it in middle age.

Notes

1. Marianne Faithful, "The Ballad of Lucy Jordan," *Marianne Faithful's Greatest Hits*, Uni/Abkco, 1969.

2. The *New York Times*, June 21, 1998.

3. The *International Herald Tribune*, Paris edition, 1986.

4. Judith M. Bardwick, *In Transition: How Feminism, Sexual Liberation, and the Search for Self-Fulfillment Have Altered America*, New York: Holt, Rinehart and Winston, 1979, p. 22.

5. The *Miami Herald*, December 28, 1997. Italics mine.

6. Julia Lawlor, "The New Breadwinner," *Working Mother*, June 1997, p. 13.

7. Elizabeth Perle McKenna, *When Work Doesn't Work Anymore*, New York: Delacorte Press, 1997, p. 124. She also cites Juliet Schor on the same page.

8. Kathleen Gerson, *Hard Choices, How Women Decide About Work, Career and Motherhood*, Berkeley: University of California Press, 1985, p. 205.

9. Some women aspire to do this indirectly, in other words, they precede it by going back to school for further training.

10. The *Wall Street Journal*, May 5, 1998.

11. These correlations are tentative because the nature of the data collected for this study did not lend itself to rigorous statistical analysis.

Chapter 4

The Redefinition of Leisure

I must have touched upon a sore point when I asked Amanda Adams to describe her leisure activities. "People think that just because homemakers are not employed, they sit around all day eating bonbons and watching soap operas. I'm a homemaker but that's so far from my reality! While I do eat candy, as you can probably tell, and I do occasionally watch a soap opera, my days are so busy and so full that I'm hard pressed to describe any leisure activities whatsoever." With this indignant introduction, Amanda took me on an odyssey through her typical day. By the end of her story, I was overcome by empathetic exhaustion although I had not moved one inch from my tape recorder.

Amanda is the mother of a nine-year-old child. She had her son late in life, after numerous unsuccessful attempts. She left her career of 15 years as a computer programmer in order to be a full-time mom. Despite the success and recognition she had attained in her field, she left her job very easily. She knew that she couldn't manage being the sort of worker she wanted to be and the sort of mother she hoped to be, so she made a choice. She chose to have what she thought would be an unhurried existence with unfettered time for her family, in the absence of the stresses and pressures that she was so familiar with in the workplace. Now, as a full time homemaker, she finds herself dealing with time commitments and management issues while performing juggling acts, just like she did before. She is moving at the same vertiginous speed as she did when she was employed.

Amanda's day begins with a jump out of bed. She has a lot to do and she gets moving right away, no point in wasting time. She gets up by 6:00 A.M. in order to read the newspaper and have coffee with her husband before their son wakes up. She then helps John Jr. prepare for school and either drives his carpool or waves goodbye to him at the doorstep. By 8:30 she has tidied up the house and possibly even squeezed in a phone call or two. If she has no pressing commitment, she takes a half hour for exercise—either walking in the neighborhood or, if she has early morning calls to make, then on the treadmill (where she can perform two tasks simultaneously). By 9:30 she has showered, dressed, and is at one of the volunteering sites where she spends some 30–40 hours per week (some days she works at the school, others at a civic organization or a local museum). She usually eats lunch on-the-go. She runs errands, such as food marketing and drycleaning, between volunteering commitments. She relies heavily on a car phone that enables her to be productive while stuck in traffic. At 3:20 P.M., without even looking at her watch, the school bell rings in her head and she heads for the most compelling of all her jobs—mothering her son. She provides a healthy snack, she drives him to his sports activity. She waits for him in the car, revising the grant proposal for state funding that is due tomorrow—yes, it will be a late night tonight! They return home, she has no energy left for cooking dinner: she'd rather spend the time coaxing John Jr. to finish his homework. A call to the local Chinese restaurant produces a dinner within the hour. By 7:30 P.M., her husband has come home, tired and preoccupied. They all have dinner together, Amanda cleans up. By 9:30, her son is in bed, her husband is snoozing in his favorite armchair, and she settles down at her desk. She completes her daily allotment of paperwork and pays some bills; she organizes, plans, reviews. She rarely manages to crawl into bed before midnight.

This is a typical day in a not-so-typical life. Amanda realizes her life is far from typical, it is fuller and more complex than that of the vast majority of homemakers. According to many indicators her life is, in fact, more similar to that of working women. The way she sees it, the only difference is that "I don't get paid for what I do. I know, I've been there!"

I asked Amanda to describe her leisure activities. "Leisure?" she says, "yeah, I guess my exercise is my leisure. Also, every once in a while I have lunch with other women volunteers. We spend part of the time talking about our work and part of it socializing. We chat, we vent, and in the process, we relax. Also, I guess reading the newspaper is leisure. Is talking to my husband leisure? If so, I guess I have about one hour of total leisure per day. The weekends aren't any better. We're always on the go. The days are just as full—they're just full of different activities, you know, child-oriented activities." While Amanda realizes that she has so little leisure because she has chosen to have so little, it doesn't change the reality that she feels her days are sometimes too hectic, too busy, too complex. "Maybe it's just my personality," she concedes with a sense of defeat, accepting that because of her personality she is unlikely ever to make more time for leisure She explains that her personality drives her to take on many projects. Indeed, no one is forcing her to be so involved in the community, no one is forcing her to be so completely available to her son and husband. Her activities are the result of conscious choices she has made. She could have chosen to sit around all day, eating bonbons and watching soap operas, but she has instead chosen to lead a different life. A life with very little leisure.

A study by Helena Lopata showed that the lives of women outside of the labor force are exceedingly complex.[1] The housework and childcare that they perform seems to grow to fill the time allotted to them. In other words, homemakers are busy and their lives full of activities even if they do not work outside the home. Is that also true for the subset of unemployed women who are upper-income and advantaged? A distorted view of women who don't have to work for pay is perpetrated by the media, by popular fiction, and to a certain extent by the academic literature. It has trickled down into mass culture resulting in the disparaging view of nonworking women that is shared by men and women alike. A joke aptly reflects this view of them.

Q: What is the source of stress for a wealthy, unemployed woman?
A: Having a hair and manicure appointment in the same day.

Yet, the evidence presented below indicates that middle-aged women with choices do not lead lives of leisure, free from all worldly concerns, in which they spend their days in a stress-free environment limited to grooming themselves and socializing. They do not all jet-set around the globe, party until dawn, and shop until they drop. All their waking hours aren't spent at the country club and at fancy ladies' events. They are not all detached and disinterested in the world around them. They are not self-indulgent, and they don't neglect their families. They are not mere ornamental appendages of their wealthy husbands.

Contrary to popular perception, the leisure component in the lives of women with choices is far more complicated and demanding than is commonly assumed. Despite their unequivocal privilege, the leisure time of women with choices is not squandered idly but rather tends to be oriented toward their families and their communities. Alternatively, leisure time is spent taking concrete steps toward their own self-improvement.

WOMEN OF LEISURE: FACT AND FICTION

According to neoclassical economic theory, leisure encompasses all activities performed during waking hours that are not work. In turn, work includes all activities that are performed for pay. In this simple binary system, the waking hours are neatly divided between work and leisure. Under scrutiny, this division proves to be inadequate in helping us understand how men and women in complex economies spend their time. While some activities are clearly work and others are clearly leisure (such as typing a memo for the boss and lying on a deck chair by the pool), most daily activities are not so easily classified. Indeed, after accounting for sleep, the diversity and complexity of residual activities make the division far from neat and simple. For example, are the following activities work or leisure: washing dishes, assisting a dying relative, driving children to their extracurricular activities, volunteering at the museum, and paying the bills? Few of these activities are considered leisure by the people who perform them, yet they do not provide an income and hence are not considered work.

In search of a more appropriate definition, some scholars have claimed that the difference between work and leisure is rooted in people's perceptions of their activities, namely, what they like to do vs. what they have to do.[2] Such a classification of activities helps explain why some people view daily meal preparation as a chore, and therefore work, while others say it relaxes them and thus is a form of leisure. However, this distinction between work and leisure fails to account for those lucky people whose employment consists of work they love to perform: they would be classified as not working. To rectify this problem, Juliet Schor developed a definition of work and leisure in which the hours of work at employment are combined with hours of work at household chores and only the residual is defined as leisure.[3] This definition, as the previous one, has the problem of classifying as work activities what people do as both chore and entertainment. Joyce Jacobsen offers yet another classification of not-for-pay activities. She states that leisure consists of recreational activities (or true leisure, including watching television or playing sports), activities that produce goods and services not traded in the market (such as meal preparation), and activities that are combinations of the two (such as shopping and childcare).[4] The range of definitions described above underscores the lack of consensus among scholars in the study of work and leisure.

American society is peppered with extremes when it comes to work and leisure, no matter how they are defined. On the one hand, there are people who engage in extensive consumption of leisure while on the other hand, workaholics abound whose addiction to work almost entirely precludes leisure.

Those who conspicuously consume leisure were first described some one hundred years ago by economist Thorstein Veblen in his book *The Theory of the Leisure Class*. He wrote about "gentlemen of leisure" who were men conspicuous in their leisure time in part because it was considered a mark of their class not to engage in work. Work outside the home was shunned as dirty, while work within the home was relegated to domestic servants. At the same time, leisure was persued very clearly for all to see because it was evidence of the ability to afford a life of idleness.[5]

Side by side with this leisure class, the working population toiled and looked upon conspicuous leisure with disdain. Such disdain existed long before Veblen described leisure. Indeed, it even pervaded the American legal system: as late as 1619, having leisure time was punishable by law in the state of Virginia.[6] Such legislation resulted from clear evidence of a positive relationship between work and economic growth. In other words, societies in which people work hard are the ones that produce more good and services. This perception was reinforced over the centuries, as the American economy benefited from increases in labor hours and labor productivity. Thus, people who have too much conspicuous leisure time have come to be viewed as lazy, uninterested, and bored. As such, they are considered virtual parasites of society.[7]

In the 1990s, the concepts of work and leisure are rooted in a strong personal sense of the importance of work. In comparing people from different countries, it has often been said that Americans live in order to work while Europeans work in order to live. This concept was elaborated by Alvin Toffler in his study of future trends, in which he claimed that Americans have a dedication to the workplace rather than having work support their private lives.[8]

Yet, this mainstream focus on work and the concomitant disdain of leisure overlooks the positive contribution of leisure and leisure activities to the economy. This contribution has two parts. First, intermittent leisure is invigorating, refreshing, and rejuvenating. As such, it serves to stimulate workers and thus to raise their productivity. Second, during their leisure time people engage in activities that often entail spending money. This consumption of leisure goods and services increases aggregate demand within the economy, contributing to a cyclical expansion of the business cycle. In other words, demand for leisure goods stimulates production of those goods, which in turn increases employment as more workers are hired to produce them. When more people work and when they work longer hours, their income increases, enabling them to increase their own consumption of all goods, including leisure goods.

Thus, according to economists, societies need both work and leisure for their economic growth while individuals need both work and leisure for their material survival. Psychologists add that people need leisure and relaxation for their psychic well-being as well. But how much of each do they need? Contemporary Americans are struggling in the search for a balance between work and leisure. Over time, this balance seems to be tipping in the direction of work as the number of hours Americans spend working is unequivocally increasing. Indeed, in the 1980s, working Americans reported that they have only 16.5 hours of leisure time per week after employment and household chores are accounted for.[9] Juliet Schor, in her study of American workers, claims that over time leisure hours have been declining rather than increasing, as it was assumed they would (since an increase in leisure time is an expected positive ramification of economic development).[10] Indeed, she reveals that since 1969, the average employee works 163 more hours per year, or an entire extra month per year. Most Americans do not feel comfortable about this encroachment of work hours into their leisure time. Notwithstanding Arlie Russell Hochschild's recent findings that professional people are working more because they prefer the workplace to the home,[11] empirical evidence from a broad spectrum of Americans reveals distress at the increased work hours. A recent survey by the Wall Street Journal/NBC News indicates that 75% of those with incomes over $100,000 feel so squeezed for time that managing their time is a bigger concern to them than managing their money.[12] Moreover, a 1993 survey of the Families and Work Institute showed that employees were less willing to make sacrifices for work and wanted to devote more time to their personal lives.[13] Finally, a Department of Labor study found that the average American worker is willing to give up 4.7% of his or her earnings in return for more free time.[14]

The encroachment of work on leisure is even more evident when the data for women are disaggregated. Recently, there has been a deluge of studies showing how little leisure time women actually have and how much work they actually perform. For example, the Chase Manhattan Bank estimated that in all their nonleisure activities, American women worked each week for 99.6 hours.[15] Arlie Russell Hochschild, who coined the term "second shift" to describe the work at home that women perform after their work outside the home is completed, found that working women have 15 fewer leisure hours per week than their working husbands. In one year they work an extra month of 24-hour days.[16]

While increases in working hours of both professional and nonprofessional males and females have increased, so have the busy hours of those who do not work for pay. Indeed, even if not employed, women with choices conduct their daily activities at a fast pace, replete with schedules and with deadlines. While these are self-imposed and perhaps by some standards unimportant (since they do not contribute to any measurable economic activity), they nevertheless are subjectively important and do contribute to the creation of a society that is time-poor and time-squeezed, both in the working and nonworking worlds.

LEISURE ACTIVITIES

Not all people spend their leisure time in the same way. Studies have found that free-time pursuits are strongly correlated with educational level, occupation, and income. For example, professionals and educated individuals tend to go to the theater, concerts, and museums; they also attend lectures and read. Unskilled laborers spend more time working on their cars, going to sporting events, and watching television.[17] Studies also show that cultural characteristics are relevant in determining leisure time activities.[18] For example, Soviets spend three times more time reading books than Americans and attend movies five times more than Americans. They also spend more time taking walks than Americans do. Americans tend to socialize and spend more time with their hobbies than the French.

There are also gender differences with respect to how leisure time is spent. An all-America questionnaire on leisure activities yielded the following responses pertaining to how women spend their leisure time (which, incidentally, many respondents associated with wasting time).[19] Sixteen percent of the women shop for leisure while only 6% play computer or video games. Whereas men tend to ride in cars for fun, women tend to talk on the phone. Women also like to travel with friends more than with their families: a national survey of women with children found that 24% of women had taken a trip with friends without family in the past two years (while another 24% said they would like to).[20]

Middle-aged participants in this study were asked about their leisure activities. They were asked to describe a typical day in their lives and to define which of their daily activities they viewed as leisure. This open-ended question yielded diverse responses. According to Maria Perez, a mother recently enrolled in graduate school, "Leisure is the time that I have for myself whereas when I do things for others, then it's usually work. Now that I've become a student, my favorite leisure activity is studying and reading." June Ellington finds her peace in the quiet of the mornings: "I consider breakfast leisure. It's the only meal that I always have by myself. It's a time when I read the paper and leisurely drink my coffee. Everyone has left the house already, yet the phone still hasn't started ringing and I don't have to go anywhere. Not yet." For Christina Garcia also, leisure is defined by solitude. When she is alone, she usually prays or simply thinks, quietly enjoying the surrounding silence. While June and Christina associate leisure with being alone, Brigitte Kelly finds relaxation in the company of her children: "I consider time spent with my children as leisure. If I just hang out with them, either as a participant in whatever they're doing or as a passive observer, I relax." Finally, Gloria Curran is very spiritual and feels that her favorite leisure activity is getting closer to God: "I enjoy going to church. It is a time to relax and to attend to the spiritual side of me. It's a side that I don't get to pay much attention to because I'm always so busy with all sorts of things. So when I get to church, I can just be quiet and turn inwards."

Women were presented with a list of activities and asked which of those they engaged in. Finally, they were asked to assess whether they viewed those activities as leisure or chores (this question underscores the subjective nature of the definition of leisure—what is fun for one person is a chore for another). The list of activities is presented in the following sections. Two points warrant mention. First, the frequency with which these activities are performed varied greatly with the particular inclinations and conditions of the respondent. Ages of children, personal health, and interests were crucial determinants in the choice and frequency of activities. Second, some of the responses to questions pertaining to leisure activities should be taken with a grain of salt. Given the nature of a face-to-face interview, the temptation to bolster the hours devoted to "worthwhile" activities (while decreasing the time devoted to others) may be very strong. In all surveys, respondents sometimes inadvertently base their answers on what they would like to be true rather than what is true. Such wishful thinking results in responses showing more hours are spent reading books than watching soap operas or more hours volunteering for the community than shopping for clothes.[21]

Social Encounters

Social interaction with friends and family is the most time-consuming of all leisure activities reported by women with choices. While the average American spends 6.7 hours per week socializing and 4.4 additional hours talking on the phone,[22] women with choices reported, on average, some 6–8 cumulative hours per week on social activities (there was a lot of variation among women: some reported a high of 15 hours per week while others claimed a low of 2 hours).

Most social encounters take the form of lunches with friends, phone conversations with friends and family, and weekend activities with family or friends. While such socializing is considered fun, entertaining their husbands' business associates is viewed as a chore by many women. Indeed, it is a labor-intensive activity that requires attention and care on the part of the woman (as it entails exposing herself, her home, and her children to bosses and potential clients) and thus puts pressure on her to perform to the utmost of her abilities.

Shopping

The consumer culture in the United States cuts across income, education, and age brackets. Large-scale concentrations of stores, all with easy access and inviting decor, dot urban and suburban landscapes in a relentless drive to entice consumption. These malls satisfy the demand for consumer goods and simultaneously create a demand for those goods. Recently they have also become centers of social activity. Yet, evidence from women with choices showed that very small quantities of time are actually spent shopping (including shopping for themselves as well as shopping for the family, but excluding food marketing). The highest reported number of hours was ten per week while the lowest was a few per month. Whether they shopped a lot or a little, the majority of women emphasized that they did not like shopping but viewed it as a necessary chore. Only two women said they enjoyed it or that it relaxed them. Clearly then, shopping, as socializing, is not purely a leisure activity.

Sports and Exercise

The evidence indicates a very strong emphasis on physical activity among middle-aged women. With the exception of two, all respondents reported to be actively engaged in sports or exercise programs at the time of the interview. While some participated in competitive sports such as tennis, sailing, and golf, the majority were drawn to solitary activities such as walking, jogging, lifting weights, and aerobics. The intensity with which such activities were pursued varied from woman to woman. Some spent as much as two hours per day at such endeavors while for others, less than two hours per week sufficed. None of the respondents classified sports and exercise as a chore. Most respondents claimed that it is the concern about health and appearance that motivates them to be so physically active.

Clubs

Ever since Alexis de Tocqueville first identified the large numbers of special-interest associations within American society, students of American culture have recognized the continuous proliferation of a myriad of clubs to suit the diverse needs of a diverse population.[23] Middle-aged women with choices reflect this national and historical trend: 26% are members of clubs, the most common of which are the specialized clubs for activities that are based on a shared interest. These include, for example, book clubs, tennis clubs, golf clubs, and wine-tasting clubs. Among the women in the sample, the book club was the most common.

Some women were also members of another kind of club, the upper-class leisure club. Exclusionary by nature, such a club plays a role in leisure activities, although it is more than a mere leisure spot. It is the place for networking as well as relaxing; it provides an environment for people with similar interests and values to meet and engage in a variety of activities. Among the respondents, only 6% reported belonging to such a club (yet on several occasions, others contradicted themselves and mentioned their participation in club activities, implying that this number is probably biased downward). Participation in upper-class clubs is viewed by respondents both as leisure as well as a necessity for their husbands' career.

Visual Entertainment

All forms of visual entertainment, including television, movies, and theater, are considered leisure activities by all women. Even though television watching is passive (and therefore easy) while theater, cinema, opera, and ballet attendance require a greater commitment of resources (time, energy, and money), the former was by far the less popular activity among middle-aged women. Most claimed to spend very little time watching television: 58% said that they watched less than one hour per week while only two respondents reported keeping the television on all the time while at home. Another was forthright about being drawn to a certain soap opera every day. Another, still, bemoaning her lack of leisure time, recalled how she saw the television show Frasier one night several months ago for the first time and really enjoyed it. While she promised herself that she would take the time to watch it every week, she has yet to see another episode. Certainly in comparison to the national average, women with choices seem to watch very little television.

Reading

While the average American spends 2.8 hours per week reading, the average middle-aged women with choices reads some 4.6 hours. The majority reported reading newspapers, books, and magazines for almost two hours per day.

Hobbies

A minority of respondents claimed to have hobbies (16%). Those who did mentioned gardening, photography, sewing, making crafts, and watercoloring. The majority said they had no inclination or time for hobbies.

Volunteering

All the women in the sample had volunteered their time and energy at some point in their adult lives. Only three claimed not to be active volunteers at the time of the interview. While this activity is discussed in detail in the following chapter, suffice it to say here that volunteer work absorbed, on average, 7.4 hours per week and was not considered a leisure activity by any of the respondents.

Grooming

While all women groom themselves, not all women spend the same amount of time, energy, and money on the activity. Most respondents reported spending about one half-hour per day on grooming. Only 19% reported having regular hair or manicure appointments. A few women viewed grooming as a leisure activity when they relaxed and slowed down. A small portion felt that their grooming activities were unpleasant and time consuming but necessary. One believed it was expected by her spouse and necessary for the image she had to uphold. Another also mentioned her husband, albeit with a different tone: "My husband wants me to spend more time on myself, you know, having my hair done and getting manicures. Not because of him. He thinks it would be good for me and that I would enjoy it."

Napping

Only one respondent said she occasionally napped during the day. Some of the others said they wished they had the time for it. Several said they couldn't even get to bed at night at a decent time, let alone sleep during the day. Thus, the vision of unemployed women taking naps in the afternoons was entirely dispelled by this sample.

CHORES

As there seems to be variation among women in what they consider leisure, so too there is variation in what they consider to be chores. Household chores, activities performed on a regular basis because they are necessary for the maintenance and functioning of the household, are often considered tiresome and boring. Yet, despite their socioeconomic position, women with choices nevertheless perform them.

Cooking seemed to be the most popular of the household chores, performed by the greatest number of women. Indeed, 68% of the respondents cook all the meals prepared at home, despite the fact that the majority of them have housekeepers. The remainder reported that they rarely (or never) cook either because others in their homes are responsible for meal preparation or because the family tends to eat out regularly (or eat-in take-out meals). Eating meals outside the home is especially popular in households where the children are older or have left home. Such a propensity to eat meals cooked by others coincides with Harry Balzer's findings that most of the meals eaten in America in the mid-1990s are cooked in restaurants.[24]

Some 39% of the respondents reported that they clean their own homes. This number is probably an overestimation because several women interpreted it to include straightening up in anticipation of the housekeeper's arrival as well as taking on complete responsibility for the cleanliness of the home.

Roughly 90% of the women interviewed did their own food marketing, irrespective of whether there was a full-time housekeeper in their home or not.

At the time of the interview, slightly over half of the mothers were responsible for driving their children. All women with children under the driving age drove their offspring to school and to their extracurricular activities, either individually or as part of a carpool (Christina Garcia: "Oh sure, driving carpools is a chore, but still, I won't let anyone else do it!"). Others either had children who had drivers licenses (or who were living outside the home). The preponderance of youthful drivers results at least in part from the financial capacity of these families to own excess automobiles for their children's use.

Parental involvement in homework declines as the school grade increases. Younger children require and are receptive to more supervision and assistance than older children. As a result, only 58% of the women participated, in some form, in their children's assignments.

Some 23% of the respondents reported doing yard work. One said that she worked side by side with the gardener "since I'm a hands-on person," while another said that she loves gardening and "wouldn't trust anyone else to touch my yard." Another said her husband took care of the yard because it relaxes him and she participates only in order to keep him company.

Mending and sewing were not popular activities among women with choices. Only one of the respondents said she mended for the family. She was also the one who reported that sewing was her hobby.

While slightly over one-half of the women said they regularly did the family laundry, less than 5% reported ironing clothes. Ironing seemed to be the least popular of all the household chores. One woman described the extent of her dislike: "I hate ironing so much I'd rather sell my body than do it!"

All of the above chores have traditionally been considered within the women's domain. Indeed, it is generally women who either perform them or oversee their performance. However, the maintenance of the household finances, including budgeting and paying bills, has traditionally not been the responsibility of married women. Yet, the evidence shows married women with choices to be very involved in household financial matters: 58% were entirely responsible for paying the regular bills while 10% shared the task with their husbands in an ad hoc manner (this coincides with the findings of a study by Bernice Kanner, according to which three out of five wives in households in which finances are pooled are solely responsible for balancing the checkbook, 56% are responsible for paying the bills, and 38% are in charge of the family budget).[25] The remainder reported that they never paid the bills as that was a chore performed either by their husbands or accountants.

Women's involvement in household finances is described by one of the respondents, Nancy Goldstein. She has strong views on the division of labor between full-time homemakers and their employed spouses. Her view extends to the financial maintenance of the household. In Nancy's family, she is in charge of budgeting and consumption, and she doesn't understand why other full-time homemakers aren't.

My husband and I both contribute to the household, although in different ways. I work in the home, he works outside the home—that's the division of labor we have chosen for our family. Home budgeting is a domestic chore, no doubt about it. So why should my husband do it? It wouldn't be fair to him if I left it for him, he's got enough work to do in the office. I do it, I'm certainly capable of it. I don't understand women who take no interest in the family budgets. Some women I know have no idea of how much their families spend on electricity and food. Their husbands just give them an allowance to cover their personal expenses. When they spend it, they merely ask for more. They are being babied by their husbands. I guess it might be nice to be so protected and to have someone else think about money for you. . . . Or no, actually it wouldn't be!

Women's involvement in financial matters seems to end with the household budgeting. The evidence indicates that women are significantly less involved in the management of investments and assets than they are in paying the monthly bills. Only 10% of the married women were solely in charge of investments, 19% shared the task with their partners, and the majority did not participate whatsoever (all unmarried women reported to be solely responsible for their wealth management, although some received assistance from paid financial advisers).

THE REDEFINITION OF LEISURE

The advantaged middle-aged woman with choices wakes up to the smell of coffee brought to her bedside on a sterling silver platter by her uniformed housekeeper. She stretches leisurely across her satin sheets while the housekeeper draws open the heavy brocade curtains and awaits instructions for morning activities. In turn, the woman inquires about her children: did they have a nutritious breakfast and did the chauffeur get little Johnny to school on time. She proceeds to eat, bathe, and carefully groom herself. Then she tackles the complex task of choosing the most appropriate outfit to wear. Her rotating clothes rack, operated by the push of a button, reveals the hundreds of ensembles suitable for her numerous moods and occasions. She dresses, at times interrupted by telephone chats with her girlfriends. Later she emerges from her quarters to give further instructions to the various hired help who have by now shown up and then speeds away, along her winding driveway, in her convertible Mercedes. She valet-parks in front of her beauty salon, where the staff await her. She emerges two hours later, confident and satisfied with the image she is projecting. She proceeds to a fundraiser luncheon with other socialite women, all donned in hats and Parisian couture, to raise money for the construction of a new wing at the local museum (of which her husband is a trustee, of course). The lunch ends, she returns to her automobile, chatting with friends on her mobile phone as she makes her way home. Should she rest for a while or should she go work out at her gym, she wonders? "I think I'll stay home, take it easy, and catch up with my daughter!" On route, her teenage daughter speeds by in her Range Rover and they wave to each other as they drive in opposite directions. "Oh well, I guess it'll be the gym, after all." In the evening, a shower is followed by yet a new choice of clothing and a peck on the cheek by her husband as they meet on their grandiose stairway. The evening ends with a lavish dinner with his business associates at the club. On the way there, husband and wife talk about their upcoming cruise and Junior's future enrollment at Princeton. After much champagne and ballroom dancing, the woman with choices settles into her oversized bed to sleep the deep and restful sleep reserved for the advantaged woman with not a care in the world.

Some respondents were given the above paragraph to read and comment upon.[26] They were asked how closely this paragraph describes a typical day in their lives. The purpose was to ascertain how they spend their leisure time and whether the lifestyle described above appeals to them. The response was overwhelming and unanimous. "Where did you get such ideas?" asked the women with choices, "Who actually lives like that?" While all respondents believed that there are women with such lifestyles, they also affirmed that they were not among them. When I probed into their personal leisure time and when I questioned them about their daily activities, it was clear that indeed they did not share the lifestyle described above. Quite the contrary!

The evidence clearly indicates that middle-aged women with choices do not lounge around aimlessly all day (indeed, many feel guilty if they have leisure or if they enjoy it: Elise Troy says "I feel guilty if I let myself rest, watch TV, or talk on the phone!"). Instead, they pursue activities they perceive to be important and they pursue many of them. Some they consider leisure, some they consider chores. Irrespective of how they view them, they pursue them with a vengeance and always with a goal. Yes, even in their leisure they strive to achieve goals. For example, gardening is done with the goal of having a showpiece garden, task photography replaces freestyle shots. Even exercising is goal-oriented (witness the motivational dashboard of the exercise machines). Women with choices have dismissed no-goal leisure as inappropriate for them and in that way they reflect the general culture to which they belong. Indeed, modern American women are part of a society that does not condone or tolerate goofing-off. There is value placed on being busy, despite the desire expressed by numerous Americans for more leisure time.

Such a negative attitude toward no-goal leisure was clearly evident from women's reactions after reading the paragraph describing a hypothetical life of leisure. Such a life held little fascination for the respondents. It did not appeal, it did not entice, it did not produce sighs of envy. Perhaps it might have produced such reactions from women with fewer advantages or women with fewer choices. For those under study, the life described in the paragraph is within their grasp. Yet, it has been rejected out of choice. These women are striving and aspiring to lead lives that will be more interesting, more challenging, and more fulfilling than what they currently have, not less. And they view the life of leisure as being less interesting, less challenging, and less fulfilling than their own.

The only element of the hypothetical life of leisure that did have some appeal was related to time—the woman of leisure had more time on her hands than any of the respondents. In contrast to her, the middle-aged women in the sample overwhelmingly felt that their lives were busy and full, and that they were perpetually overcommitted (as noted in Chapter 2, 77% lamented that they had to juggle too many commitments). Thus, it is no wonder that the concept of time was at the forefront of women's responses about leisure. Time, or the lack of it, is a burning issue for them. In that way, women with choices apty reflect the times in which they live. It is an age in which the general American population feels it lacks time as much as money. While those with lower incomes are primarily pressed for money, those with income above $100,000 are primarily pressed for time (indeed, 75% of people in that income bracket claim to be acutely time-poor).[27] The fact that the activities women with choices are involved in are not for pay but rather are performed out of choice does not negate the fact that they nevertheless make women time-poor. Indeed, only 6% of the respondents reported occasionally waking up in the morning and having nothing to do that day (one overstretched woman said, "I wake up in the morning and don't know what to do first!"). Thus, for unemployed women with choices, the words of Franklin D. Roosevelt's ring so true: "Never before have we had so little time in which to do so much."[28]

Notes

1. Helena Z. Lopata, *Occupation: Housewife*, New York: Oxford University Press, 1971.

2. See, for example, Chris Rojek, *Capitalism and Leisure Theory*, London: Tavistock Publications, 1985. For a feminist approach, see Rosemary Deem, *All Work and No Play? The Sociology of Women and Leisure*, Milton Keynes: Open University Press, 1986.

3. Juliet Schor, *The Overworked American*, New York: Basic Books, 1992, p. 13. This, she claims, is an objective approach since it is measurable.

4. Joyce Jacobsen, *The Economics of Gender*, Cambridge, Mass.: Blackwell, 1994, p. 154.

5. Thorstein Veblen, *The Theory of the Leisure Class*, New York: Mentor Books, 1953 (first published 1899), p. 46.

6. The Virginia Assembly legislated the following statute: "No person, hawseholder or other, shall spend his tyme idely or unproffably, under such punishment as the court shall thinke meet to inflicte." Paul Rice, *Timesource*, Berkeley: Ten Speed Press, 1989, p. 144.

7. The *Harvard Business Review* in 1959 wrote, "Boredom, which used to bother only aristocrats, has become a common curse." cited in Schor, p. 4.

8. Alvin Toffler, *Future Shock*, New York: Random House, 1970.

9. Schor, p. 4.

10. Schor furthermore describes how the question of working hours was crucial since the 1700s and that the work week had been declining over time until some 50 years ago, when it simply dropped out of the debate between labor and employers. While it was assumed that over time, with economic development, there would be a decrease in the working hours of workers, that did not happen and instead there was an increase.

11. Arlie Russell Hochschild, *The Time Bind: When Work Becomes Home and Home Becomes Work*, New York: Metropolitan Books, 1997.

12. The results of the *Wall Street Journal*/NBC News Survey were published in the *Wall Street Journal*, March 8, 1996.

13. *Washington Post*, September 3, 1993, p. A2.

14. Labor Department study cited in Eugene McCarthy and William McGaughey, *Non-Financial Economics: The Case for Shorter Hours of Work*, New York: Praeger, 1989, p. 275.

15. Michael H. Minton with Jean Libman Block, *What Is a Wife Worth*, New York: McGraw-Hill, 1983, pp. 59–60, cited in Naomi Wolf, *The Beauty Myth*, New York: Anchor Books, 1991, p. 24.

16. Rice, p. 148.

17. Rice, pp. 146–148.

18. Rice, p. 147.

19. The *Wall Street Journal*, March 8, 1996.

20. The *Wall Street Journal*, February 9, 1996.

21. This section includes very few quotes from women since the interview questions pertaining to activities necessitated merely a yes or no answer, as well as a numerical assessment of the time devoted to the activity.

22. Geoffrey Godbey and John Robinson, *Time for Life: The Surprising Way Americans Use Their Time*, College Park: Penn State University Press, 1997.

23. Alexis de Tocqueville, *Democracy in America*, New York: HarperCollins, 1988.

24. Harry Balzer, president of the National Public Diary project in Port Washington, New York, cited in the *New York Times*, August 17, 1997. Also, see Elizabeth Perle McKenna, *When Work Doesn't Work Anymore: Women, Work and Identity*, Delacorte Press, 1997, on issues pertaining to cooking in the life of the modern woman.

25. Bernice Kanner, *Lies My Parents Told Me*, discussed in the *Miami Herald*, March 27, 1998.

26. Not all participants in the survey read this paragraph. Given that the interview took over an hour to complete, I omitted this section if I determined that the respondent was getting too tired.

27. The *Wall Street Journal*, March 8, 1996.

28. Quoted in the *Wall Street Journal*, March 8, 1996.

Chapter 5

The Reevaluation of Volunteer Work

Tory Cohen has worked for years in prestigious organizations, she has raised hundreds of thousands of dollars, she has directly managed hundreds of people, and she has led and inspired several times that many. Tory is neither a corporate CEO, nor a director of development, nor a personnel director, nor a religious leader. She is a volunteer. A volunteer who has held office in civic, educational, and cultural institutions for over a decade and who spends anywhere from 20 to 40 hours per week on volunteering activities.

Tory doesn't remember a time when volunteering wasn't a part of her life. She has distinct memories of her mother volunteering on a regular basis and her father doing so sporadically. It was a way of life for them. She would be no different, she decided as a young adult. She remembers being interested in the community while still in high school, in an era when volunteering was neither required in schools nor particularly recognized. After she finished college and began working as a marketing executive, she tried to stay involved as much as her time permitted. It wasn't until she left the labor force to be a full-time homemaker that she could really turn her attention to service work.

However, over the course of the past two years, Tory seems to have petered out. She lost interest, she became disillusioned. She became restless and yearned for change. There was no single factor that led her to pull back from her volunteering activities, rather a combination of several forces narrowed her focus so that she is currently only involved in her children's school. She expects to continue with that activity until her girls go to college. Then, she expects to quit volunteering altogether.

Why? Were the places where she volunteered inappropriate for her? Were the women she worked with not to her liking? Has she changed? No, no, and yes. During the interview, a profile emerged of a middle-aged woman who wanted to do something new. Tory had done volunteer work for so long and she had accomplished so much that she was simply ready to move on. "You see, I have the choice to move on. I can do something new, if I want. At 42, I'm still young. There are still so many things that I want to do and that I believe I can do. I've acquired so many skills and so much experience during my volunteering, I can't believe that I won't be able to use it somehow." She feels that its OK to stop volunteering, despite her family tradition. "My mother didn't have the choices I have. In her time, it wasn't considered appropriate for ladies of her class to work for pay. That's the difference. Now it's OK for women like me to be employed. And anyway, my mother didn't want to work whereas I do!"

All across the country, American women spend hours and hours of their time, energy, and labor in a variety of activities. They create, organize, sell, cajole, fundraise, drive, sew, motivate, and bake. They do this work in cultural institutions, colleges and universities, health organizations, social welfare and charitable organizations, botanical gardens, religious institutions, and schools. The nature of the work they do ranges from holding leadership positions to answering telephones in the front offices.

Whatever they do and wherever they do it, volunteer women's efforts are not formally recognized as economic activity. Indeed, volunteering activities are omitted from every measure of national economic activity. Measures of economic performance such as gross national product and national income all fail to include the goods and services produced by the volunteer. As such, volunteer work is an invisible economic activity. The reason why services in civic duty, in schools, in museums, and in politics are all uniformly excluded from national income accounting is because they are performed for free.

Since volunteer work is free labor, there is no evidence of transactions between the worker and the institution. No pay stubs, no W-2 forms, and no tax returns are produced for volunteering. In the absence of such formal evidence of work, volunteer labor does not show up in national income accounting. Moreover, since volunteer workers are unpaid, their participation does not show up in labor force statistics describing the labor market. In sum, their work is a mirage by macroeconomic standards and their participation is unrecognized. It follows, therefore, that it is valueless!

Yet, if volunteer hours were included in the assessment of national economic activity, the gross national product would be greatly increased. According to a Gallup poll in 1991, more than 94.2 million adult Americans (51% of the total population) volunteered their time to a variety of organizations. The time, on average, was 4.2 hours per week, amounting to 20.5 billion hours. Some 15.7 billion hours of this total were in the form of full-time work equivalent to those worked by 9 million full-time paid employees. In order to value these hours, one must attach a dollar sign to them. But how does one put a dollar value on volunteer time? United Way has valued one hour of volunteer time between $5 and $14.50; the National Points of Light Foundation in Washington values one hour at $12.45; the Independent Sector, an organization that tracks volunteer efforts and publishes Giving and Volunteering in the U.S., prices one volunteer hour at the "non-agricultural salary rate" of $12.57.[1] Thus, the volunteer time equivalent of 9 million full-time employees mentioned above would, in dollar terms, be worth some $176 billion![2]

If we disaggregate by gender and shift our focus to female volunteers, we learn that women's volunteer work amounts to some $18 billion per year![3] According to Marilyn Waring, women's total free labor, including volunteering as well as work in the home, amounts to some 20 to 40% of the gross national product.[4] She estimates that the economies of the Western countries would collapse if women didn't do the work they do for free, including volunteering.

The women interviewed for this study all engaged in volunteer work at some point in their lives and did so over a long period of time. They cumulatively spent an average of 300 hours per week on activities they didn't get paid for.[5] Taking only one year into account, their efforts amounted to 15,600 hours per year, which roughly translates into 7.8 full-time positions. If we were to assign only minimum wage to these workers (namely $4.25), their cumulative services would contribute $66,300 to the gross national product. Since most of these women are college trained and most have years of professional work or volunteering experience, a valuation of $12.50 per hour seems more appropriate.[6] In that case, their cumulative contribution to the economy may be valued at $195,000. Yes, the labor of unemployed women with choices, outside the home, is worth more than zero dollars!

The purpose of this brief introduction has been to identify the positive monetary role of volunteering in the American economy. It also serves to accentuate the crucial identifying characteristic of volunteering, namely, that it is done for free. To understand the phenomenon of services rendered without payment and to appreciate the basis for its proliferation in this country, it is necessary to understand the women (and men) who participate in such activities and who derive satisfaction from them. This chapter will focus on the role of volunteering in the lives of women with choices and will explore if and how that role is being reinterpreted in middle age.

BACKGROUND ON VOLUNTEERING: WHY DO IT FOR FREE'?

Despite the clear economic contribution of female volunteers, volunteer work has often been negatively stereotyped in American culture. Just as numerous female professions have negative connotations (indeed, female flight attendants and waitresses have worked hard on dispelling some unflattering images), so too volunteer women are viewed as silly, aimless, and lazy (because, the argument states, if they weren't, they'd be in the paid labor force). Alternatively, volunteers are viewed as rich, trying to climb the social ladder, and interested in persevering elements of their upper-class lives (because, another argument states, if they weren't, how come volunteering isn't more prevalent among members of other socioeconomic groups?). Furthermore, the world simply does not view volunteers in the same way as paid labor. Society views volunteer work with little respect and status because labor is valued according to how much it pays. It is a basic tenant of neoclassical economic theory that the value of labor is equal to its wage. It follows that if the wage is zero, then the value of labor is zero.

It is only recently that commentators on social conditions, policymakers, and even presidents of the United States have begun to extoll the value of volunteering.[7] President Bush attempted to boost volunteering efforts by his One Thousand Points of Light campaign and President Clinton introduced AmeriCorps, in which young people are encouraged to do community service, albeit to earn their college fees. In 1997, a bipartisan effort brought together three ex-presidents and one sitting one in the President's Summit for America's Future to draw attention to the need for volunteering at the local level. In this spirit, numerous companies, viewing volunteering as good business, have made large commitments of their staff's labor.[8] At the same time, recent academic literature has begun to dispel some of those negative stereotypes and reveal what many women volunteers have known all along.[9] Among the volunteers, a large proportion are women who are truly motivated by altruism, who are exceedingly hard workers, who put in many, many hours of work, and who cheerfully agree to work overtime and on weekends when up against a deadline. The character of these women is described by the words dedication, organization, and motivation. Over time, these women have become organized, efficient, and skilled. They can handle large commitments and responsibilities. The jobs they perform have challenge and potential.

Volunteering thus entails the paradox of hard work and no pay, little recognition, and only sporadic appreciation. Despite this paradox, volunteering has been a traditional alternative to the paid labor force for a long time in America. Indeed, as far back as the 1700s, Alexis de Tocqueville recognized the sense of community that Americans have and noted how people are willing to give of themselves in order to foster that sense.[10] Why do women do it? Why do they volunteer their time and labor for free? The reasons are many. Volunteering provides a way to be useful to the community. It provides women with an outlet for their creativity and energy. It provides them with an environment in which to develop social connections and friendships. It enables them to be involved in projects that they otherwise wouldn't be involved in. Volunteer work is a way of life. It is often a family tradition. Volunteerism builds class networks among the rich. It has even come to be recognized by employers as a skill-enhancing activity, and employers accept their employees' engagement in company-approved community involvements where they can learn new skills (and simultaneously enhance the company's image).[11]

There is a distinction between income groups and classes with respect to the quantity of time they can allot to volunteering as well as the nature of the work that volunteers perform. With respect to time, women who are employed working 9 to 5 simply have less time available for nonwork activities than unemployed women. Moreover, if they are also actively raising children, their residual time and energy is often insufficient for additional commitments such as volunteering. Thus, volunteering tends to be associated with upper- or middle-income women who are either unemployed, working part time, or have support at home to ease the burden of domestic chores (in fact, Joyce Jacobsen found that the stereotypic volunteer is middle-aged and works part time).[12] Alternatively, it is associated with women in professional occupations that are more likely to be flexible in time and location and therefore more conducive to accommodating volunteering commitments.

With respect to the nature of the work that is performed by volunteers, there is a further subdivision between the more rich and the less rich. The more rich tend to be involved in civic leadership activities; they are rarely involved in direct service volunteer work. Upper-class women are drawn to leadership positions in which their primary task is fundraising. Given their social position in society, these women know who has money to contribute and they know how to mobilize them to contribute. Upper-class women who are engaged in civic volunteering are able to get involved in the social power structure in the same way that their husbands are in the paid economy. They are able to direct policy and make important decisions. They play the role in the volunteer world that their husbands play in the real world. The less rich women, on the other hand, tend to be involved in volunteering activities that are closer to their home and their lives, notably in their schools and their religious organizations. They are in service volunteering, that is, they come into direct contact with the recipients of their services. They are the ones who bake for the bake sales at school, who make deliveries for the art association, and who type for the local church.

VOLUNTEERING IN THE LIVES OF WOMEN WITH CHOICES

Women with choices were asked how much time they spend on volunteering activities during an average week. Three of the respondents said they were not actively volunteering at the time of the interview although they had volunteered in the past. Others said that their volunteering was seasonal: during low periods, they only put in a few hours per week while during peak times, such as just before an event, they worked full time as well as evenings and weekends. On average, women with choices in Miami put in between 3 and 40 hours per week in volunteering activities.

Women were asked why they volunteer. The most common response had to do with the personal sense of fulfillment that they derived from it. Joanna Flex said, "Volunteering fills a gap in my life, it gives quality to my life." Laura Carleson's response was similar, "I counsel and I tutor at-risk teens. It gives me an enormous amount of pleasure to think that I may have made a difference in their lives." Isabel Gutierrez added, "I volunteer with abused children. Ever since I got divorced and my children left home, I've turned to these kids. I feel they really need me—they are my family now." Elise Troy said "volunteering is my calling."

The second most common reason why women volunteer is that it enables them to work—to be productive, to reach goals, to be creative, and to be responsible outside the home and on their own terms. Specifically, it allows them to be flexible with respect to their time input and their commitment. It allows them to stay home with their children when they are ill; it allows them to accompany their husbands on a trip when they travel; it allows them to take the slack for household members when they are overburdened. In short, it allows them to respond with flexibility to events in the household in ways that paid employment, with its inherent rigidity and structure, does not. Jennifer Thomas describes this sentiment: "I wanted to do something outside the home. Volunteering was a way of working on my terms and on my schedule. If I were on a professional career path, I wouldn't have had flexibility and so wouldn't have been available to my children when they needed me."

Another attraction of volunteering is that it enables involvement in activities women otherwise wouldn't have access to. For many, volunteering provides the opportunity to be involved at the top levels in policy making and decision making that they would rarely be in in the working world. Indeed, on the basis of their previous training and work experience, many volunteering women would be considered unqualified to do, in the labor force, the work they do for free in the volunteering world. They perceive volunteering to be the best that they can do, given previous life choices. Melissa Donovan says:

Volunteering enables me to be involved at top levels in both a health program as well as in the arts. I used to work in a hospital, I was a nurse. My husband is a physician and we spend a lot of time in the medical community. I know it well and I feel that I can contribute to it. Volunteering is a way to do it. Another side of me is drawn to the arts. I love art and I love to go to museums and to study what artists have done. I sometimes wish I had studied art history instead of nursing. These two fields are so diverse, yet by volunteering, I can be in both of them. In that way, I feel like I got the best of both worlds.

Jennifer also thinks volunteering enabled her to do what she otherwise wouldn't have done: "I was able to participate in a large variety of activities which I never would have been able to do or to experience had I stayed in my career. I used to be an accountant, and working full time and coming home to a family with small children didn't leave much time for volunteering. Now, I can be involved in the arts and I can be involved in education. These are both areas that I'm very interested in, much more than accounting." Julia Schuman's view is similar, "I'm really interested in advocacy. I've been an advocate volunteer for several years now." She chuckles and adds "you see, I have an opinion about everything and volunteering gives me an opportunity to express it."

There were other miscellaneous reasons why women volunteered. Some noted that it was a way of meeting people, others said they liked doing good, and some said it was a status symbol and a mark of privilege. One respondent claimed to volunteer because her husband supports it (or possibly insists on it?). Helen Barkey explains: "I have accepted the chairmanship of the Hospital Ball this year only because my husband really wanted me to. Throwing a party for 900 guests is a lot of work, but he thinks it would be valuable for him, given that he is a doctor at that hospital" (her comment coincides with David Potter's findings that it is the women's husbands who reap as much benefit from their wives volunteering as do the women themselves.[13])

When asked if they learned anything from their volunteering experience, most women responded affirmatively. The overwhelming majority said they acquired skills they didn't possess before. The following phrases offered by women describe the skill-enhancing effect of long-term sustained volunteering:

"I have learned to do fundraising. I have learned to make people feel good about giving money." "I have learned to lead a group through a project and I've developed better people skills." "I have learned to communicate with people. I have learned how to talk to people and how to listen to what they have to say." "I've learned to juggle and I've learned to manage. I have learned to do three things and keep five thoughts going at the same time. I can have the world crashing around me and smile sweetly and have it get back on track in no time." "I have learned to budget; I can set goals and I can meet those goals." "Volunteering has taught me public speaking. It has killed off any shyness I had. Now I can talk to the president of the United States or a room of 2,000 people if I need to." "I have learned to organize large activities and large numbers of people." "I have learned to plan events." "Volunteering has strengthened my interpersonal skills, as well as organizational skills." "I have learned how to run programs, small and large."

There were, however, a few dissenting voices from women who didn't feel that volunteering had any effect on their skills and abilities. Nancy Goldstein said, "Volunteering hasn't really taught me anything I didn't know before." Laura Carelson voiced a similar opinion, "I'm probably better at some things, but not many."

THE REEVALUATION OF VOLUNTEERING

The fact that all but three women were actively volunteering at the time of the interview indicates that they must be getting something from it, in other words that the benefits continued to exceed the costs. However, when pushed to make an overall assessment of their volunteering activities, many women did reveal that they had reservations about their activities. When asked whether they had negative volunteering experiences, affirmative answers focused on their perceptions of the difference between volunteers and paid workers. Overwhelmingly, women who volunteer say that it is qualitatively different from paid labor. If a job is not completed, they will work into the night to finish it while paid workers might just go home. Many feel that they are better workers and much more motivated than those who get paid for similar work. They also feel that they are more responsible and more committed. They go the extra mile, while paid workers often try to do as little as they can get away with. As much as the paid workers may look down upon the volunteers because they perceive them to be rich women filling their days with idle activities, volunteers view some working women with equal contempt. According to Martha Ross: "When I was in charge of planning the annual school fundraiser, hired workers would leave at 5, without a care in the world, while I stayed late and then brought work home with me to do over the weekends. I understand that our motivations for working on the event are different, but still I can't help thinking that they get paid and I don't and yet they show so little commitment and enthusiasm."

Francesca Layten concurs with this feeling after a decade of high-level, high-profile volunteering: "I feel that we volunteers are not appreciated and we don't get enough respect. We're expected to take on enormous projects, such as to put on an art festival, organize tours, and raise a lot of money. And there is rarely a blueprint. There is no one telling us how to do it or what steps to follow. Volunteers have to be creative and rely on each other, on other fellow volunteers. And in the end, no one really knows just how much work went into creating what we've done. No one except other volunteers who have already done it before us."

There is a minority opposing view pertaining to the difference between paid and volunteer labor that is shared by a minority of the respondents. Nancy Goldstein, for example, is disappointed with the volunteer workforce. She compares volunteers to office workers and concludes that in an office setting, slackers aren't tolerated the way they have to be in the volunteer workforce. Volunteers are doing it for free, so its difficult to demand from them more than they are willing to give. "Volunteers aren't accountable to you, so you have to spend a lot of time trying to motivate them. I find that in my volunteer work, over the years I have come to delegate less and less and to do more and more myself. I found that I was carrying an enormous amount of responsibility. Some volunteers simply aren't serious and just shouldn't be there if they don't want to work hard."

Opening the door to expressions of dissatisfaction with volunteering led to the exploration of women's retrospective and prospective assessments of their lives. Specifically, women were asked if they had any regrets about the years that they spent volunteering, and then they were asked about their future plans pertaining to volunteer work (namely, do they expect to continue doing it into the future). With respect to the former, none of the women seemed to have any regrets. Asked if they would volunteer again if they had to do it over, they all said that they would. That response is strikingly different from what Susan Ostander heard when she interviewed middle-aged women in the early 1980s. In her study, women were asked what they would do differently if they had their lives to live over again and a large number responded that they would change their life choices with respect to work. One-third of the women she interviewed would not volunteer if they could live their lives again.[14]

The most revealing aspect of women's responses had to do with their future plans. Despite the overall positive experiences that women had in their volunteering activities, when asked about their future plans, most allocated very little time to volunteering. These middle-aged women are in the process of reevaluating their volunteer activities. While they are not doubting the value of volunteering in general, they are re-evaluating the purpose that volunteering serves for them at this time in their lives.

About three-quarters of the women said that volunteering had stopped providing the personal gratification that it once provided. They claim that volunteer work no longer satisfies the needs that they had when they began such activities in the first place. Alternatively, their needs have changed. They attribute this to new developments in their lives: they have outgrown their previous roles, they are ready to move on, and the conditions that led them to choose volunteering in the first place have changed. A clear example of this is volunteering in children's schools. All respondents expected to cease their school involvements after their children graduated and to vacate their spots for the new incoming mothers. Indeed, they viewed graduation day of their youngest child as the end of one era and the beginning of another. Joanna says, "I've been volunteering during all the years that my children were in school. Now that the last one is about to graduate, I have to start thinking about what else I'll do. I don't want to volunteer anymore, I want to get a real job. You see, now I can give up some of the flexibility that I needed before. In anticipation of their leaving, I've started pulling out of school volunteer activities already. I don't want to go cold turkey next year."

For June Ellington, volunteering is tied to her children's school and she too expects to stop volunteering in the future: "I spend about two and a half hours per week in Julia's school. I work in the classroom and help the teacher do whatever she needs to have done. I'm not really big on volunteering, I just do it for my kids since they really like to see me there. I also do it so I can see what's really happening in the class. When they leave school, I'll leave school! It'll be the end of my volunteering at their schools. I may or may not volunteer someplace else after that, we'll see. If I start working, then I certainly won't."

While the majority of the respondents share Joanna's and June's views, a small minority do plan on volunteering in the future. Whether they pursue other avenues of fulfillment or not, whether they enter the labor force or not, they claim to plan on volunteering. They view volunteering as a part of their lives and they believe that they can continue to volunteer, possibly at a slower pace, while also doing other things.

It is clear that in their choice between continued volunteering and moving on to new goals, all the participants in this study are rationally reviewing their options and attempting to maximize their overall satisfaction. Those who move on will be doing so because they find greater fulfillment elsewhere. While they might be better off, society will certainly feel their loss. Although it might be argued that the loss of their labor will be offset by the inflow of other volunteer's labor, it is not clear that the future will have such a dearth of women (and men) willing and able to work without pay. Studies have shown that there has been a decrease in overall volunteering hours between 1974 and 1989 (and that the decline is far greater for women than for men)[15] and given macroeconomic conditions, this trend is likely to continue.

Notes

1. Marie Stiefel, *Report on Volunteer Hours 1995–96*, Ransom Everglades Parents' Association, Miami, 1996.

2. Virginia Hodgkinson and Murray Weitzman, *Giving and Volunteering in the United States: Findings from a National Survey*, 1992 Edition, Washington, D.C.: Independent Sector 1992, p. 2. Also cited in Jeremy Rifkin, *The End of Work*, New York: G. T. Putnam's Sons, 1996, p. 241.

3. Yvonne Roberts, "Standing up to Be Counted," *The Guardian*, London, 1989.

4. Marilyn Waring, *If Women Counted: A New Feminist Economics*, San Fransisco: Harper and Row 1988, p. 69, cited in Naomi Wolf, *The Beauty Myth*, New York: Anchor Books, 1991, p. 23.

5. Assuming that the 30 women worked on average ten hours per week. The other assumptions that underlies the calculations in this paragraph is that 2,000 hours per year is considered a full-time position (40 hours/week for 50 weeks of the year).

6. Susan Ellis, who has written extensively on volunteering, claims that the work volunteers do is not minimum-wage work. Considering the type of work they do as well as their experience, the value of their labor is at least double the minimum wage (*Philadelphia Inquirer*, March 21, 1996).

7. See, for example, Rifkin. Presidents Reagan and Bush were especially forthcoming in commending volunteer work for its role in American society.

8. In 1996, 75% of companies had an employee working full time on community relations, up from 9% in 1987. Nearly 80% of companies now have a volunteer program and one-third give time off for volunteer work. Pledges for the President's Summit for America's Future include the following: Kimberly-Clark Corp. will invest $2 million to support community playgrounds built by its employees; Blue Cross and Blue Shield will offer $20 worth of free health coverage to uninsured children; Time Warner is pledging to increase its volunteer hours of literacy tutoring to 1 million by 1998. (*Miami Herald*, April 26, 1997).

9. See Susan A. Ostander, *Women of the Upper Class*, Philadelphia: Temple University Press, 1984 and Arlene Kaplan Daniels, *Invisible Careers, Women Civic Leaders from the Volunteer World*, Chicago: University of Chicago Press, 1988.

10. Alexis de Tocqueville, *Democracy in America*, New York: HarperCollins, 1988.

11. "Tony Lee, "Doing Good Works Can Also Benefit Career and Company," The *Wall Street Journal*, October 10, 1995.

12. Joyce Jacobsen, *The Economics of Gender*, Cambridge, Mass.: Blackwell, 1994, p. 143. Jacobsen uses economic analysis to explain why this is the typical volunteer.

13. David M. Potter, "American Women and the American Character," in Eliot Freidson, ed., *American Character and Culture*, Deland, Fla.: Everett Edwards, Inc., 1964, pp. 65–84.

14. Nearly half of the women she interviewed had expressed regret that they had not had more practical education that would have enabled them to work in the paid world and that they had not worked in paid employment before their marriages. Ostander, pp. 122–123.

15. Jacobsen, p. 143.

Part III

CONDITIONS

Chapter 6

Women in the Labor Force: Changes in Who, What, When, Why, and How

Female employment is one of the most complicated issues of our time. Society both condemns women who are in the labor force and disrespects those who are not and thus denies them all the support they so desperately need. Working women find themselves juggling the demands of employment, marriage, and children in a frenetic struggle for daily survival and long-term happiness. Women work for the money, women appreciate the stimulation, and women yearn for the respect that employment provides. Nonworking women find themselves shunned by society because they are "just housewives" or "just moms" while struggling with their own dilemmas pertaining to responsibilities, self-fulfillment, and the meaning of life. Smart and skilled women make the choice to stay at home and raise children; loving mothers make the choice to enter the labor force. We are living in a time of transition and change, and employment choices still elicit very animated defenses from women both in and out of the labor force, as well as their spouses, parents, and children. Decisions pertaining to work and home in the lives of average women are reflected in the debate, accusations, and praise that are voiced when public figures make employment choices: witness when Blanche Lambert Lincoln, a democratic candidate for senator in Arkansas, left the House of Representatives in 1996 because she wanted to be home full time with her twins or when Susan Molinari, the former republican congresswoman from New York, resigned from her House seat in 1997 to take a less demanding job in order to have more time with her daughter. The literature on parenting and the work vs. home dilemma is just as contradictory and inflammatory, including those who take the position that women must work at all costs and those who claim they must not work under any circumstances.[1]

To many women, the grass is greener on the other side, no matter what side of the employment divide they are on. Among those who are employed, complaints pertaining to incessant demands and overwhelming time pressures abound. Working women fantasize about future peace and tranquillity, usually associated with the absence of full-time employment. Among those who are not employed, voices expressing the desire to do "real work," to be "out in the real world," and to earn their own income are heard. Whether women perceive they have too much work or insufficient work, dissatisfaction permeates large segments of the female population, and middle-aged women everywhere seem to want to change some aspect of their work lives. In order to understand the possibilities open to unemployed middle-aged women, it is helpful to assess the nature of the working world they would be entering. Specifically, who is in the labor force, what kind of work do they perform, when in their life cycle do they perform it, why do they work, and how do they manage to work and tend to their families? The answers to these questions, as well as an assessment of how those answers have changed over the two decades since women with choices left their jobs to become full-time homemakers, are described below.

There was a time in the not-so-distant past when the employment of married women was considered undesirable. Those who worked were pitied, vilified, and otherwise regarded as eccentric.[2] All personal satisfaction was to be derived from motherhood. At that time, it was a status symbol for men to have a wife who did not work outside the home. Indeed, being able to support the entire family on one paycheck was as much a symbol of success as the make of the car, the address of the home, and the destination of the family vacation. Much has changed over the past few decades. Women of all ages and inclinations have entered the labor force in increasing numbers. Not only are some 75% of women aged 35 to 55 already employed, but most aspire to a life that combines marriage, career, and children.[3] A poll of young women indicated that only 8% agreed with the statement: A husband should earn and a wife should stay at home.[4]

If the current trend in women's labor force participation continues, it is estimated that in the closing years of the twentieth century, 51% of the new entrants in the American labor force will be women.[5] It has been said that "the economic vitality of this nation's women is the single most important edge the U.S. has over its major industrial rivals in the race to build a 21st century economy" and also "American women will create the most profound change in our society since the emancipation of the slaves."[6] The gap between male and female employment in industrial countries has already narrowed as all industrialized countries have witnessed an increase in the proportion of women who enter the workforce. Moreover, there have also been changes in labor market conditions and it is likely that women will profit most from these changes. All these changes are of relevance to the middle-aged women who are poised to become part of the trend.

WHO IS IN THE LABOR FORCE?

Throughout history, women have worked in and around their homes. They toiled in economically productive activities such as sewing the family clothing, heating the home, growing the food, preparing the meals, and so forth. It was only after the Industrial Revolution, with its concomitant technological changes that necessitated labor specialization, that the worlds of home and work became separated for women. While continuing to perform household chores, increasing numbers of women were drawn to jobs outside the home. This trend continued so that today, 46% of the workforce is female, as compared to 17% one century ago.[7]

Several trends in labor-force participation of American women are particularly relevant for this study. These trends have all resulted in new social concerns pertaining to the balancing acts that working women, especially mothers, must of necessity engage in. First, the average white family in the 1950s and 1960s consisted of five people: mother, father and three children. They were supported entirely by the remunerations of the father who worked in the labor force while the mother toiled in the home. At the time, only one-fourth of wives were in the labor force. By 1990, two-thirds of married women were in the labor market.[8] Thus, married women who work outside the home have become a majority over the past two decades. While more single women (who were never married) are in the labor force than those married (with spouse present), in both groups there was higher participation in the 1990s than in the 1940s. However, the rise for married women was the most acute (from 20.4% in 1948 to 58.8% in 1991).[9]

Second, the greatest rise in labor-force participation has been among married women with young children. The rate has more than tripled during 1960 to 1991 for women with preschoolers. But labor-force participation has risen among other women also. More single women tend to be employed. In 1991, 66.5% were in the labor force, as opposed to 58.6% in 1960. The numbers among the divorced, separated, or widowed women also rose from 41.6% in 1960 to 46.8% some 30 years later. The participation of married women went up from 31.9% to 58.5% during the same period.[10]

Third, more women at all levels of education are in the labor force in the 1990s than they were in the 1940s. However, the rise is least acute among women without a high school diploma (from 43.0% in 1948 to 46.0% in 1992).[11] Today, as in the 1940s, women with a college education are the most active in the economy. Indeed, some 81.3% of college-educated women are in the labor force.

Finally, there has been a downward movement in the male labor-force participation coupled with an upward movement in the female participation rate.[12] While this trend is evident in a variety of age brackets, it is most prominent among the middle-aged population. Indeed, the portion of men ages 60 to 69 who work has declined during the 1980s, while the proportion of women ages 55 to 64 who work has increased during the 1980s.[13]

WHAT WORK DO WOMEN PERFORM?

What do secretaries, shop assistants, cashiers, nurses, kitchenhands, and nannies have in common? They are all predominantly women. In the United States, 50% of all employed women are concentrated in four relatively poorly paid female occupations: registered nurse, clerk, retail-sales worker, and teacher.[14] Most women remain in these female-dominated occupations where they have relatively low pay and little scope for advancement. No doubt about it, these are generally dead-end jobs.[15] As in most industrialized countries, a dual labor market seems to exist in the United States, according to which most women tend to be segregated into "women's jobs." In virtually all economic systems, a gender-based division of labor has occurred, according to which women perform jobs that are compatible with maternity while men perform jobs that require strength, aggression, and mobility.[16]

Some women, notably the college-educated, have successfully elbowed their way into male-dominated occupations. During the period between 1960 to 1990, women lawyers and judges increased from 7,500 to 180,000; women doctors increased from 15,672 to 108,200; women engineers increased from 7,404 to 174,000. The number of women in local elected office tripled to 18,000. Women today fill 50% of entry-level management positions, 25% of middle management, and are half of the officers and managers in the 50 largest commercial banks.[17] Despite this seeming success, other statistics indicate that women still have a long way to go: for example, a professional women's support organization recently found that women make up 5% of senior management even though they amount to 50% of the labor force.[18]

The fact that women are spreading into various occupations shows that there has undoubtedly been a change in their work opportunities. The formerly female-dominated occupations, such as clerical, service, sales, teachers, nurses, and librarians, are now attracting only 70% of the total female labor force, while only 53% of the college-educated are going into these professions. The traditionally male-dominated occupations, business and administration, draw 19% of the total and 26% of college-educated females, while law, medicine, and other male professions draw 11% of the total and 20% of the college-educated.[19]

More jobs are open to women as a result of the structural transformation of the economy that accompanies long-term economic growth, the kind that the United States experienced over the past two centuries. An integral part of this transformation is the changing importance of the three business sectors (agriculture, manufacturing, and services). As economies grow and mature, the importance of the three sectors with respect to the labor force changes. Specifically, the relative importance of agriculture declines (namely, the proportion of total jobs that are in the agricultural sector declines) while the importance of manufacturing and services increases (namely, the proportion of total jobs that are in those sectors increases). In the early stages of growth, the manufacturing sector experiences the greatest expansion; in mature economies, it is the services sector that grows the most and therefore absorbs the most labor.[20]

How does this structural transformation of the economy affect the distribution of work by gender? More women than men work in services, while more men than women work in manufacturing.[21] In manufacturing, manual labor is the norm, giving men an advantage as a result of their (often) superior physical strength. As manufacturing jobs begin disappearing in mature, post-industrial economies, men begin losing their jobs. At the same time, the service sector is expanding, providing jobs for men as well as women. In this sector, brains rather than physical strength are required, and therefore the competition between men and women is more equal. Women have thus been the main beneficiaries of the structural transformation of the economy because it has increased work possibilities in those fields in which they can compete more easily.

WHEN DO WOMEN WORK?

When in their life cycle do women participate in the workforce and when do they leave it? In 1992, 49.2% of young females between the ages of 16 and 19 were in the labor force, up from 38% in 1963. This number rises dramatically during women's early twenties, when 71.2% of women participated in the labor force. However, it is in the middle years that the largest number of women participate in the workplace—78.2% of the women aged 40 to 44 years (in 1963, this number was only 47.8%). The number drops to 75.6% and 75.8% respectively in the five years preceding and five years following that age bracket.[22]

There is evidence that increasing numbers of women are staying in their jobs later in life then men. The labor-force participation rates indicate that while the number of working men 55–64 years of age is decreasing, the number of working women in that age group is increasing (in 1978, 41% of women in that age bracket were in the labor force while in 1993, 47% were. For men, the numbers were 73.5 and 66.5%, respectively).[23]

WHY DO WOMEN WORK?

Women work for pay for the same reasons that men work for pay: they either have to (in order to earn sufficient income to satisfy their consumptive and savings needs) or they want to (because it provides them with psychic benefits, it satisfies their need for stimulation, it is a vent for their creativity, it makes them feel good about themselves). Most people work for some combination of these two reasons.

The question of whether women have to work for pay is complex. As discussed in Chapter 2, its complexity is rooted in the subjective nature of the determination of economic necessity. What one woman considers choice in employment, another does not; a household income that one woman perceives to be sufficient to free her from the labor force is viewed as insufficient by another. The minimum threshold of household income that enables women to feel they do not have to work varies, and therefore the economic forces that push them out of the home and into the workforce also vary.

Despite the subjectivity involved in determining whether one can afford to stay at home, empirical evidence from across the United States indicates an important trend that affects the perception and reality of family wealth, purchasing power, and standard of living. Over time, there has been a clear decline in the rate of growth of the real wage: indeed, the growth rate averaged

2% during the late 1950s and 1960s, 0.5% during the early 1970s, and dropped to -0.6% during the late 1970s.[24] Since wages are not growing as they did in the past, the purchasing power of families is also not growing as it once did. It follows that the number of women who feel that they can afford to stay out of the labor force is decreasing. In order to maintain the standard of living they had in the past, families now need two earning adults instead of one. Empirical evidence from two economic studies supports this.

First, Lester Thurow argues that currently two incomes are necessary to sustain a comfortable, middle-class standard of living.[25] While his contention is disputed by other studies that claim that the baby-boomer generation lives better than its parents did,[26] there is no doubt that the additional income provided by women's work enables families to consume more, consume bigger, and consume better. Second, in order to maintain the same household income, it is necessary to work more hours than in the past. Or, as a study by the Census Bureau points out, workers are working longer hours for the same pay, and to the extent that their incomes are rising, it is because they are doing more work, not because they are being paid more.[27]

While the above may explain why women work for economic necessity, it sheds no light on why women who have no economic necessity work. The answer to that question is the principal theme of this book.

HOW DO WOMEN WORK?

How do working women in America manage? How do they manage to raise kids, work outside the home, work inside the home, be supportive and desirable spouses or partners, care for their elderly relatives, and maintain their sanity? The balancing and juggling acts performed by millions of American women have been the focus of numerous books, studies, conferences, and discussions. In essence, the answer to how working women manage to juggle home and work consists of two possible solutions: either "something's gotta go" or "someone's gotta come."

"Something's gotta go" has two components. First, there is a reduction in the overall standards of quality with respect to the performance of selected chores. Cleanliness, perfection, and order are given up so as to save time and energy. For example, bedsheets are washed bimonthly instead of weekly; children watch television in lieu of receiving parental attention; take-out food replaces home-cooked meals, and so forth. Moreover, all activities deemed unnecessary are replaced by chores deemed essential for household survival. For example, the Monday night book-club meeting is eliminated, the lunch with the girlfriends is skipped, and the husband's shirts aren't touched up with the iron. Thus, the "something's gotta go" refers to the reduction of both quality as well as the range of activities that women engage in.

The second component of the "something's gotta go" solution refers to homemakers who leave the home and go to work. In order to manage their responsibilities and demands at home, some homemakers are drawn to the labor market in the hope that their earnings will enable them to alleviate some of their pressures. Indeed, although employment increases the pressures in women's lives, the income it generates enables the purchase of amenities and services that more than offset the increase in pressures and thereby make their lives more manageable. Alternatively, women are drawn to the workforce in order to escape the chaos and the incessant demands of their homes. In these cases, while income remains the primary reason for working, additional hours of work are taken on as a way of managing by escaping. As Arlie Russell Hochschild argued in her recent study of an American corporation, employees often work overtime because home has become work while the workplace offers the rest, relaxation, and support that the home used to offer.[28]

The second solution to women's overwhelming responsibilities entails the concept of "someone's gotta come." According to this solution, additional pairs of hands are brought into the household to alleviate the pressures on the primary caregiver. Just who do those extra hands belong to? The answer depends on the socioeconomic background of the household. Among women with high household income, "someone's gotta come" usually refers to hiring assistants with specific tasks to alleviate stress in any particular area. This includes housekeepers to clean, babysitters to care for children, drivers to transport children, laundresses to wash laundry, and so forth. Among women with low household income, hiring household help is not a realistic option. Instead, they tend to engage in barter arrangements in which they exchange services with friends and neighbors: the I-care-for-your-child-while-you-do-my-groceries syndrome is thriving in many neighborhoods across America. In addition, the extended family is harnessed to help out and share the burdens of daily life. Indeed, three-generational living arrangements have been known to serve numerous functions, as older generations care for the young, younger generations make the old feel useful, and together they free the middle generation to work outside the home for pay. Also, the single aunt, the widowed mother, and the unemployed brother all might get room and board in exchange for helping out with household chores. Alternatively, middle- and low-income women participate in cooperative arrangements in their neighborhoods or workplaces that provide services such as babysitting, carpool driving, and after-school care that are repaid in kind rather than money.

Women manage by juggling and setting priorities and by constantly reevaluating those priorities. Those who attempt to retain quantity and quality in all their activities, and who do not get help to relieve their pressures, are likely to burn out sooner and faster than others.

WOMEN WITH CHOICES AND EMPLOYMENT TRENDS

This brief description of the what, when, where, how and why of female employment has served to indicate the principal trends that are emerging in this country. However, they are just that—trends. As such, they describe the big picture for the majority of women. Women with choices, a subset of American women, are outside most mainstream trends. Given their small number and their unique characteristics, they are on the fringe of several bell-shaped curves, be they ones that measure household income, wealth, or education. Nevertheless, a study of overall employment trends is useful insofar as it provides an overview of the world into which these women will be entering and which will ultimately shape their long-term prospects and possibilities.

Notes

1. At one end of the spectrum of the home vs. work debate are writers such as Joan K. Peters, *When Mothers Work: Loving Our Children Without Sacrificing Ourselves* (Reading, Mass.: Addison-Wesley, 1997) who advocates that mothers should work outside the home. At the other end of the spectrum are those who argue that women should remain outside the labor force (see, Cindy Ramming, *All Mothers Work: A Guilt Free Guide for the Stay At Home Mom*, New York: Avon Books, 1966).

2. However, this trend varies by class. Indeed, lower-income women have been working outside the home for much longer than upper-income women.

3. The majority of the 3,000 women surveyed for the Virginia Slims Opinion Poll expressed this desire (*Working Mother*, April 1996, p. 18).

4. Natasha Walters, *The New Feminism*, London: Little Brown, 1998, p. 186.

5. Walter Mead, "Domestic Saints in the Next Revolution," *Worth*, April 1994, p. 41.

6. Mead, p. 41.

7. *Economist*, March 5, 1994, p. 80.

8. Juliet Schor, *The Overworked American*, New York: Basic Books, 1992, p. 25.

9. Joyce Jacobsen, *The Economics of Gender*, Cambridge, Mass.: Blackwell, 1994, p. 114.

10. Jacobsen, p. 43, 44.

11. Jacobsen, p. 114.

12. Single women participated in the labor force at the rate of 66.5% (Jacobsen, p. 42).

13. N. Tuma and G. Sandefur, *Trends in the Labor Force Activity of the Elderly in the United States* (Reprint #587) Madison, Wisc.: Institute on Research on Poverty, 1988.

14. Elizabeth Markson, "Older Women in Labor," in Elizabeth Markson, ed., *Older Women*, Lexington, Mass.: Lexington Books, 1983, p. 73.

15. Especially marked is the dead-end phenomenon for older women. See Ellen Rosen, "Beyond the Sweatshop: Older Women in Blue-Collar Jobs," in Elizabeth Markson, op. cit., pp. 75–91.

16. See Shirley Burggraf, *The Feminine Economy and Economic Man*, Reading, Mass.: Addison-Wesley, 1998, p. 16.

17. Ruth Sidel, *Women and Children Last: The Plight of Poor Women in Affluent American*, New York: Penguin Books, 1987, p. 60 (cited in Naomi Wolf, *The Beauty Myth*, New York: Anchor Books, 1991, p. 25).

18. However, 85% of female executives said they were optimistic about their prospects for promotion. This is due to their success at developing styles that men are comfortable with (namely, playing golf and holding their own in corporate politics). It also entailed having time-management skills, above average physical stamina, and supportive husbands. Then, they claim, they can have both a child and a job. These are the results of a CATALYST study (a women's professional support organization). See *Philadelphia Inquirer*, February 28, 1996.

19. Kathleen Gerson, *Hard Choices, How Women Decide about Work, Career, and Motherhood*, Berkeley: University of California Press, 1985, p. 81.

20. This industrial classification of the labor force changes because of the nature of the three sectors: services tend to be labor-intensive and are thus most likely to absorb

workers; manufacturing tends to be more capital-intensive and so absorbs relatively fewer workers; agriculture experiences a net overall decline in the quantity of labor that it requires.

21. *Economist*, March 5, 1994, p. 80.

22. This number is only slightly lower than for men: 53.3% and 52.9%, respectively. *Working Women, A Chartbook*, Bulletin 2385, cited in Jacobsen, p. 114.

23. The *Wall Street Journal*, September 1, 1994.

24. Jacobsen, p. 136.

25. Lester Thurow, "The New American Family," *Technology Review*, August-September 1987, pp. 26–27.

26. In 1993, a study by Richard Easterlin, Christine Schaeffer, and Diane Macunovich said that the economic status of young Americans was higher, on average by two-thirds, than that of their parents when they were the same age. Another study by the Urban Institute and Congressional Budget Office said that baby boomers in 1989 had 55% higher pre-tax income than their parents 30 years earlier. Both studies are cited in the *Wall Street Journal* January 25, 1996.

27. The *New York Times*, October 5, 1997.

28. Arlie Russell Hochschild, *The Time Bind: When Work Becomes Home and Home Becomes Work*, New York: Metropolitan Books, 1997.

Chapter 7

The Accommodating Work Environment

Alternative work arrangements have become a dominant theme of the 1990s. The press is discussing them, television is exhorting them, Hollywood is depicting them, and all are guilty of exaggerating them. Such arrangements have been presented by governments, policymakers, and academics as the panacea for the overstretched, overworked, and time-squeezed American worker. They are touted as the new trend in labor relations; they carry the promise of worker salvation. According to this view, alternative work arrangements bring workers a step closer to workers' paradise because they will decrease their overall stress, increase the time available to spend with their children, subdue their marital disorders, and improve their general health. They will also improve the bottom line for businesses by increasing worker productivity, total output, and ultimately even profits. Finally, they will improve the overall macroeconomic picture because they will stimulate economic growth and thus increase the gross national product. Since individuals as well as societies at large will be significantly better off when alternative work arrangements permeate the economy, whoever thought up the concepts should be nominated for the Nobel prize for economics and possibly also for world peace!

Alas, there is no such simple solution to the labor problems facing contemporary Americans. While the benefits of alternative work arrangements as a universal solution for all workers' problems are wildly exaggerated, undoubtedly some benefits to some workers and some employers in some occupations cannot be denied. Women with choices are among those for whom alternative arrangements, in their many forms, have both promise and potential. They stand to benefit from the newly accommodating work environment because of their particular circumstances and conditions.

ALTERNATIVE WORK ARRANGEMENTS

Flexibility is a key component of alternative work arrangements. What exactly does flexibility in the workplace mean? It means tailoring work conditions to fit the particular worker. It means having the option to change those conditions as circumstances change. It also means accommodating the nonwork demands that regularly pressure workers. Flexibility may translate into taking time off from work to care for a dying relative, to address child-related emergencies, and to engage in personal growth activities. It may also entail choice with respect to the physical space in which workers perform their duties (including work-at-home options). Moreover, flexibility may provide workers with a choice in the scheduling of their work activities (such as condensing a 40-hour week into four days).

Flexibility underlies all the forms of worker accommodation that have emerged in the American work scene. Numerous permutations, options, and possibilities for workers exist in the 1990s and new ones are arising every year. Changes in the workplace occur in response to changing conditions, demands, and expectations. Just like the work environment of one hundred years ago had none of the worker protection that currently exists, so too today's accommodating programs will seem inadequate by tomorrow's standards. Indeed, some one hundred years ago, the capitalist economy rarely accommodated its workers' needs. Workers had few rights and even less protection. Over time, the nature of capitalism underwent a fundamental transformation so that presently, social, health, and welfare concerns of the workforce are at an all-time high. It is likely that the capitalist system will continue to accommodate its workforce. It will do so because there will be both a demand for such accommodation and because it will be possible to supply it, as discussed in this chapter.

Today, there is no single package of accommodations that is available to all workers, no single blueprint that is universally applied across all occupations. In her study of work, Elizabeth Perle McKenna said that there can be no one single model of work that works for everyone.[1] Instead, work-related policies and programs have had to take into account the very diverse composition of the modern workforce, complete with its very diverse goals and needs. Moreover, Stephanie Coontz studied the workforce and showed how the profile of the American family changed drastically over the past few decades and how a changing family requires a change in the nature of work.[2] American households, she notes, have changed so profoundly that they can no longer be defined by one simple definition. The typical family of the 1950s, which included a breadwinning father and a homemaker mother, is not so typical anymore. Indeed, that family profile is now a minority, given that the single-parent households, the dual-income families, and the adult-without-minors homes have become more common. Single parents, unwed mothers, mothers with small children, and husbands with working wives are the new workers of the contemporary labor force, and a changing profile implies changing needs. Those needs are as diversified as the workers themselves. How does the workplace currently accommodate workers' demands and what forms of accommodation are available to them? What are the alternatives to programs designed with a certain type of family in mind, the type that is now a rarity? Some possibilities that accommodate particular needs of particular workers are described below.

Part-Time Work

The 40-hour work week has been the standard in the American workplace for some 60 years. During that time, a parallel alternative developed: part-time work. Today, it is the most common alternative to the 9 to 5, 40-hour per week job. It is defined as work for less than 35 hours per week. According to this definition, over one-quarter of all employed women work part time, while only slightly more than 10% of men are part-timers.[3]

The general trend for men and women alike is an increase in part-time work. Indeed, in the 1970s, the number of part-time jobs increased by 68%, and by 1980, almost one-fourth of all jobs were part time.[4] Macroeconomic conditions (such as those associated with recession) undoubtedly contribute to this increase, resulting in a rise in workers who search for full-time work but cannot find it. At the same time, microeconomic conditions in the labor market, embodied in the nature of demand and supply of part-time work, also explain the observable increase. More employees are demanding part-time work and more employers are supplying part-time jobs.

What is the attraction to employees and employers of part-time work? Workers pursue it because it offers them more free time than they would have in full-time employment. This free time, to be spent in household, leisure, or moonlighting activities, enables a balancing of work and family that is desirable to many workers, especially women.[5] Employers want it because it reduces their total wage bill in two ways. First, it allows them to employ workers only when they need them, rather than maintaining people on their payrolls during slack periods. Second, part-timers cost less on an hourly basis than full-timers in part because they do not qualify for fringe benefits such as paid sick leave, holidays, or occupational pensions.

Lest the labor-market analysis described above conveys too rosy a picture of part-time work, it should be added that it is by no means a panacea for working women. Indeed, a study of some 188 Fortune 500 manufacturing firms in 1990 found that while 88% of them offered part-time work, only 3 to 5% of their employees made use of it.[6] Why? Clearly, the attraction of the free time associated with part-time work should be viewed in light of the numerous negative connotations that make the personal costs of part-time work very high. These costs include the fact that part-timers are likely to have no benefits as well as lower incomes and lower status than full-time workers.[7] Moreover, part-timers tend to be excluded from promotions and are ineligible for high-level positions. They are also often on the fringe of social activities of the workplace and suffer discrimination at all levels. Part-timers may be viewed with disdain by full-time workers who perceive they are unjustly carrying an unfair share of the total work weight. Finally, the stress level of the part-timer does not decrease with the number of hours worked. Indeed, a recent survey by *Working Mother* magazine found that women working 32 hours a week or less have roughly the same overall stress levels as women who work full time, although a higher percentage of their stress comes from the home rather than the workplace. This is due to the fact that more demands are put on them by family members who perceive their part-time work as incidental and therefore fail to take it seriously. Indeed, both family and bosses underestimate what women working part time do.[8]

In an effort to further dispel the notion of part-time work as a universal panacea, it is noted that not all occupations lend themselves to shortened work hours and reduced responsibility levels, therefore part-time work is not even a choice for most workers. For example, it is unlikely to find a CEO of a corporation or a high-level manager working part time. The type of occupations that tend to be part time and the type of people who prefer to work part time do not necessarily coincide. This results in a paradoxical situation across the American labor scene: many workers are looking to work part time, while many of those working part time are searching for full-time employment.[9]

Alternative Work Schedules

Increasingly, workers have been demanding the right to choose a work schedule that is more closely aligned to their particular needs and conditions. In order to meet this demand, employers have offered several forms of alternative work schemes. None are universally available and all are in a state of flux as policies and guidelines are in the process of dynamic transformation.

Flextime, the term associated with flexibility in working hours, offers employees the possibility of varying their work schedules to suit their needs. In the least, flextime entails changes in starting and quitting time and at the most it includes altering the number of hours worked per day or per pay period. Compressed workweeks are an alternative for workers who opt to work 40 hours in less than five days a week. This usually entails putting in four ten-hour days. Paid time off (PTO) allows employees to pool their vacation, sick, and personal days together and to use them however they please, with no questions asked.[10] Moreover, it allows them to carry over their free days into the next year. Finally, leave banks offer employees the possibility of borrowing extra days off, over and above their regular sick leave, in order to cope with their own or a family member's medical emergency. They borrow from days that other workers have donated.[11] While it may seem incredible that some workers would donate their vacation days, such magnanimous behavior has indeed been observed (especially in cases in which donations are extended to friends in need).[12]

Just how widespread is time flexibility in the workplace? Years ago, the economist Paul Samuelson noted: "In contrast with freedom in the spending of the money we earn, the modern industrial regime *denies us a similar freedom in choosing the work routine* by which we earn those dollars."[13] While some firms do offer flextime, most employers do not offer the possibility of a tradeoff between time and income. To the extent that employees increase their labor productivity, this increase is passed on to them in bonuses and in raises, but not in flexibility.[14] Nevertheless, by 1987 some 43% of U.S. firms offered it in some form to their workers.[15] However, while there is no doubt that some time flexibility is being offered, there is also no doubt that it is not getting the response that was expected. In her study of how families balance their work and home time, Arlie Russell Hochschild focused on a large corporation that had the reputation of being extremely family friendly. Focusing on its flextime program, Hochschild notes that while it was the single most popular of its worker friendly programs, it was only used by one-quarter of all workers and one-third of working parents.[16] Hochschild was not alone in her findings—a study of Fortune 500 firms indicates that while 45% of sampled manufacturing firms offered it, only 10% of their employees used it.[17]

Despite its slow penetration into the workplace, flextime is considered the most significant recent change in the American labor scene. It represents the first major questioning of the standard workweek and workday that has occurred in 60 years. As a result of its potentially enormous impact on the way in which people work and produce, various interest groups are taking strong positions, and the discussions of its pros and cons are likely to persist into the future.

Alternative Work Location

In some occupations, employment no longer necessitates confinement to a single work location such as a desk in an office. It is clear that one's job can be performed, one's responsibilities carried out, and one's deadlines met from a variety of locations. As a result, numerous employers are offering flexplace, a program allowing workers to work from any location in addition to their office.

The most common of these alternative locations is the home. Evidence shows that the home office is moving into the mainstream of American work life. It has become popular not only for self-employed individuals but also for employees of large and small firms. This trend is due to a myriad of social and economic changes, not the least of which are the realities of corporate downsizing and the desire of parents to combine work and family life. The home office has been enabled by the advent of affordable computers, modems, and fax machines. By keeping in touch with one's office through telecommuting, workers have the freedom to work when they want. For women with family obligations, the home office has provided the freedom to work at night and over the weekend. It is for this reason that Paul Saffo, director of the Institute for the Future, said, "The workplace turned into a work space when we added a new dimension to the office: electronic communications."[18]

The possibilities of working at home and being connected electronically to the office are growing not only because workers want it but also because employers want to offer it. Due to their concern with worker retention, employers are motivated to keep their valued workers happy and so indulge those who want flexibility in their work location. Also, in their concern with the bottom line, employers are motivated to cut their overhead expenses (which they can if workers work at home). As a result, 30% of the one hundred companies nationwide surveyed by *Home Office Computing* had a telecommuting program in place.[19]

However, despite its increasing proliferation, the virtual office poses problems both for the worker as well as the employer. Workers who work at home encounter difficulties in separating work and leisure. Many have found that work has a way of creeping into what was traditionally leisure time, and the lines have become at the least blurred and usually altogether obliterated. Moreover, some have difficulty concentrating and keeping focused as the forces of distraction are greater at home than in an office environment. From the employer's point of view, workers who work at home are more difficult to control and supervise. They are not part of the team and they fail to develop the camaraderie that comes from sharing a physical space with other workers. As a result, they often fail to develop the loyalty to the workplace that comes from sustained daily contact.

Obviously, not everyone can nor wants to work at home. While 47% of workers report that they would like to have a job in which they could opt to work out of their home, the number that actually can do it is small.[20] Working at home is possible only in a small number of occupations. According to the U.S. Bureau of Labor Statistics, those who work at home tend to perform white-collar jobs. Incidentally, they also tend to be white males (although among those who work only at home, and nowhere else, women outnumber men more than two to one).[21]

The number of people working at home at least some of the time, whether for themselves or someone else, was 41.1 million in 1993 (33% of the adult labor force). This number is growing 8.9% per year.[22] Of these workers, 42% are female, 78% are married, and 66% have children. Of the men and women combined, 7.6 million work as telecommuters—company employees who work at home part or full time (this is the fastest growing category). Another 9.2 million bring their work home from the office with them.

Job Sharing

Job sharing entails splitting one position among two people. The most common form of job share comes from husband-wife teams who view it as a single job that enables one parent to be with the children at all times. Alternatively, it is a form of work that appeals to women who share interests and skills and who prefer the free time associated with what is in effect part-time work for each of them. The appeal of job sharing is due to the fact that it can overcome some drawbacks associated with part-time work: for example, a single position may be promotionable, it may be at a high level, and it may entail benefits, while a part-time position is not.

While job sharing might sound appealing to some, it has generally not been very popular. Howard Hayghe showed that only 16% of firms across America offered the opportunity for job sharing.[23] The assessment is even more dismal according to a study by the Families and Work Institute, which indicated that while job sharing was offered informally by 48% of surveyed companies and formally by 6%, only 1% of workers made use of it.[24] Clearly there remain many unresolved issues, both on the demand and supply side. Although the concept of job sharing is still sufficiently innovative to prevent a clear assessment of its benefits, some difficulties have made it less than appealing from the employee's point of view, such as the fact that job sharing raises the sensitive question of how to divide the paycheck, sick time, vacation time, and pension benefits. Because this is an internal matter to be negotiated between the job sharers, the employer offers no solutions and takes no mediating stands.

Family-Related Benefits

Standard benefit packages for employees, including health care, retirement, and life insurance, were conceived when the typical family consisted of a male earner and a female homemaker. Given the diversification of the labor force over time, additions and modifications to standard benefits were needed to coincide with its evolving demands.

Two types of family benefit plans are currently in existence. One involves the allocation of a specified amount of money, predetermined by the employer, for employee benefits. It permits covered employees to select from a specified assortment of possibilities (known as dependent care). Another type of plan involves the use of money taken out of paychecks on a pretax basis, which may be used by employees for particular job-related expenses, such as care of dependents (known as pretax set-asides). About 13% of American workers are covered by one of these two plans.[25]

Family leaves, introduced under the Family and Medical Leave Act,[26] are a novel form of accommodation that appeals to workers who must care for family members. These come in several forms, including maternity leave (often consisting of six weeks paid leave and six months unpaid leave), paternity leave (often up to six weeks paid leave with one week granted for each year of employment), adoption leave to care for an adopted child, family care leave to care for a seriously ill family member, and foster care leave to care for a foster child who enters the family (all these family leave benefits are only available to full-time workers).

Moreover, when working for someone else, some employees are likely to be offered some of the following programs: on-site daycares, transition time, and spouse relocation programs.

On-Site Daycare. Given that mothers with small children constitute the largest increase in the labor force, childcare has come to demand the attention of employers as well as policymakers. Employers are finding that by providing a childcare solution, the stress workers feel during the separation from their infants decreases and thereby their productivity increases. As a result, both large and medium-sized enterprises have been installing or considering on-site facilities for their workers' offspring.

Transition Time. Offered by some companies, transition time allows a post-partum woman to phase back into her job on a part-time basis for a limited time period, before she returns to full-time work. This program, also known as "phase-back," allows new mothers to temporarily adjust the balance between work and children more in favor of children. By making use of this benefit, the working mother keeps in touch with her job, stays in line for promotions, and is present when salary increases occur. Thus, she remains "attached" despite her absence.

Spouse Relocation. Firms that relocate a member of a two-career family may accommodate the employee by helping find employment for the spouse. It is an increasingly common form of aid that enables two-career families to manage their lives in light of career moves. In the past, when a geographical conflict arose, it was usually the women's career that was disrupted or sacrificed in order to enable the move. With the increasing need for two incomes, coupled with the increased assertiveness of working women, families are either not willing to move (and thereby the husband sacrifices his promotion) or one of the two workers resorts to commuting. In order to ease the pain of either of those solutions, employers are undertaking a more active role in finding employment for the spouse. Nepotism rules are falling by the wayside as jobs within the company are seriously considered.

SELF-EMPLOYMENT

Self-employment, an alternative to working for an employer, may entail working alone or hiring other workers and being a boss.[27] Self-employment is increasing in popularity across America. Both men and women are turning to it as a viable alternative form of employment. An assessment of the trend in the labor force over the past two decades reveals that for male civilian workers, the proportion who were self-employed in 1963 was 11.6%, it dropped to 8.2% in 1973 and then rose to 10.7% in 1992.[28] Women also experienced a decline and a rise during the same period: from 6.2% in 1963 to 4.4% in 1973 and to 6.0% in 1992. Generally, self-employment rates for men and women move together, with the male rate higher than the female rate.

Among possibilities in self-employment, setting up one's own business has been both popular and prominent. In 1995, American women have come to own eight million businesses (one-third of the total), and their numbers are growing at double the rate of firms owned by men.[29] The number of women employed in female-owned companies of over one hundred workers is rising more than twice as fast as the average for all such American firms. Moreover, women-owned firms also have more staying power than the average firm: three-quarters of those that existed in 1991 are still in existence, as compared with two-thirds of all American companies.

Self-employment, as any other form of employment, has both positive and negative aspects. Time, money, and motivation are key considerations in its overall assessment. Generally, self-employment is considered a less desirable form of work because it is riskier, it is harder to establish benefits such as health insurance, and there is no consistent and dependable salary. It entails an enormous time commitment and imparts upon the worker an enormous responsibility. The self-employed worker often has difficulty staying focused and motivated, as well as managing her time. If working on her own, she has to deal with isolation from colleagues. Moreover, she might have difficulty finding start-up capital. Despite these considerations, self-employment has consistently appealed to many because of its numerous advantages over working for others. While the time commitment is enormous, it is largely self-determined. While the hours are long, working for oneself offers freedom and flexibility that is unavailable under the eye of supervisors. Self-employed workers are more easily motivated since they do what they want to do and they do not need to share the benefits of their labor with others. If self-employment takes place in the home, then other advantages kick in. For example, the home offers tax breaks for those who use part of their home space regularly and exclusively as an office. Also, as noted by *the Home Business News Report*, the benefits of self-employment in the home also include one-minute commutes and blue jeans.[30] As a result of these considerations, in 1993, 12.2 million people ran full-time businesses from home, while some 12.1 million worked part time from their home office.[31]

In response to questions of why women have left their employers in order to be self-employed, three out of four self-employed workers said that being their own boss gives them a sense of security, achievement, and recognition for doing a good job.[32]

If self-employment is viewed as a less desirable option for women, then the fact that it is increasing in popularity might be a reflection of the declining opportunities in employment with firms. However, if self-employment is considered a desirable alternative, then its rising rate is a reflection of the fact that more and more people are opting for it as a way of increasing their total work satisfaction.

DEMAND AND SUPPLY OF ALTERNATIVE WORK ARRANGEMENTS

A flexible and accommodating work environment holds enormous appeal to all workers, especially those who are primary care-providers to their families.[33] It is women who usually fill that role, and in order to fill it better, they want to increase their options for balancing their work life with their home responsibilities. When the household demands for their attention do not coincide with the 9 to 5 workday, flexibility in work scheduling, work location, and work conditions all increase women's options. The greater their options, the lower the stress associated with worry about the possible future needs they may have. Women want the peace of mind that comes from knowing that they can, if needed, more effectively juggle their home and work responsibilities. Flexibility in work time, for example, is crucial for working mothers who are sensitive to the amount of time they spent commuting to work. If they have the option of avoiding rush-hour traffic, most will gladly take it. Flexibility in workdays is also important because it enables women to shuffle, condense, and compartmentalize their work in ways that suit them and their families. It enables them to better control the time they can devote to nonwork activities, be they personal leisure or family-related chores. Moreover, if they can have the peace of mind associated with taking their baby to an on-site daycare where they can pop in during the day, they will appreciate it.

While it may seem obvious that women want an accommodating workplace, it is less clear why employers provide it. There are, in fact, several reasons why it makes sense for a profit-maximizing firm to accommodate its female (and male) workers. Those reasons have become so compelling that the Wharton School at the University of Pennsylvania has created a special master's degree program that trains people to advise employers on how to accommodate their workers.[34] Some of those reasons are discussed below.

Capacity

Employers accommodate workers because they can! Technological advances have enabled work styles and work relationships to permutate in ways that may have seemed impossible only a decade ago. The spread of modern technology has increased the possibilities in the relationship between work and worker in many types of jobs. Telecommunication makes it possible to work in a variety of locations and remain electronically connected to the office by way of fax machines, modems, and electronic mail. In other words, the capacity for flexibility in schedule and location has increased and continues to do so.

Profit

Employers accommodate workers because by doing so they can maximize their profits. Profit maximizing businesses carefully consider the costs and benefits of accommodating their workers. To the extent that they adopt family-oriented policies it is because they perceive that the benefits of doing so outweigh the costs. How do they in fact measure those costs and the benefits? Costs for the employer take the form of out-of-pocket expenses, as well as expenses associated with scheduling problems, hiring of replacements, and reformulating existing policies. These costs have to be adjusted when employers trade wage increases for some family benefits. Incidentally, studies have shown that the most cost-effective strategies for employers are programs such as flextime, job sharing, and part-time hours, while on-site daycare is the most expensive.

Benefits, on the other hand, may include increased attractiveness of their firm in the recruitment process, as well as greater appeal to workers that will reflect itself in high retention rates. Indeed, workers who might have quit work for family reasons often decide to stay on if they work in an accommodating workplace. With high retention rates, employers save on turnover costs, which are often significant.

Firms also accrue benefits associated with increased worker productivity. Indeed, accommodation of worker's needs has proliferated in part because employers realized workers are more productive when they are satisfied. The happier they are, the more and better they will work. So in their desire to maximize labor productivity, employers have made adjustments to the workplace that suit workers (and indirectly benefit themselves). It is for this reason that some large employers have introduced, for example, on-site daycare facilities. They have also responded to health demands of their workers: the workplace has become transformed as no-smoking regulations have cleared the air, gyms have provided an opportunity to maintain fitness, and on-site medical facilities have brought health care to the employee. Cafeterias have also come to provide better and healthier food. Finally, workplaces are involved in increasing diet awareness by offering various programs that teach about and modify nutritional behavior of their employees.

Productivity increases also result from better morale and a reduction in absenteeism in accommodating firms. When employers help resolve a workers family-work dilemma, it gives rise to worker loyalty, higher morale, and therefore higher productivity, according to a new body of research. A 1994 survey by Work/Family Directions found that workers in family friendly businesses exhibited reduced absenteeism and superior job performance.[35] Direct reports from selected companies claim that programs such as PTOs (paid time off) can cut unscheduled absences by 40%.[36] Moreover, employers who offer PTOs, for example, have the benefit of scheduled days off, as opposed to unscheduled absences, which are much more expensive. Workers who used to call in sick when they went to a parent-teacher conference cost the employer more than if they had arranged to take a day off weeks in advance. Thus, initiatives to help employees balance work and family responsibilities are saving companies millions of dollars per year.

Government Pressure

Despite the evidence that few employees actually make use of the family friendly programs companies offer, pressure is mounting from both the republican and democratic leadership to set policies that are aimed at making workers happier. This is especially true with respect to flexibility in scheduling work. In the mid-1990s, both republican and democratic leaders claimed to give top priority to such flexibility. In 1996, President Clinton proposed sweeping changes in the concept of flexible work time. His two-pronged approach included allowing all workers to take up to 24 hours per year without pay to participate in children's school activities and to take family members to the doctor. Moreover, the plan included an allowance of up to 80 hours per year to be taken as time off (instead of overtime pay) by workers who prefer time over pay. Labor unions, surprisingly, responded to these changes with criticism. They worry that changing the Fair Labor Standards Act would give employers too much power. They fear that employees might be pushed into working longer hours at less pay.[37]

Social Pressure

Employers accommodate workers because they are under social pressure to do so. As social conditions change, so do the social pressures that act on firms to modify their behavior. Vocal groups, representing various interests within society, have the power to focus attention on burning issues. As more women enter the labor force and as more mothers rise into upper-level positions, pressure is exerted for accommodating change. Moreover, as more men become involved in family life, there will be more pressure to change family-leave policies. Also, as more corporate wives and daughters enter the labor force, corporations will begin to pay attention to family issues in the workplace.[38]

There is already evidence that some companies have responded to social pressures by increasing programs that accommodate their workers. Wells Fargo gives personal growth leaves and Xerox offers social service sabbaticals. Job sharing is possible at Hewlett Packard, Black and Decker, TRW Vidar, and Levi Strauss. Control Data has a part-time program that includes benefits. Body Shop gives its employees one paid half-day per week to engage in volunteer activities. Moreover, First Tennesse National in Memphis sometimes gives paid time off as a reward for finishing a project or meeting a special goal.[39]

Given that firms have realized employees prefer to work in caring firms, they compete to be named on the lists of "Family-Friendly" companies. *Business Week* has joined *Working Mother* in rating employers according to their attention to family issues. The Families and Work Institute in New York publishes a list of family friendly companies[40] and the federal government, through its Women's Bureau in the Department of Labor, also evaluates firms. A growing number of community groups and agencies are starting to pay attention to family friendly policies of firms. Indeed, there are even community awards given to firms that are especially family friendly.[41]

FLEXIBILITY IN THE WORKPLACE AND THE STRUCTURAL TRANSFORMATION OF THE ECONOMY

Flexibility in scheduling and location is not feasible in all occupations. Clearly, assembly line production cannot function efficiently if its members come and go as they please. Administrative assistants also must adhere to the confines of their boss's work schedule in order to effectively perform their duties. On the other hand, jobs entailing relatively solitary work that can be linked to coworkers via telecommunication are less dependent on coordinated schedules and face-to-face encounters. Flexibility in time and location has characterized several types of work for a long time already. For example, university faculty have always had flexibility insofar as they can choose when and where to prepare their lectures, grade their exams, and conduct their research. Also, flight attendants have the option of altering the number of hours that they work per pay period by declining trips in excess of a minimum number per month. Thus, the degree of flexibility that can be offered to the worker is determined by the nature of the work that he or she performs.

Given that flexibility is determined by occupation, in order to understand possible future trends in flexibility, one must hypothesize about the future occupational structure of the United States. While looking into the future is best left to fortunetellers, the structural transformation of the economy (mentioned in

Chapter 6) can shed some light on the possibilities American labor might be faced with. This transformation, consisting of fundamental and structural changes that occur in all growing economies, has been studied at length by economists so that its properties are by now quite clear. The pioneer in this field, Nobel laureate Simon Kuznets, showed that over the past hundred or so years, there has been a shift in the occupational structure of the U.S. economy characterized by a movement toward white-collar jobs and away from blue-collar jobs.[42] These occupational changes reflect the increased relative importance of the service sector (in which jobs tend to be white collar) coupled with the decreasing importance of agricultural and manufacturing jobs (in which jobs are largely blue collar). In other words, the relative share of total employment in agriculture is decreasing a lot, the relative share of employment in manufacturing is decreasing little,[43] and the relative share of employment in services is increasing a lot. This does not mean that the absolute number of jobs in agriculture and manufacturing are necessarily decreasing, but rather that the relative distribution of jobs is changing across the country (indeed, employment rates and job creation are at an all-time high in the mid- to late 1990s).

This changing structure of the labor force in the United States is best understood in light of new trends in the international division of labor. In the mid twentieth century, the United States was the undisputed global center for manufacturing and industrial development. Then, as its economy matured, the services sector increased its relative share in national income and ultimately began to dominate the economy. At the same time, manufacturing began to proliferate in regions outside the U.S. borders, as previously agricultural countries began to develop their industrial bases. By the mid-1960s, Japan overtook the United States with respect to the share of manufacturing in its national income. However, as its economy matured, it was displaced by countries such as Taiwan, Hong Kong, Singapore, and South Korea where manufacturing took off. By the mid-1990s, another tier of states (including Malaysia, Thailand, and Indonesia) emerged as countries with the most dynamic manufacturing sectors. Since maturing economies become increasingly service-oriented when they lose their manufacturing advantage, it follows that most new job creation occurs in the service sector. This is indeed what occurred in the United States. A greater share of the national product is now produced by services, and a greater share of employment occurs in that sector. According to all indicators, we have moved into the post-industrial phase in which the service sector will continue to play an increasing role in the economy.

Such a long-term trend in the global division of labor and the national sectoral distribution of jobs has implications for the future of work flexibility. To the extent that future job creation is in the service sector, overall work flexibility is likely to increase because flexibility is most likely and most possible in the white-collar service jobs.

ACCOMMODATION BY GENDER AND INCOME

While overall both men and women think they have insufficient choices with respect to work issues, men feel they have even fewer than women. In particular, men with dependents do not feel they have any choices at all with respect to work. Yankelovich Partners conducted a survey on choices in the workplace for *Fortune* magazine and report the bitter complaints of a male executive: "Men have responsibilities and women have choices!" he said.[44] The polled men feel that some women have the choice not to work for pay or at least not to work full time, while they do not share that choice. Moreover, these men do not feel that they can realistically make use of the accommodating programs offered by their companies. Indeed, they feel they do not have the luxury to partake in programs such as job sharing or compressed work weeks because the price they would pay with respect to their career would be too large to sustain, especially in their capacity as breadwinners. Since most men view themselves as the primary wage earners, they feel they do not have the option to stay home or embark on a new (risky) endeavor.[45] The MORI Socioconsult survey also found that 31% of working men under 35 said that they would like to work partly at home.[46] Moreover, women can ask for part-time work and family leave at their firm while men cannot because they feel they would be penalized much more than women. In the end, it comes down to who is the main breadwinner in a household: as long as women have a husband or partner who is the primary source of income, they have options that men do not have.

To the extent that male workers perceive themselves to have fewer choices than female workers, they are focusing on the choice of whether to work at all. If that is their focus, empirical evidence supports their view: working women are more than four times more likely than working men to leave their workplace.[47] However, men's perception of having less flexibility than women is not supported by data for the overall workforce: a higher proportion of men than women have flexible schedules (13.2% vs. 11.1%, respectively).[48] It is likely that this is due to differences in occupations among men and women. In Chapter 6, it was noted that 50% of all employed women are concentrated in four occupations: registered nurses, clerks, retail sales, and teachers. Few of these occupations lend themselves to flexibility in time and space: indeed, a teacher cannot start her workday at 10 A.M. and a salesperson cannot work from home. Men, on the other hand, tend to be concentrated in occupations where flexibility is possible.

Accommodation in the workplace also differs across socioeconomic groups. Professional women (with higher earnings) are more likely to be in more accommodating work environments than unskilled women stuck in dead-end jobs. The higher the income, the more professional the job and so the greater and broader the range of options to accommodate workers. The jobs that pay little tend to be in unskilled occupations that least lend themselves to accommodation. Indeed, employers in manufacturing or the petty service sector, such as fast-food establishments, are less prone to offering in-site daycare or flextime. Moreover, professional women are more educated and thus have a greater ability to negotiate accommodating work conditions than women in low-skill, menial jobs.

TRADEOFFS FOR WORKING WOMEN

When women consider making use of programs that accommodate their needs, such as switching to working part time or working flexible hours, they carefully examine the costs and benefits of their choices. In this personal cost-benefit analysis, working women have to consider possible tradeoffs in their choices. Tradeoffs, an ever present component of every decision-making process, involves allocating priorities among different outcomes since, as discussed in Chapter 1, one cannot have them all, one cannot achieve them all, one cannot do them all. The biggest tradeoff working women face is between home and work. When women ponder the relative importance they want and can give to family versus to their work, they take into consideration just how seriously they want to pursue their career, how much time and energy they want to devote to it, and what they are willing to give up in order to succeed in that career.

Womens' deliberations about their tradeoffs have resulted in a variety of combinations of family and career. Some women have chosen to excel at their careers and forgo family life altogether; others have excelled at work but have chosen to juggle family and to pay the price of that juggle. Toward the other end of the working spectrum, women have chosen to forgo career advancements in favor of more time and energy for their families; others have decided to forgo their careers altogether.

This range of possibilities brings to mind the pioneering and highly controversial research by Felice Schwartz, which resulted in the phrase "mommy track."[49] The mommy track has come to be associated with settling for a less ambitious job, with lower pay and lower status, but one which would have sufficient flexibility to enable women to adequately combine work and family. This is to be distinguished from the other track in which women devote themselves to their careers while forgoing having children (or at least actively rearing them). Schwartz defined these two tracks because she perceived a need to address a recurring problem: professional women were being torn between the demands of their job and the demands of their family, and as a result some dropped out of the employment race altogether. In so doing, they have conveyed to employers an erroneous impression that all women will behave that way. One of the results of this impression is that investment in the female labor force, in the form of promotion and training, is a wasted effort because they will leave anyway, as soon as they get pregnant. The solution to this inappropriate view, according to Schwartz, is for women to choose which track they want to follow in their work-family lives.

By speaking openly about this issue, Schwartz thought that both women and employers could make the necessary adjustments. Opposition and protest to this exposition of the possible tradeoff between work and family life was vehement and is ongoing, despite the passing of a decade. Opponents to Schwartz's view state that it is not right to force women into making such decisions so early in their careers, for once labeled on one track, retracking becomes more difficult with each passing year. Women, the arguments continue, should have the right to change their minds and not be penalized for earlier choices.[50] Moreover, forcing a track choice on women underscores the stereotyping of men and women according to which women are the only ones responsible for parenting. Such a stereotype reduces the role of the father to mere observer status, to a nonparticipating entity.

Despite the negative connotations associated with tracking, there is no doubt that some women are happy to have the option of the mommy track. These women include many middle-aged homemakers with choices. The options within the mommy track and their relevancy for middle-aged women are discussed in Chapter 10.

Notes

1. Elizabeth Perle McKenna, *When Work Doesn't Work Anymore*, New York: Delacorte Press, 1997, p. 184.

2. Stephanie Coontz, *The Way We Really Are: Coming to Terms with America's Changing Families*, New York: Basic Books, 1992.

3. Joyce P. Jacobsen, *The Economics of Gender*, Cambridge, Mass.: Blackwell, 1994, p. 44.

4. Susan Feiner, ed., *Race and Gender in the American Economy*, Englewood Cliffs, N.J.: Prentice-Hall, 1994, p. 4.

5. This free time may also be used for performing a second or a third job, as some 5.9% of women moonlight (Jacobsen, p. 45).

6. Cited in Arlie Russell Hochschild, *The Time Bind: When Work Becomes Home and Home Becomes Work*, New York: Metropolitan Books, 1997, p. 27.

7. For example, part-time workers receive less earnings than one-half of a full-time person (indeed, a full-time associate professor at a liberal arts university typically teaches six to eight courses per year and earns an annual income in the range of $45,000–55,000. That translates into over $5,000 per course per semester, assuming an eight- course load. However, a typical part-time professor teaching one course earns in the range of $1,800–2,500 per course. This differential in earnings is actually significantly underestimated since it fails to include the fringe benefits that the full-time employee earns.

8. *Working Mother*, July/August 1996, p. 22.

9. Indeed, the fraction of the labor force that is seeking full-time work has increased seven times during 1969–87. Schor calls this "enforced idleness" (Juliet Schor, *The Overworked American*, New York: Basic Books, 1991, p. 39).

10. A 1994 survey conducted by Hewitt Associates showed that nearly 17% of 360 companies had already instituted such plans, while another 13% indicated they would in all likelihood follow suit (*Working Mother*, July/August 1996, p. 28).

11. In fact, the term "borrowing," while used in this context, is inappropriate because workers in fact never have to repay those days. Employers limit the number of such days that a worker can withdraw within a given period of time. However, if the bank reserves are low, then the employee's request may be denied.

12. According to the chair of the leave bank committee at the Bureau of National Affairs, Inc., donations of vacation days creates goodwill among workers. Workers make

such donations because they care about their coworkers and hope to have days available to them when they are in need (*Working Mother*, July/August 1996, p. 31).

13. Paul Samuelson cited in Schor, p. 128. Italics mine.

14. Schor says, "Employers rarely have the chance to exercise an actual choice about how they will spend their productivity dividend" (p. 3).

15. Francine D. Blau and Marianne A. Ferber, *The Economics of Women, Men and Work*, 2nd Ed., Englewood Cliffs, N.J.: Prentice-Hall, 1992, p. 184 .

16. Hochschild, p. 26.

17. Hochschild, p. 27.

18. Gloria G. Brame, "Seismic Shifts: How Technology Will Change the Way You Work," *Working Woman*, June 1996, p. 31.

19. The *Miami Herald*, December 13, 1993.

20. The *Miami Herald*, February 10, 1997.

21. The *Miami Herald*, December 13, 1993.

22. LINK Resources, 1993 Work At-Home Survey cited in the *Miami Herald*, December 13, 1993.

23. These data refer to Howard V. Hayghe, "Employers and: What Roles Do They Play?" *Monthly Labor Review*, 111, no. 9 September 1988, pp. 34–44.

24. Galinsky et at., *The Corporate Reference Guide to Work-Family Programs*, New York, Families and Work Institute, cited in Hochschild, p. 263.

25. These are workers in the middle to large range of companies. Bureau of Labor Statistics, *Employee Benefits in Medium and Large Firms*, Washington, D.C.: GPO, 1988.

26. This is a federal law requiring employers with 50 or more workers to give up to 12 weeks of leave to new parents. Also, for details see Commission on Family and Medical Leave, *A Workable Balance: Report to Congress on Family and Medical Leave Policies*, Washington, D.C.: GPO, 1996.

27. Two alternative forms of self-employment have been particularly popular in the recent past, namely freelancing and franchising. Freelancing entails hiring out to others to do temporary and finite tasks (translating a document, trying a single case, editing a book, illustrating a brochure, typing a term paper). Franchising entails having ones own business without having to set it up and begin from scratch. This is a popular alternative in the United States: some 2,100 franchises exist, with more than 478,000 outlets and six million people employed (Richard Nelson Bolles, *The 1996 What Color Is Your Parachute?* Berkeley: Ten Speed Press, 1996, p. 124).

28. Jacobsen, p. 51.

29. *Economist*, August 10, 1996, p. 13.

30. *Home Business News Report* is published by the Home Career Opportunity Conference organizers who offer courses on starting home businesses.

31. The top home-based businesses in 1993 are listed below, along with the proportion of them that are home-based (*Home Office Computing*, 1993 Reader Survey, cited in the *Miami Herald*, December 13, 1993). Business support services (28%), consulting (11%), programming/computer services (9%), communications (8%), secretarial/word processing (7%), financial support services (5%), graphic/visual/fine arts (5%), marketing/advertising (4%), medical services (4%), and real estate (4%).

32. *Working Mother*, July/August 1996, p. 10.

33. This does not mean they will all make use of the programs that they have. Indeed, studies have shown that programs are not always made use of to the extent expected. Women have the possibility of taking six months unpaid absence at the birth of their child, yet they don't. They have the possibility of working part time, yet they don't take it. Various arguments have been offered to explain this behavior. The most widespread

explanation is that women cannot afford to reduce their work time. Alternatively, they worry about their reputation as workers and that their bosses will think they're not serious about their jobs. Possibly women simply don't know about the policies that are available to them. Or possibly the policies are just window-dressing by the companies, and no one is really serious about letting workers make use of them without penalty. Finally, the possibility exists, as Hochschild (1997) has recently stated, women (as well as men) don't make use of accommodating programs because they prefer to be at work than at home.

34. It is a program that combines study of business at the Wharton School of Business with the Graduate School of Education, providing students with a background not only in marketing, finance, and policy but also in early childhood development (in order to enable informed decisions about on-site daycare and other child-related benefits). *Working Mother*, February 1997, p. 12.

35. *Working Woman*, July/August, 1996, p. 55.

36. *Working Mother*, July/August, 1996, p. 30.

37. The *Miami Herald*, February 1, 1997.

38. Katherine Wyse Goldman, *If You Can Raise Kids, You Can Get a Good Job*, New York: HarperCollins 1996, p. 100.

39. The *Wall Street Journal*, September 16, 1998.

40. Goldman, p. 99.

41. The *Wall Street Journal*, August 21, 1996.

42. These findings are the result of research by Simon Kuznets in his analysis of modern economic growth (*Modern Economic Growth*, New Haven: Yale University Press, 1966). There are two reasons why this occurs: one is the result of changes in personal income and the other is due to technological change.

43. In the early periods of economic development, the employment share of manufacturing increased.

44. These insights were revealed at a Focus group conducted for *Fortune* magazine by Yankelovich Partners (*Fortune*, September 18, 1995, p. 72).

45. See also Robert Moffitt "The Tobnit Model, Hours of Work, and Institutional Constraints," *Review of Economics and Statistics*, 64, no. 3, August 1982.

46. Cited in Natasha Walters, *The New Feminism*, London: Little Brown, 1998, p. 162.

47. Thomas J. Stanley and William D. Danko, *The Millionaire Next Door*, Atlanta: Longstreet Press, 1997, p. 182.

48. Blau and Ferber, p. 184.

49. Felice N. Schwartz, "Management Women and the New Facts of Life," *Harvard Business Review*, 67, no. 2 (January–February 1989), pp. 65–76.

50. Opponents to this view are expressed in the letters to the editor in response to Schwartz, *Harvard Business Review*, 67, no. 3, May-June 1989, pp. 182–214.

Part IV

CAPACITIES

Chapter 8

Advantages to Be Harnessed:
Human Capital and
Shadow Skills

Most middle-aged homemakers recognize the depth and breadth of the skills they have acquired while tending to their homes, raising their children, and volunteering in the community (namely, in their second career). They are aware of how demanding their job of homemaker really was, especially in view of their proclivity to apply the same standards of perfection to the home as they applied to their former careers (namely, their first careers). They are also aware of how challenging their volunteer work was, given the often overwhelming managerial, supervisory, and fiscal responsibilities they took on. But most of all, women know how demanding their job of "just mom" really was, requiring them always to be on call, always ready to negotiate, and always ready to lend a comforting shoulder to the many people who expect it. It was a job they performed for 24 hours per day, with no realistic way to "get away from it all." Indeed, most middle-aged women who raised children know that the job description of a mother is one that would fetch an enormous salary if it were offered on the open market. Imagine, for example, the following ad:[1]

Wanted, responsible mature woman who is willing and able to satisfy the intellectual, emotional and physical needs of a varied group of people, and who must at times perform the functions of doctor, driver, banker, cook, electrician, manager, judge, exterminator, and mediator, among others. This position entails a lifetime commitment and once the job is taken, resignations cannot be accepted. The working hours are: 24 hours, 7 days per week, no vacation time for at least 17 years. Moreover, the job entails no pay and no retirement package.

Even though the demands described above are overwhelming, 3.9 million American women answered such an ad in 1994 alone! They did so even though most jobs they might have taken in the labor market were bound to be easier, less stressful, and less demanding than what they will do as mothers. Despite the difficulties entailed in mothering, when women reach middle age, they look back to their mothering, homemaking, and volunteering years as ones in which they acquired numerous important and useful skills.

Many middle-aged women with choices believe they have acquired valuable and attractive skills during their years outside the labor force. However, they also believe that employers fail to recognize them. A discussion of the skills and women's views on marketing them follows.

SHADOW SKILLS: SKILL ACQUISITION IN THE SECOND CAREER

It has been claimed repeatedly that housewife skills are difficult to convey and market to employers. In her study of American women, Judith Bardwick claimed there is a widespread denial that "experience in childcare, household logistics and volunteer organizations has anything to do with management, making decisions, directing people or solving problems."[2] Yet, as most mothers will assert, having children, rearing children, organizing a household, and coordinating activities for all members of the household develop skills that women were not born with. While women have no genetic predisposition to learn to perform such tasks, instinctual survival, goal attainment, and love drive them to develop certain skills that are not significantly different from those required and rewarded in the world of paid employment. Whether a woman volunteers to organize the annual museum ball, whether she manages five in household help, or whether she home teaches a single child, she has had to learn to manage, to juggle, to advise, to make decisions, and to budget her time. Over years of practice, she has become trained and her abilities have become sharpened. Indeed, Cokie Roberts, a newscaster who covers the U.S. Congress, said "the best preparation for covering Congress is being a mother because they [congressmen] all behave like a bunch of two year olds."[3] Similarly, women in their fifties interviewed for the *New York Times* "Review of Women at Work" said that they had trained for the workforce through years of "juggling children, households, graduate school and the occasional work."[4]

This emphasis on homemaking skills is not to deny the importance of formal skills acquired in the formal educational sector (including schools and training programs). Instead, it is meant to underscore the reality that workers have different types of skills and different valid sources for their acquisition. Richard Nelson Bolles, the writer of the immensely popular *What Color is Your Parachute?* wrote that it is a great misconception to think of skills as only what one learns in a structured, formal setting and for what one receives a diploma. Instead, one must think of skills in terms of transferable, functional abilities. Transferable skills are those attributes of an individual that can be transferred from one job to another.[5] Bolles says these are skills with people, skills with information, or skills with things.

Building upon Bolles's contribution, I have identified the skills women acquire in their second careers, and I have divided them into the four categories described below. Women develop and perfect these skills day in and day out in their roles as homemakers, mothers, and volunteers. They are survival skills for the contemporary urban world in which most American women live. While not all women learn the same lessons from their experiences, most develop similar ways of dealing with their complicated daily lives. The skills they acquire can be called *shadow skills* because they are overlooked, they are underestimated, and they are not formally valued by society. They are skills learned in the home classroom, which neither grants degrees nor certification. Shadow skills have questionable value in the labor market because there is no examination nor test that one has to pass in order to prove proficiency or possession of the skill. For example, the raising of a couple of children into adulthood, with all their limbs intact, with no long-term drug use, with a completed college degree, and without a teenage pregnancy would certainly be considered an achievement by most mothers. But it is not an achievement that will provide them with the certification necessary to impress a prospective employer.

Skills in Human Interaction

In their roles as mothers, homemakers, and volunteers, women interact with children, teachers, spouses, household helpers, covolunteers, and others. Over time and with the benefit of experience, women have learned how to make their human interactions most effective and how to maximize the benefit they derive from them. First and foremost, they have learned to be clear about their values and their expectations in order to successfully convey them to others. They have acquired insight into human nature, which helps them to understand, classify, manipulate, and pacify the personalities they deal with. They have learned to supervise people and to tell them what to do. When people become distracted and wander off track, women have had to refocus them to bring them back on track. They have perfected the best way to keep those around them on schedule. They have learned to have patience with people and to adjust when expectations are not met. When dealing with their families, women have had to learn tolerance since they cannot fire nor replace those they work with.

As a result of their mothering experience, many women have undoubtedly become more intuitive, adaptable, sensitive, and compassionate. They have become more nurturing and loving. They have learned to sympathize and empathize. As mothers, they had to listen and to understand, often performing the functions of a priest. They had to provide attention and care when someone was ill or unhappy. They instinctively protected those for whom they are responsible. They also learned to be loyal above all else.

As a result of their diverse human interactions, women in their second careers have developed problem-solving skills to put to use when the occasion demands it. They have also acquired leadership skills in order to provide guidance to the people for whom they are responsible, be they at home or in their volunteer sites. They now have the ability to perform balancing acts when they need to. They have learned to take responsibility for the entire group and keep track of what is ultimately most important for all members. They have also had to become good at learning by doing as well as making decisions by the seat of their pants.

To the extent that they were not flexible before, homemakers had to adapt quickly. They had to learn to take a large share of the family slack and to bend with the demands of the household. In the least, this included being adaptable in their daily activities (for example, adapting their schedule if their child were ill). At the most, women developed flexibility in their life choices (for example, picking up and moving when their husbands' career demands relocation).

With experience, women have learned to inspire, to motivate, to persuade, and to cajole. In their communications with family and friends, they have had to give, guide, help, and intuit. Women have become trained to be advisors and councilors and judges. They have learned to arbitrate, advise, decide, guide, influence, inform, and persuade. They have had to make and to partake in big decisions with far-reaching ramifications. They have thus learned to be responsible and to take responsibility for their actions.

"What do you think you've learned over the past decade or so?" was the question posed to the participants in this study. Then, "Specifically, have you acquired any skills from your experiences as mothers, homemakers, and volunteers?" Women overwhelmingly responded in the affirmative. They consistently described learning, developing, and improving. Despite differences in focus, the overall characterization of homemaking was that it taught women to be all things to all people. The vehemence of women's positive responses points to a strong conviction about the value of their second careers.

June Ellington focused on the lessons she learned from mothering her two little girls. She tells how "being with children has taught me to become more patient. How else would I have survived being at home with little kids so close in age? But there's something much more important that I've learned from them—I've learned to strive to do things better. Raising kids has brought to light all those things that I could do better, if I tried. It's gotten me to push myself closer to my limits, in everything I do." Rebecca Miller believes that being a mother has taught her how to listen to others. Also, she says, "it has taught me to put myself in someone else's shoes and to try to think like they do and feel like they do." Brigitte Kelly describes how "having children and being in touch with children has developed my people skills and listening skills so much more than anything I ever did before. I think if I had no children, I never would have learned these skills." Elise Troy reports that her experience as a mother and volunteer has taught her to motivate and delegate. She explains, "I delegate responsibilities, then I praise and watch people blossom. I motivate others to be the best they can be. I never criticize, instead I pitch in and help. These are rules that I learned from the Junior League and they are the rules I apply to my family."

Francesca Layten reports that after some two decades of mothering, she has become adept at providing solid and consistent support to people. Within her household, she is the pole around which her family gravitates and against which they all lean:

I have learned to keep other people's lives from falling apart. I know that sounds a little arrogant, but it's true. When my children and my husband have problems, I am there to stabilize them. My husband is an attorney and sometimes he has real problems, big problems. At those times, I have to stand behind him and keep him from falling apart. I guess I've learned to be a personal assistant: I've learned the job so well that I think I should be paid by his company. In fact, I think all wives of professional men should get paid by the man's company. I really do. Wives provide such an important stabilizing service to the company yet they are rarely recognized for it.

Several respondents focused on the people skills that they acquired in their second career. Curiously, former professionals were particularly vociferous in their claims that homemaking often increases communication skills more than the labor force. Both Amanda Adams and Rebecca Miller compare how people interact inside and outside the labor force and describe how their capacity at interacting with people in general has broadened during their hiatus from employment. Amanda says: "When you work in a corporation, as I did, you get a very narrow view of how to deal with people. In a corporate environment, people are more or less alike. They have such a narrow view of the world and there is so much political blabla. You can't use that style outside the corporation. As a mother, I encounter so much variety among people and I've had to learn to deal with all sorts of individuals and personalities. I simply didn't have that people-skill before I became a full-time mother."

Rebecca, a former accountant, also perceives a dichotomy between human interactions inside and outside the labor force: "When you work as a CPA, you are mostly surrounded by CPAs and therefore you only communicate with people in one way. As a volunteer and a mother, you have to communicate on so many different levels. Not everyone you come across will have the same background as you, so you have to relearn how to speak in order to reach a wider audience."

Elise Troy is even stronger in her condemnation of her first career people skills. She describes how she became socially adept only as a result of dealing with the mothers of her children's friends and volunteer people, namely, in her second career. She claims "when I worked as an attorney, I was blunt and efficient in all my human interactions. I used what I call 'working briskness' even with people outside of work. It was just the sort of person I had become. Then, when I became a full-time mother and volunteer, I quickly realized I couldn't be so blunt. I had to learn how to be more gracious with people because otherwise no one would have tolerated me. You just can't be nasty while motivating other mothers to work on a school project!"

Finally, Ileana Diaz also reported that her people skills improved over time, despite her premarital professional background. In her case, the improvement was due to the demands of her role as the wife of an important community leader. "I have learned to interact with human beings because that was expected of me in my marriage. I had to become a lot more social than I naturally would have been. My husband forced me into social situations I would have otherwise avoided. Over time, I have learned to be comfortable in them, but it was really hard at first. Now I'm very grateful to him for having had social expectations of me because now I've become more confident and I can interact with a large variety of people with a lot of poise."

Skills in Conveying Information

Homemakers had to develop teaching skills in order to effectively convey information to the many diverse individuals with whom they regularly interact. They had to learn how to explain, to advise, to show, and to define. They had to help their children and other members of their household imagine and discover. In order to do that, they had to coach, inform, lecture, and mentor.

The conditions under which women convey information are often more varied than those experienced by most professional teachers. It is because mothers are their children's role models that their behavior is used as an example. No matter where they are and what they are doing, their values are absorbed by their children and their actions are imitated (since children do as their mother's do rather than as their mothers say). In this way, mothers are always teaching and their behavior is always under scrutiny.

Women also have to convey information using a variety of mediums, most of which professional teaching does not encompass. They teach through play, through song, through drawing, and through imitating. In the process, women perform the functions of storyteller, singer, artist, and actor. In all their actions and all their activities, women have to convey information while simultaneously influencing, motivating, and inspiring.

Ileana Diaz, currently a graduate student in architecture, describes how mothering taught her teaching skills: "In the last ten years, I've become a natural teacher. I never used to be like that before I had children. Now they're telling me that I'm always lecturing, that I'm always teaching them things. I guess it's because I view every day as an opportunity to show my children something new. So it became very natural for me to lecture on architecture and art as part of my volunteering. I've learned to be an effective teacher and to convey knowledge in a way that people actually understand."

Roberta Martin beams with confidence because, she claims, she has learned how to teach people what she knows. She believes she acquired this skill gradually, over the past decade or so that she has been volunteering. "Now, if I have something to say, I don't hesitate to say it. I believe in my views and I seem to be able to get them across to people. Even in public, I'm no longer intimidated or embarrassed as I was before."

Skills in Producing Final Products

In order to fulfill their daily obligations, homemakers are responsible for the production of numerous goods and services for themselves and their families. They have had to become adept at completing a task and at getting a job done. In the process, they have learned that a job half done is not good enough: a meal half cooked, bills half written, a carpool half driven, and a fundraiser half organized are simply not good enough. To the extent that their tasks are not completed and the final products are not evident, no credit accrues and no benefit is derived.

"I now have the confidence that I can produce just about anything!" June Ellington responds when asked if she learned any skills during her second career. She describes herself as a hands-on person who rolls up her sleeves and takes charge both in her home and in her volunteer sites. She spends her days producing things—be they meals for the family, brochures for the church function, or backdrops for the school play. Her abilities sharpened with experience, and she now evaluates, with amazement, the benefit of her learning-by-doing. She explains, "What I have been through and what I have had to learn to do in order to help my kids get through school has taught me to do a lot of things and to see them through to the end. I guess parents who are ambitious for their children will self-teach themselves anything in order to help their kids. And then, long after their kids leave, what they learned stays with them forever."

Skills in Managing and Juggling

In classifying women's work in the home, the World Bank uses the term *home management*.[6] That term was chosen because of the managerial nature of the economic functions that a woman provides in the home. Women with choices, as all women worldwide, have had to manage not only their own lives but also the lives of their household members. Many run households in isolation of their husbands or partners at least some of the time, making numerous decisions on their own (indeed, Patricia Houck Sprinkle claims that over half of American women are home alone much of the time.)[7] They also manage the work activities of hired household helpers such as babysitters, housekeepers, and gardeners. Often without realizing the magnitude of the task, women easily manage some four part-time workers. In the world of work for pay, a very small portion of the labor force manages that many people.

As a result, women had to develop organizational abilities. They had to learn to allocate responsibilities, to administer, and to negotiate. They had to master thinking on their feet and thinking quickly. They had to decide how to allocate time and resources among competing ends. They had to know how to use their power, since much power is exerted in running a household.

Women had to develop the ability to manage groups. That includes judging situations and determining when to get involved in the squabbles of others and when to stay away and let them fight it out. When the individuals in their households stray out of line, women had to become corrections officers. When household members had nothing to do, women created jobs for them.

With experience, women learned not only to be managers but also to be quick managers, often having to respond instantaneously to situations as they arise. Of necessity, they became flexible and adaptable in their management styles.

Homemakers also had to develop and perfect their time-management skills in order to juggle the numerous duties and activities that fill their lives and those of their dependents. They had to learn to plan and to organize both their daily activities as well as their long-term obligations. They learned scheduling and budgeting their time in order to maximize their efficiency, or else bear the consequences of not getting it all done. Thus, they have become adept at multitasking, namely, combining several tasks and performing them simultaneously.

Robin Bifflow, the mother of two high school daughters, says: "I have learned all about management and logistics and supervising. I've also learned to prioritize and to plan and to execute things. It's only in the past decade that I've learned all these things. You see, it wasn't required of me when I worked [for pay]. Being a mother sort of forces you to become a manager, if you know what I mean."

Jennifer Thomas has two children who are straight-A students. She is also a very active volunteer in a major local cultural institution, in which she holds office. "The most important lessons that I've learned from my experience as a homemaker and a volunteer have to do with organization," she says. "I wasn't very organized before, when I worked full time. But I had to become organized in order to survive my current lifestyle. I'm trying to teach my children to become organized at an early age because it will make their responsibilities so much easier to handle. I really believe that organization is the key to life, at least the way we live it."

The estate of Ileana Diaz spreads over a large territory in an exclusive part of town. She manages the maintenance of that property, as she manages her large family. Her husband's career entails a lot of entertainment, all of which she is responsible for. As a result of all the demands she faces, Ileana has become exceedingly efficient. "As a mother in a big family, you learn to be efficient in every gesture, in every movement. If your kids leave things downstairs, you start lining them by the stairs so every time you go upstairs, you take something. That's just a little example of how you have to constantly be thinking about saving time and cutting corners. You just have to figure out how to do everything you need to do to keep it all going, without an enormous amount of time. You have to figure out how to be 100% efficient, all the time."

Being full-time homemakers forces women to function under conditions of "chopped time." According to Amanda, chopped time refers to "the way the day is chopped up for mothers and homemakers. It's so different from the concept of time in an office environment. When I was employed as a computer programmer, I worked on one project at a time. As a full-time homemaker, I have tens of projects ongoing simultaneously. There is never sufficient *consecutive* time to devote to any one of them. My day is all chopped up. It's much harder to function under those circumstances than if you have all day to work on one single thing."

Finally, in her discussion of the management skills acquired by homemakers, Tory Cohen focuses on the experience of women who survived Hurricane Andrew, which hit Miami with full force in August 1992. She explained how dealing with the aftermath of the storm was a major formative experience for many of her female peers, forcing them to become adept at a large number of tasks. She described the conditions under which women acquired the skills they didn't have before and sharpened those they had.

After the total devastation of the hurricane, our husbands went back to their workplaces where they had to collect the pieces of their offices. We wives were left with doing the same at home. Many of us had lost our houses and our belongings, many of us moved our families into hotels or temporary apartments. Over the next year or two, we negotiated with contractors and we negotiated with insurance agents. We had to figure out how to articulate our goals and plans in terms that others could understand. The post-hurricane period was really a major learning experience for me and now I feel ready to take on any negotiation process whatsoever.

ADVANTAGES OF WOMEN WITH CHOICES

In addition to the gender-based advantages that have been identified by feminist anthropologists,[8] women who have acquired the above shadow skills in their second career have advantages in their future job search relative to other unemployed women (especially those who have not had the same experiences or who have not learned the same lessons from those experiences). To the extent that they are also women with choices, they have additional advantages due to their particular socioeconomic background.

First, women with choices have the advantage of a financial safety net so that they do not have to be employed. As a result of their spouse's income or their own independent wealth, they are not desperate to enter the labor market in order to pay their bills and sustain their lifestyles. They can be choosy with respect to what job they take, when they take it, and on what terms. In other words, they have choices with respect to work. According to Christina Garcia, the fact that she is financially secure will help her when she ventures into the business world: "When I set up my own business, I won't have to scrape and if it doesn't work out, I won't lose my shirt."

Second, despite their insecurity about the market value of their shadow skills, women with choices have the advantage of self-confidence. Part of that confidence is rooted in their socioeconomic position and the social status that their household enjoys. Another part is rooted in the education they have acquired (despite the fact that they haven't formally used their degree in many years) and the work experience they had (despite their hiatus from the labor force). Middle-aged women with choices derive confidence from two more sources, both of which are common to numerous other women. Those who are mothers derive confidence from the children they have reared—they become confident when others look to them for advice and for answers. Thus, the experience of motherhood gives them emotional strength and balance, contributing to what Daniel Goleman described as emotional intelligence.[9] Also, as discussed in Chapter 1, many women derive confidence from their age, since in their forties and fifties they finally know who they are and what they want. They have matured and they have "been there, done that." In her study of older women, Cleo Berkun found that many women considered themselves to be more attractive in their midyears than they had been earlier.[10] Such feelings undoubtedly contribute to their overall sense of self-confidence.

Third, women with choices have the advantage of a realistic possibility to reeducate and retool. They have two crucial requirements for such an endeavor—time and money. They have the time since they are not employed and their children are grown (so their mothering duties have decreased). They also have the money to pay for tuition, fees, advice, tutoring, and other expenses entailed in reeducating themselves.

Fourth, while retooling and later while working, women with choices can lighten their load by hiring people to help them or to replace them. Buying services in the form of additional housekeepers, laundresses, and gardeners frees women to pursue their aspirations while maintaining the standards of household order and organization that the family is accustomed to. In so doing, women with choices are exploiting their comparative advantage, since they are presumably more productive in activities other than housework.[11]

Fifth, women with choices who are also mothers have the advantage of a firsthand source of information. In addition to teaching their parents how to be humble (when they ask questions parents can't answer), offering fresh perspectives on old problems and requiring a high degree of compassion and patience, children can also be the source of concrete information. They have acquired this information in their own subculture, one dominated by innovative and dynamic technology. Women looking to penetrate the world outside their home, such as an educational institution or the labor market, can benefit from familiarization with this subculture. Indeed, their future employment is likely to be technology-intensive, and who better to introduce them to that world than their own children, who certainly know more than they do in this area? In this way, women who recognize the potential embodied in their teenage and adult children and who capitalize on it undoubtedly have an advantage over other women.

Sixth, middle-aged women with choices have learned the value of time through years of multitasking and juggling, all of which require getting someplace and finishing something. They have survived numerous school projects and planned numerous volunteer events, all of which entailed serious time constraints. In a workplace environment, these women would have the advantage of recognizing time pressures and knowing what it means to work against a deadline. They would know how to value their time as well as that of their coworkers.

Seventh, women with choices tend to have husbands who are well connected in the business or professional world. Such connections provide a sound basis to begin their own networking and job search. They have access to advice on how to look for work and they may also have access to preferential consideration in job opportunities, should they choose to avail themselves of such options.

All of these advantages are a function of the socioeconomic position of women with choices. Indeed, having a well-connected husband, having a financial cushion, and having the option of hiring household assistants are not advantages shared by women of other socioeconomic backgrounds. To a certain extent, even learning from children is class-biased since low-income families are less likely to have children exposed to the computerized world either in the particular schools they attend or in the homes where they live.

REPACKAGING: HOW TO TRANSLATE SHADOW SKILLS AND ADVANTAGES INTO MARKETABLE ASSETS

While performing their mothering duties and managing their households, women with choices were not paid. An application of market analysis, according to which the wage is a reflection of how much their work is valued by society, indicates clearly that since women's work in the home is not paid for, it is not valued at all. Indeed, an attorney who left her practice to raise and educate her children, who is instilling them with ethics and human values and who is teaching them to be caring individuals and leaders of tomorrow, is valued less by society than a high school dropout who holds a minimum wage job in a fast food chain. Under these circumstances, middle-aged women with choices are wondering how to market themselves in order to compete in the labor market.

Tory Cohen was astute in identifying her current position vis-a-vis the workforce: "The key for women like myself lies in learning how to reframe what we've been doing so as to effectively market it to prospective employers." She is right. Helen Barkey speaks out about marketing her experience as a volunteer: "I think it won't be so hard [to find work]. As a volunteer, I've been associated with some very important associations and when I put that on my resume, I think it'll look great!" She too is right.

The skills that women with choices have acquired during their second career are real and tangible. However, they require manicuring and refinishing before they can be successfully marketed in the world outside the home. In addition to skills, the maturity and experience that have molded and shaped middle-age women also need to be carefully integrated to create a more marketable persona. This repackaging is not only useful but rather it is necessary in order to ensure success in the job search. In the labor market, many recently returned mothers with children are viewed as women with baggage. The stereotypic view is that they will work little, leave work early, produce less than men, renege on their responsibilities, and will not be around for long. It is up to these women both to change the stereotype and to turn whatever baggage they have from negative to positive. The shadow skills that are a part of that baggage, coupled with the advantages they derive from their socioeconomic background, provide women with possibilities to repackage and reformat themselves. Furthermore, when they integrate the training and experience acquired in their first career, women's appeal to potential employers increases manifold.

In order to repackage themselves, there are several steps middle-aged homemakers would benefit from taking. First, they must clearly formulate their goals for the future and they must identify a strategy for achieving them. Second, depending on the nature of their goals, some women must retool and reeducate in order to acquire new skills or renew the ones they previously acquired. Third, they must seek out their family's support because without it, a new beginning will be difficult.

Identification of New Goals and the Strategy for Achieving Them

The lives of homemakers are full of big goals, little goals, and medium-sized goals. The little ones are often not even recognized as goals, yet they are crucial for the daily functioning of their households. They include getting out of bed each day, making the children's breakfast, driving the carpool, marketing for food, returning the neighbor's phone call, and getting to their volunteering activities on time. Medium-sized goals are less routine, take more effort, require more organization, and are accompanied by greater hurdles. They include servicing the automobile, identifying nursing care for an elderly relative, and completing a photography project. Then there are the big goals, the ones that profoundly touch women's lives: for example, chairing the museum fundraiser, having a baby, or moving to a new city, or pursuing a degree, getting a job, or starting a business in middle age.

As a result of their experience with goals big and small, women with choices have recognized the importance of having goals. They have learned that goals satisfy, give impetus to life, and contribute to feelings of happiness, fulfillment and motivation. Therefore, it is imperative to construct such goals, to have many of them, to work on them, and to achieve some of them. While setting goals motivates women into action, the achievement of those goals provides relief, satisfaction, and the push to pursue ever more challenging goals.

But as women's life circumstances change, so do their goals. As women mature and pass through different phases of life, their requirements of themselves change, as do their requirements of their environment and their relationships. When they reach middle age, some women with choices are ready to formulate new goals. They may want to become employed, they may want to pursue a degree, or perhaps they may want to set up their own business. However, the process by which women formulate goals is not the same for all. Some women are simply goaloriented by nature. They are conscious of frequently formulating goals and they are conscious of the satisfaction they derive in attaining them. They are addicted to the process of goal formulation and achievement, and they move from achieved goal to proposed goal with ease. Such goal-oriented personalities cut across cultural, educational, and income demarcations. Contrast this with the lack of goals and the lack of ability to formulate them that characterizes some women's lives. Such women have often relied on others to provide them with direction. Indeed, first parents told them what to aim for, then their religions, their spouses, and their governments stepped in to formulate and guide.

Whether goal oriented or not, women with choices would benefit from applying some of those techniques of home management that helped them achieve household and childcare goals over the past decade or two. For example, in order to attain their new goals, they must stay focused and self-disciplined (taking care not to stray from their ultimate goal). They must value completion (if they don't finish what they start, they might as well not start it). They should break up tasks into manageable segments (a large task, such as finding a suitable job, is paralyzing if faced in its entirety. It must be broken up into small, attainable steps so that the achievement of each small step provides the impetus to embark upon the next). Finally, they should increase the efficiency of their time management.

Retooling: The Acquisition of New Education and Skills

While some women with choices would benefit from retooling, it is not a universal recommendation for all. Whether such an endeavor is necessary depends upon the particular goals for employment, the training and education acquired in the first career, and the shadow skills acquired in the second career. If women received previous training in the field they currently want to pursue or if their shadow skills complement that training, then retooling is minimal and relatively simple. As women prepare to remarket themselves under the new market conditions, they first need to review their skills to ensure that their field has not significantly surpassed them. If indeed their old skills have become obsolete, they must retool by becoming reacquainted with their field. That may entail renewing links with people in their particular area, aggressively networking, and even taking a course or two in subjects whose content has changed during their hiatus.

Women with employment goals in fields unrelated to their previous training and women with no previous training require more extensive retooling and reeducating. Depending on their employment goals, such retooling may, in the least, involve refocusing, which may be limited to the coherent evaluation of who they are, what they can do, and what is best suited for them, and repositioning themselves for the most appropriate entry into the labor force. However, if their goals entail entry in a new field that requires certification, then the amount of education and new skill acquisition will be extensive.

Such education must be pursued in schools and institutions that grant certification, in other words, in the formal sector. Formal education differs from informal education in numerous ways, not the least of which is the way in which it is acquired: women acquire informal education (including shadow skills) from life experiences while they acquire formal education in schools. While informal education has been emphasized for middle-aged women with choices, that emphasis does not negate the important role formal education plays in their job search.

Formal education is important for a variety of reasons. It provides a structured conduit for the acquisition of information; it offers a single venue in which a wide variety of topics and issues can be explored; it provides an environment that stimulates women's intellect and enables their imagination to soar; and it brings them into contact with people who can shape and form their creative development. In short, it offers the conditions conducive to the maturation and stimulation of women's intellect (as well as a structure for social and emotional development).

On a more pragmatic level, formal education serves some utilitarian functions for the women who pursue it. First, it opens doors to women because it gives certification without which certain jobs cannot be performed. Indeed, medicine cannot be practiced without a certificate; kindergarten teachers cannot teach without a certificate; divers cannot scuba dive without a certificate; people cannot drive a car without a license. Western society has introduced strict regulations pertaining to its internal division of labor. This division, institutionalized by an intricate system of certification, determines who is allowed to perform certain tasks. The certification states that its holder has studied the necessary material, has been tested, and has satisfied a body of judges that he or she can successfully and safely work in a particular field. Thus, formal education opens the doors for employment because it provides assurance of competence.

Second, formal education empowers women. The more they know, the more powerful they become because knowledge sharpens their ability to discern, to judge, to decide, and to recognize. More importantly, it sharpens their ability to think and to apply that thought process to a variety of situations. With knowledge and information, a woman is more likely to accurately recognize the boundaries of her possibilities. She is more likely to be cognizant of her limits as well as her rights within society. She is also more likely to understand her civil, legal, economic, and social place within that society.

Third, formal education offers women greater choice. Knowledge gives information pertaining to choices, it also gives the capacity to make informed decisions.

Finally, formal education is usually the key to wider choices in lifestyles. In most cases, education determines occupation and therefore it also determines income. Income in turn determines lifestyle: what kind of home people live in, what they do for entertainment, who their friends are. The lifestyle people can afford is the lifestyle they can earn. Earning capacity is determined by the work one does; and the work one does is determined by the educational certificate that one has. Therefore, the quantity and quality of education determines the nature of the lifestyle one can aspire to. However, exceptions exist. For example, as a result of marriage or inheritance, some women can enjoy standards of living that are unrelated to their employment or education.

The Indispensability of Family Support

A survey recently conducted by CATALYST, a professional women's support group, cites spousal support as one of the three most important components in a woman's success in the professional world.[12] All women are dependent on their husbands and children for support in their endeavors. When considering entering the labor force in midlife, those women who have supportive husbands or significant others, ones who accept with enthusiasm what they propose to do, who believe in them, who offer their help, and who listen to them, are already ahead of the race. They have the springboard from which to leap into the working world. They have the sympathetic shoulder to fall on if they fail and the proud arms to embrace them when they succeed.

If women have to battle their families in order to achieve their goals, then the sum total of the obstacles encountered may be overbearing and insufferable. To the extent that women can harness family support, they will be more successful in marketing themselves in the labor market.

Notes

1. The following paragraph is based on a concept developed by Katherine Wyse Goldman, *If You Can Raise Kids, You Can Get a Good Job*, New York: HarperCollins 1996.

2. Judith M. Bardwick, *In Transition: How Feminism, Sexual Liberation, and the Search for Self-Fulfillment Have Altered America*, New York: Holt, Rinehart and Winston, 1979, p. 44.

3. Goldman, p. 88.

4. The *New York Times*, November 28, 1994.

5. Richard Nelson Bolles, *The 1996 What Color is Your Parachute?* Berkeley: Ten Speed Press, 1996, pp. 180–185. Elizabeth Perle McKenna, in her study of women and work, called portable skills those that women can take with them when they change jobs or move in and out of the labor force (*When Work Doesn't Work Anymore*, New York: Delacorte Press, 1997, p. 247).

6. The World Bank, *World Development Report 1995*, Washington, D.C.: The World Bank, p. 25.

7. Very often women run households in isolation of their husbands, who often are on business trips for much of the time. As a result, women must learn to be responsible and to make decisions on their own (Patricia Houck Sprinkle, *Women Home Alone*, Grand Rapids, Mich.: Zondervan Publishing House, 1996).

8. See, for example, Elinor Lenz and Barbara Myerhoff, *The Feminization of America: How Women's Values Are Changing Our Public and Private Lives*, New York: St. Martin's Press, 1985.

9. Daniel Goleman, *Emotional Intelligence: Why It Can Matter More Than I.Q.*, New York, Bantam, 1995.

10. Cleo S. Berkun, "Changing Appearance for Women in the Middle Years of Life: Trauma?" in Elizabeth Markson, ed., *Older Women*, Lexington, Mass.: Lexington Books, 1983, p. 29.

11. Although formerly professional women with choices are not employed, they retain a high opportunity cost of their labor. They remain more productive in other activities than in housework.

12. CATALYST, cited in the *Philadelphia Inquirer*, February 28, 1996.

Chapter 9

Obstacles to Be Overcome: Inertia, Discrimination, and Many More

"Why would anybody hire me? I'm just a mom. And anyway, I'm 47 years old. No one wants to hire people my age," said a mother of two grown children who organized over ten charity balls serving thousands of people.

"I can't even look for a job because I don't feel that I have anything to offer. I've forgotten everything I learned in college and graduate school," said a veteran volunteer who devoted over a decade of her life to organizing museum and synagogue functions.

"I didn't really do anything over the past 20 years and I don't really know how to do anything. What kind of job could I possibly get now, at 49? " said the mother of three healthy, happy, and successful adult children.

"I'd have to compete against people who have so much more work experience than I. What I've done doesn't count to working people. They have no respect for those of us who haven't worked for pay," said a woman who raised a son while serving as president of the PTA and principal organizer of several fundraising campaigns that raised some million dollars.

Atlas holding up the world? Hercules pushing a rock uphill? Finding one's way out of the Mycenean labyrinth? By comparison, none seem as daunting a task as that faced by middle-aged homemakers who aspire to enter the labor force. Despite their conviction that the skills they acquired in their homemaking careers have value, many middle-aged women are nevertheless apprehensive and skeptical about their transition into the working world.

Part of that apprehension stems from the knowledge that there are obstacles to be overcome before their employment goals can be achieved. These obstacles can be divided into two categories—internal and external. Internal obstacles stem from the women themselves, their own insecurities, their inability to formulate clear goals, and their proclivity to procrastinate. External obstacles, just as real and menacing, include family pressures at home and discrimination in the workplace, as well as concrete impediments such as inappropriate education, obsolete skills, or insufficient work experience.

INTERNAL OBSTACLES

Elizabeth Perle McKenna, in her study of professional women leaving the labor force, described their feelings as follows: "It's as if the whole group of us were standing on the bank of a river looking at different lives on the far shore. But none of us wants to jump in the water. . . . We tell each other all the scary things about the water. 'Its cold, it's wet, the current is swift, there are things that bite in there. . . .' We resist risk, we resist the change. We resist leaving the security of the identity we know. How human."[1]

Confidence falters at the prospect of looking for work after years outside the labor force. Poised, mature, and secure women show more than a hint of insecurity when considering their future options as well as the obstacles entailed in achieving them. Although women with choices are often content with their lives and are self-confident with respect to their positions within their families and communities, their self-confidence plummets when exploring possibilities for a new beginning.

Most women are aware that before facing the outside world, they must first face inward. They realize that before achieving their goals, they must come to grips with those personal characteristics that produce powerful resistance to change. They must face the demons that scare them and prevent them from constructively working toward their goals. Women lack confidence and so they vacillate with respect to their goals; they are scared of failing and so they procrastinate. The more they vacillate and procrastinate, the lower their self-esteem becomes and the harder it is to muster the energy and the confidence to break out of the paralyzing cycle of insecurity and indecision. The more their self-esteem suffers, the more imperative it is that they break out of that cycle. Yet, that is exactly when women have the greatest difficulty in forging ahead.

What are the most common internal obstacles to goal achievement among middle-aged homemakers? According to the women in this study, the following obstacles were cited, in descending order of importance.

Lack of Clear Goals

With respect to future plans, women fall into two groups, those who know exactly what they want to do in their third careers and those who know they want something new but have no concrete idea of what it is. Clearly those in the former group are better off. Since they have clear goals, they can immediately proceed to the next step, namely, dealing with other internal obstacles or mapping out their strategy for goal achievement. It is those who lack clarity and direction that have an additional obstacle to overcome. Before they can even begin to ponder a strategy, they have to identify their goals. That in and of itself is often a daunting task. Barbara Sher wrote about this problem in her inspirational book entitled *I Could Do Anything If Only I Knew What It Was*.[2] She identifies lack of clarity and inability to formulate concise goals as the two principal impediments to bringing about life changes.

Among the middle-aged participants in this study, 36% knew exactly what they wanted to do in the future. Whether their direction was longstanding or whether it only crystallized over the recent past, these women are clear both in their goals as well as the strategy they must pursue to achieve them. A poignant example of such clarity was provided by Maria Perez, 44 years of age. Her dream to study psychology and to open a private practice as a clinical psychologist sustained her for the past two decades of full-time homemaking and childrearing. "I've wanted to study psychology for so long," she explains, "now that my children are no longer infants, I've enrolled in a graduate program. I have very clear ideas about what I want to do afterwards, and it makes me very happy to be getting closer to achieving my goals." Like Maria, Elise Troy envisions her transition out of full-time homemaking with clarity. "When my children get a little older, I want to return to practicing law. I even know the organization for which I want to work. Although I'm not ready to take that step yet, I am very focused on it and I plan for it."

The clarity of vision that Maria and Elise report is not common among homemakers. While many feel the urge to change their lives, they have little more than nebulous ideas. The possibilities they ponder are at once both endless and limited. They know neither how to narrow their options nor how to search for inspiration. These women are having difficulty defining their interests and identifying their passion. They want to make a commitment but they have no idea what to commit to. While they want to achieve a goal, they do not know what that goal is. They understand instinctively that they must love whatever they do in order to overcome the barriers and obstacles inherent in goal achievement. But they cannot identify what they love. Clarity of vision keeps eluding them. One confused mother describes her dilemmas. Joanna Flex is trying to identify what she wants through a process of elimination, first by identifying what she doesn't want to change in her life. What remains, will, by definition, be the focus of change and ultimately the source of a new beginning. She says, "In the past few years, I've started feeling that I want something new, that I want my life to change in some way. It's not that I want to change husbands, I love my husband. I don't want to change homes—I love where I live and I'm happy in Miami, with all my friends and relatives. But I want something that I can't put my finger on. I'm pretty sure that this something has to come from within me and that it has to be something that I do during the day, something having to do with how I spend my time. . . . That's why I want to start working. The problem is that I don't know what work I want to do or what I can do."

The most frequently cited explanation for the lack of clear goals is ignorance pertaining to future options. Middle-aged homemakers claim to have insufficient information about the world outside their homes and the possibilities it holds (or doesn't hold) for them. This lack of information often has a paralyzing effect. It is compounded by the embarrassment middle-aged women feel about asking for guidance and direction, given that they are so used to doling it out to others. Asking for help conveys powerlessness, a state of being they are not accustomed to. Some women are also embarrassed to admit to others that they are not entirely happy with their current lives. Even if they successfully overcome embarrassment, they still do not know where to turn for help. There are few role models they are close to and whose confidence they enjoy. They are reluctant to seek advice from career women since, given the underlying mommy wars, such a step might be misconstrued as admitting they made a wrong choice a few decades ago. They cannot seek advice from their friends outside the labor market because they are often equally uninformed. Anyway, many of their friends have no understanding of their desired change of life. The best source of information is from other middle-aged women who have just recently made the transition. "However, I don't know any of them!" June Ellington concedes.

Lack of Self-Confidence

Advantaged women with choices are at the pinnacle of society with respect to family wealth, class, and privilege, and they know it. At the same time, these women lack recent work experience and up-to-date skills, which translate into clear advantages in the labor market, and they know that too. Part of their self-doubt stems from the realization that outside of their comfortable environments (such as in the competitive world of the labor markets), the benefits and advantages they are used to having are less relevant. Indeed, in their home environments these women are "somebodies." They are important. They have authority, people listen to them, they have rights over other individuals, and they can shape the behavior of spouses and children. Alas, the labor force holds no such secure tenure, no such clear power, and no such love and devotion. It offers no forgiveness for mistakes. All of this makes entering the labor force a terrifying prospect mired in uncertainty and anxiety.

One woman in the sample gave the impression of strength and poise in her verbal responses to the questionnaire and conveyed self-confidence with her body language. She was intelligent, beautiful, articulate, and wealthy. She had devoted children and was respected as a volunteer. Yet, she broke down when asked about her confidence with respect to the labor market. Isabel Gutierrez said, "Going through a divorce was difficult for my self-confidence. The thought of trying to find a job brings back all the feelings of insecurity that I had when my husband left. I know that prospective employers won't focus on those characteristics that my friends love and value in me. Instead, they'll just mercilessly probe into those areas where I'm the weakest. I don't know how I will bear it."

Inertia and Procrastination

Inertia, the force that keeps us rooted in place, was perceived as an overwhelming obstacle by many middle-aged homemakers. In the absence of some compelling reason for change, it is very difficult to wake up one morning and say, today is the day! Today I will change my life! Indeed, it is so much easier to stall than to actively take charge. It is so much easier to adhere to the status quo than to initiate turbulence. It is so much easier to continue with one's leisure activities, volunteering work, and childrearing, despite their declining benefits, than it is to muster the energy, the confidence, and the momentum necessary to fundamentally change one's life. So therefore, change is best put off until a later date. Inertia takes an enormous amount of energy and motivation to overcome. Procrastination is so easy.

Denise Bentley identified inertia as the major obstacle in achieving her goals. While cognizant of its hold on her, she cannot seem to liberate herself. When she worked as a professional, part of her job requirement was to motivate workers to overcome their inertia. Yet, she seems unable to apply the lessons she taught others to herself. "For some reason," she says, "I'm stuck in place. I'm sure that once I get some momentum, I'll keep on rolling. But I can't get the momentum. The beginning is always the hardest, isn't it?" Denise wonders if it wouldn't be easier to overcome inertia when a concrete event precipitates it, like a divorce or a death. Possibly, Denise thinks, having her last child leave home may provide the necessary push to break out of the inertia that shackles her. She has to wait a few more years to find out.

Oftentimes procrastination applies only to specific tasks, while motivation abounds for others. Some women, while professing to want to prepare their resume or begin networking but just can't seem to get around to it, seem to have no trouble getting around to other tasks. June Ellington talked readily about such selective procrastination. For several years now, she has been thinking about returning to work. However, she has yet to embark upon a serious job search. She can't seem to get around to it! She described an ongoing battle with herself; she described feelings of inner conflict and struggles with resolutions that she is unsure of. The demons she has to fight are so large that she keeps coming up with even bigger excuses to postpone her job search. June says, "Several times in the past few years I decided that the time has come for me to go back to work. I want it, my husband wants it, the kids are ready for it, so it should happen. But just as I'm about to start polishing my resume and planning my networking strategy, I decide that there's something else that just has to be done. And then, my attention is diverted." She goes on to describe those diversions. "Last year, for example, I just had to redo the entire landscaping on our property. We were putting our house on the market, so I just had to make some cosmetic improvements. That took a lot of my time and attention. This year I have a new project: I want to sort out all our old photographs. All of them—decades of photographs. I have to do it because they'll be ruined unless they get mounted on bonded paper. Do you see a pattern here? I do. Every time I get close to seriously looking for work, something comes up that demands my attention. I think I'm procrastinating." Finally, with a shy smile and an almost ashamed demeanor, she whispers that she is considering having another baby. First she admits that doing so is probably a cop-out, but then she reconsiders. No longer shy, she takes a deep breath, pulls her shoulders back and thinks outloud—maybe she really does want to have a three child family. . . . Or maybe not? . . . "If I had a small child, then I couldn't work, right? The only valid reason for not using my MBA is to be with my children. If I'm not with them, then by definition I need to be working." Long pause. "Do you understand what I'm saying?"

Homemakers know they have to overcome their proclivity to procrastinate in order to pursue (and ultimately achieve) their goals, yet they continue to procrastinate. Such behavior reflects the dominance of short-term concerns over long-term ones and the dominance of emotional responses over rational ones. The pressing demands of the short term, such as mounting photos onto bonded paper or relandscaping the yard, take precedence and simultaneously offer the necessary rationalization for putting off a long-term goal.

Fear of Failure

Dr. Seuss's book *Oh, the Places You'll Go!* has been on the best-seller list for years in part because of the many mothers who have read it, over and over again, to their children. Despite the courage they tried to instill in them and the cautioning that life doesn't always turn out well, many women failed to learn Dr. Seuss's lessons. Today many of them feel sheer terror at the prospect of stepping out of their sheltered home environments. They fear the step into the working world where they may be told that they are not wanted, that they are too old or too uneducated, that their skills are obsolete, or that there are other women who have so much more to offer than they. The possibilities for rejection seem endless, while the courage to voluntarily expose oneself to such risks is in short supply.

There are several concrete steps entailed in entering the labor force that produce the sense of impending failure. For some women, the mere thought of calling strangers on the phone produces anxiety. Others fear writing letters and getting no responses. Others yet shudder at the prospect of networking. Polishing the resume often churns stomachs—what should a homemaker put on her resume to explain her primary activity during the past decade or two? Driving carpools? How can women make a case on their behalf to prospective employers if they cannot make a case to themselves?

The fear of competing in the labor market was prominent in the minds of many middle-aged homemakers. Their greatest fear is the youth of their competitors, their eagerness, and their skills. Especially feared and envied is the technological advantage of the young competitors who are almost universally computer literate (while few middle-aged women are comfortable with new technologies). Joanna Flex certainly fears the ramifications of this disadvantage, despite that fact that computer-related conversations have dominated her dinner table during the past few years. She describes her feelings: "I don't know the latest trends and methods, especially the use of electronic equipment such as the computer. I'm just starting to understand the meaning of network and World Wide Web. And the only reason I sort of understand these terms is that my children talk about them and I force myself to understand in order to participate in their conversations. So imagine trying to enter the workforce, and competing with some young person, a few years older than my kids, who has grown up comfortable with the computer! How can I possibly compete?"

Fear of failure is also linked to fear of losing face. Trying to get a job after a hiatus entails going out on a limb. If the limb breaks, everyone might say, "I told you so." Of particular concern is the possibility that husbands and children will witness women's failures, possibly with repercussions on their credibility in the home.

There was one exception to the litany of fears about failure. Tory Cohen is a strong, confident woman who worked in marketing for 17 years before her hiatus. Despite the fact that she voluntarily left the labor force to care for her twin daughters, she always stayed busy with projects as a community activist as well as a volunteer in her daughters' school. All her projects consumed her body and soul. Whatever she did, she gave fully of herself. That's just the way she is—"it's the beast within me"—that's how she describes her dedication to whatever she does. When asked if she was afraid of failing in her future job endeavors (in her case, starting her own business), Tory's response was different from the others: "No, I don't have fear of failure, I have fear of success. What if I succeed in my business idea and it really takes off? I know myself. I get absolutely absorbed in whatever I do. I'll get so absorbed in it and I won't realize what's happening until it's too late. I'll be enjoying it too much and not realize the cost I'll be paying with respect to my family. That's what I'm afraid of."

Limited Options

Paradoxically, the socioeconomic background of women with choices decreases their range of occupational options. For example, they will not even consider numerous jobs in the menial and unskilled labor categories. Yet, in some cases their work experience and their lack of up-to-date skills make them prime candidates for such jobs. Women with choices aspire to interesting and professional jobs. In order to entice them out of their homes, their future work environment must be attractive. In other words, it must be suitable to their particular needs and tolerant of their particular conditions.

Robin Bifflow describes how she faced this dilemma. "I really want to start working again but I don't think that I'll ever find a job. You see, I don't think there are any jobs for me. My liberal arts degree of 20 years ago didn't really prepare me for any particular job. I've got no significant work experience. So what kind of work can I do now? What I want, I can't get; what I can get, I don't want. There's such a big gap between what I'm qualified for and what I want to do." Anna Moore, a former banker, is grappling with similar sentiments. In reviewing her options for reentry into the labor market, she identified the university setting as her favorite: "I'd really like to work at a university. I love the environment and I believe I would have a lot to offer to it. However, I think that because of my hiatus and my skills and my age, I would have to enter at a low level, probably as a typist or a low level clerk, if I'm lucky. I'm not willing to do that, so I have to drop the university as a possibility altogether."

Fear of Collapse of Safe Environment

Rhona Mahony studied working women and found that many had put so much time and energy into their households that they developed strong territorial feelings. Consequently, they became reluctant to allow others to perform some of their duties for fear that their territoriality will be threatened.[3] One manifestation of this territoriality is the fear, shared by one-quarter of the women in this study, that if they withdraw their undivided attention from their households, their households will fall apart. Their home will collapse because no substitute could possibly take care of it the way they did; their supervision is so crucial that family life will be completely transformed if they leave home to enter the labor force.

Based on her past experience, Elise Troy expects that her house would fall into disrepair when she starts working. "Before, my job as an attorney was so demanding that I simply couldn't keep our home in the condition it's in now. When I stopped working, there were at least fifteen things that desperately needed repair. When I go back to work, I expect that house projects will pile up again, although probably not as much as before since I won't be working full time." June Ellington laughed when asked if she worried that her family might fall apart if she went to work. She said, "Even if I realize that it might not really be true, it certainly does provide me with a convenient excuse not to work, doesn't it? If my family would die, so to speak, without me, then how can I possibly leave home?" Francesca Layten also found the question amusing: "Do I think my home environment would collapse without me? Well, I think it would serve my family right if it did. If they had to start taking care of themselves, they might learn some responsibility. And they might start to appreciate me more!"

The majority of women felt that their absence from the home would be compensated for very easily in several ways: additional household help would be hired, overall standards of order and cleanliness would decrease, and family members would take more responsibility for the functioning of the household. Most women seemed to feel comfortable with any of these outcomes and believed their families would be too.

Fear of Disapproval

A small number of respondents worried that their family and friends will disapprove when they begin to work. Their husbands might put up a resistance and thus deny them the support they will need; their children might respond in unanticipated ways, possibly masking their disapproval, anger, and disappointment with behavioral problems.

Middle-aged women with choices opened their hearts and minds when asked about potential (and actual) disapproval. Maria Perez, who hopes to finish graduate school and open a private practice, expressed concern that her family, especially her husband, might not support her. She knows that achieving her goals will be harder without an encouraging family with whom to share her fears, her hopes, her successes, and her failures. With dismay, she says, "I don't think my husband really approves of my desire to work. He just can't understand why I would want to work. I'm going ahead with my plans anyway, but I am worried about his reaction when his life changes, as inevitably it will if I'm out of the house for long periods of time. And if he doesn't support me, that means that all my goals will be harder to achieve."

The question of disapproval struck a cord with Isabel Gutierrez. She explained her emotional reaction by recounting parts of her life history. She wanted a career but her husband disapproved of her goals. She had stopped studying when she got married because he expected her to be a full-time homemaker. He insisted that she would have no use for her degree since she was expected to spend her time raising children (of whom he wanted many) and performing wifely duties (which would be extensive). It is not surprising that when he recently left her, after 21 years of marriage, she immediately went back to school. While she is currently not under his influence, she cannot forget her experience in part because her girlfriends' lives are constant reminders of what she went through:

I have girlfriends with whom I meet once a month. We have formed a sort of club. We are (or were) all wives of relatively important men, you know, wealthy men with a position of status within the community. I'm divorced now, but I was in the same boat these women are now in. They exist to cater to their husbands. They continue to do it because they're afraid if they don't, their husbands will leave them. They see what happened to me and they don't want it to happen to them. In reality, so many of them would like to do something other than run errands for their husbands and organize parties for their colleagues. They'd like to study, to start up businesses, to do something for themselves. But they're too scared of the consequences!

Disapproval emanating from extended family and friends is just as disturbing as that from a spouse. Parents, in-laws, and friends may feel threatened when a woman begins to work, having learned to rely on her consistent and reliable behavior. Employment entails new rules, new schedules, new roles, and new demands, all of which they may dislike.

Francesca Layten, a loving and sociable person, is genuinely concerned about the effect of her job search on her friendships. She has girlfriends whom she cherishes yet she has reason to doubt the longevity of their bonds.

I have a few close girlfriends with whom I've been inseparable since our children were in lower school together. None of them work. I'm the only one who wants to. While they don't want to meddle in my life, I know by their comments that they don't understand why I want to work. I think they see it as a rejection of them and their lifestyle, of our lifestyle, the one we shared for so many years. I feel so bad about this. I'm not rejecting them at all. My desire to work has nothing to do with them. I really value our friendships, but I want more from my life. They're not looking for more from theirs. We all know that the nature of our relationship will change if I start working: I won't be spontaneous any more, I won't have time to do all those things we used to do together. I'm upset about losing their friendship. On the other hand, I sometimes get angry when I think about it: it's not fair that they're pressuring me not to change.

Unlike Francesca, Ann Bowden encountered no disapproval from her friends. However, her husband's family became a source of consistent negative feedback about her employment. After Ann enrolled in graduate school and subsequently began working, her relationship with her extended family soured. Ann recalls with bitterness how she and her husband regularly socialized with the local members of their large families. "Does my extended family disapprove? Of course they do, especially my sisters-in-law. Before we were getting along just fine, we were all women at home, tending to our families. Now that I'm out of the home, even if its just part time, they feel threatened. I am now a professional, they're not. Now they compete with me in ways they never did before. It has completely changed the way our families interact."

EXTERNAL OBSTACLES

To an outsider, the labor market seems like a treadmill with no stop button. Its perpetual motion prevents women from mounting easily and at their own pace. Then, in the aftermath of their first step, they must work extra hard to learn the ropes and to adjust to the movement. Only after a time lag can they relax somewhat since they will have started to go with the flow. Women aspiring to enter the labor force must overcome the obstacles posed by the treadmill's speed and must understand its cycles before they make their attempt to get on. Understanding those cycles entails understanding the obstacles that they will face with respect to both institutional and discriminatory factors.

For middle-aged women with choices, the labor market is simultaneously a sellers market and a buyers market. It is a sellers market because these women can exert their choice in employment since they do not have to work in order to survive. They can outright dismiss certain jobs and occupations, they can refuse conditions that do not suit them, and, to some extent, they can set their own terms. At the same time, the labor market is a buyers market because employers are faced with increasing demand for work from increasingly qualified individuals. Indeed, more and more young women are opting to work rather than stay at home, so the overall competition between potential female employees is growing. Moreover, there is widespread pent-up demand for employment among women who have taken a hiatus from work. Together, these demand and supply factors combine to make the labor market a complicated institution for women with choices to understand and wade through.

In trying to assess the external obstacles they will face in their job search and later in their workplace, middle-aged women with choices focus on the way they will be perceived by employers and coworkers. How will coworkers respond to them, knowing that they don't have to work for a living? How will their boss deal with the fact that they are older than he or she, or that they have more household wealth? Women worry that they will encounter discrimination, a lot of it and for a lot of reasons. Their worries are well grounded in the academic literature on labor markets. Indeed, numerous economists and sociologists use discrimination to explain occupational and pay differences that are not accounted for by productivity differences.[4] While the early literature on discrimination focused on race, increasingly scholars are finding that women as a group are also victims in both overt and covert ways. For women with choices attempting to break into the labor market, such potential discrimination is an uncomfortable obstacle to be overcome; for those who have just recently succeeded in finding work, discrimination on numerous grounds remains a problem they contend with daily.

Discrimination Against Women in General

After graduating from top law schools, Ruth Bader Ginsberg and Sandra Day O'Connor were offered jobs only as legal secretaries. They discovered a wall of resistance, a clear sign of discrimination against them because they were women.[5] Employers discriminate against women for a variety of reasons. Some believe that women are not as productive as men, that they are less committed to their job, that they are not in for the long haul, and that they do not have loyalty to the workplace. Some think they aren't as smart, nor as well trained, nor as resistant, nor as competitive as men. They fear women will get pregnant and leave, they think women will take too much time off, they believe that women are weaker than men, and that they will resign if their child gets ill. The list goes on and on.

On the basis of such views, many employers are generally reluctant to hire women. Such discrimination makes women disadvantaged from the start. Even in preparation for the labor force, there is evidence that boys are given preference in schools in hard (read: important) subjects such as math and science (Bernice Sandler found that females are often singled out for different treatment or simply ignored in class,[6] resulting in disparities in learning between males and females). Then, in the workplace, women performing the same job tend to receive lower pay (according to a study by Blau and Ferber, gender differences at least in part explain why equally qualified people receive different earnings).[7] When it comes to promotions to more lucrative and higher status jobs, women tend to be overlooked in preference to men. Women are discriminated against when they apply for business loans and when they try to raise capital; they face discrimination when they need to deal with clients or when they are renting office space. In other words, a woman has to be much better than a man in order to receive the same treatment from her employer. Yet, clear evidence exists that women are as serious about their work as men (one study even shows that women take shorter coffee breaks and lunches than men in the same jobs).[8]

Only a small proportion of the respondents in this study said they worried about encountering discrimination in the workplace against women in general (many more worried about specific kinds of discrimination, as described below). Those who expected to encounter it were of Hispanic heritage: "Most men don't like to see women working and they certainly don't like to hire them. Yes, I think I will experience discrimination because I'm a woman," was the gist of the response from most Hispanic respondents.

What did women think who had just recently started working? Sixty-eight percent believed there was no discrimination against them merely on the basis of their gender, although they did experience it in some of the other forms discussed below. One respondent, Alexandra Jones, had an experience that, she believes, would not have happened to a man. She recently started working after a decade-long hiatus. Within a few days, hurtful rumors began circulating her workplace: the only reason she got her job was because she was sleeping with the boss. Otherwise, it was said, how could she possibly get such a good job, having been a full-time homemaker for so long? One (male) coworker was blatant in his accusations, even confronting her to her face (and continued to do so until her boss firmly put an end to it). So yes, Alexandra is convinced that there is discrimination against women in the workplace.

Discrimination Against Mothers

Mothers with children are viewed as having baggage (also known as maternal responsibilities). This baggage acts as a red flag, an alert signal, for employers. They associate this baggage with women leaving work early when the babysitter fails to show up, decreasing their productivity because of worries at home, and taking many days of sick leave. Such discrimination against mothers is pervasive, despite Arthur Emlen's conclusive study that having children in no way affects a person's attendance record at work.[9]

Most women with choices did not worry that they would not be hired because they were mothers only because their children were no longer so young as to warrant their absence from work. Indeed, since most respondents had children in high school or in college, their mothering commitments were unlikely to interfere with their work. Isabel Gutierrez, with only one child of 17 remaining at home, said "for all purposes at work, I'm no longer a mother! I won't have to leave work because my child is sick or resign because I'm needed at home!"

However, a different kind of discrimination against mothers was expected by Julia Schuman—discrimination from other women in the workplace. She explains, "Women who didn't have children as well as women who did but chose to have careers and delegate childcare to others have no idea of what life is like as a full-time mother. . . . They don't think homemakers have acquired any skills and they don't value what we've been doing. These women are unlikely to hide their attitudes in the common work space." Her view was formed by her own experience. When she worked as a young attorney in a major law firm, she did not feel that the women in her firm were very supportive of each other nor that female solidarity was very pervasive. In fact, she found that "a lot more women wanted to take my head off than support me." As a result, Julia expects no less discrimination from other women than she does from men.

Discrimination Against Age

Pat Schroeder, who is planning to leave Congress because at age 55 she wants to begin a new career "while still young," is unlikely to suffer age discrimination in her endeavors.[10] However, less-known and less-accomplished women are likely to be faced with it to some degree. It is a fact that employers are not motivated to hire women who they consider to be chronologically old. How old is old? While old has different meanings to different employers, their economic reasoning tends to be uniformly the following. Older workers are less likely to learn as quickly as younger ones. They are less likely to be malleable and manipulatable. Their personality and work habits cannot be formed by employers since they are already formed. The employer is less likely to invest in the older worker in the form of training because the payoff period before retirement is shorter. The older worker is more likely to get sick, which will decrease her productivity since she will either take time off work or be concerned about her health while on the job.

In considering middle-aged women, employers are further aware that menopause is an upcoming physical condition whose effect on each particular worker is unknown a priori. They have visions, based on negative stereotyping, of raving crimson-faced middle-aged women in fits of hot flashes whose hormonal disturbances prevent them from controlling their tempers. A comparison of that vision with the middle-aged, distinguished, and calm male worker is surely to produce a tilt in favor of hiring a man.

Moreover, sometimes employers simply want to be surrounded by youth. Naomi Wolf, in her book *The Beauty Myth*, describes a 54-year-old woman whose boss fired her without warning because he told her that he "wanted to look at a younger woman so his spirits could be lifted"![11]

Several participants in this study shared their experiences with age discrimination. Maria Perez, at 44, is among the oldest women enrolled in her master's degree program. As a result of her age, she feels that both students and professors treat her differently: "There was the general sense that I wouldn't make it, that I would never finish the program. Teachers, students, and administrators all acted as though I couldn't finish because I was too old." Given that kind of discrimination in an educational environment, Maria feared even more in the labor market. Ann Bowden would say that her fears are well founded. She recently went through the hiring process. She had many interviews and although no one said anything openly to her, she always felt that her age was an issue. "Age is really a deficit when reentering the labor force. I know it, I experienced it. When I interviewed for work, I had so much more life experience than the people who were interviewing me. I was intimidating and threatening to the younger people. And that's a problem if you want them to hire you."

Not all women share Maria's and Ann's experience. There are some occupations, as Anna Moore attests, that are more forgiving of age than others. While age might not be venerated in these occupations, at least it isn't a hindrance. Anna bases her view on her own experience. At 49, she recently reentered the labor force as a real estate agent. "Age discrimination doesn't happen in all jobs. In real estate, for example, it doesn't seem to matter if you are male or female, young or old. However, I'm sure that age discrimination exists in other areas, such as finance. Women my age who try to enter or reenter the financial world are sure to encounter resistance. I know from experience."

Discrimination Against Wealth and Social Position

Employers may feel uncomfortable hiring a woman who is obviously advantaged, who is of an upper-class background, or whose husband is wealthier and more successful than they. A woman's wealth and social position may accentuate an employer's personal discomfort because it can produce an imbalance in the office—either there is equality where hierarchy is expected or, if there is hierarchy between boss and worker, it is reversed. Employers also consider the possible negative repercussions on office dynamics if an advantaged woman joins the workforce. On the basis of education, work experience, or skills, such a woman may have more in common with the general staff; on the basis of her socioeconomic position, she may be more comfortable with professionals. If the advantaged woman were to accept a menial job, the ensuing confusion pertaining to her identity and role is unlikely to have a positive effect on group dynamics.

Employers also worry about questions of productivity when they hire wealthy women. Will they be hiring a prima donna, a woman who is used to having her way, who will not work hard, who thinks that she does not have to pay her dues? Moreover, will the negative effects on group dynamics, described above, negatively affect the productivity of resentful coworkers?

All these concerns are reflected in direct or indirect discrimination, as some of the respondents can attest to. Sarah Bond, 49 and divorced, recently completed a master's degree in social work. Her graduation requirements included several internships meant to give her real-world experience. It was during these internships that Sarah worked with a variety of supervisors who discriminated against her because of her wealth. She remembers clearly how one of them said to her, "Why are you doing this [studying and interning]? You know you'll never work. You'll never have to! You did better in your divorce than I do in my job."

Ann Bowden also completed a master's degree in social work and now works part time. She lit up when I asked if she suffered discrimination because of her socioeconomic position. "I certainly do! I know that my boss is tough on me because of my economic position. He resents the fact that he and I do the same type of work, yet he is the male in his household and the sole breadwinner. He knows that the male in my house is a successful attorney. As soon as I noticed his resentment, I was quick to make adjustments. For example, I now drive an old car to work, never my new Lexus. I specifically bought a used car so that I could blend in at work. I know I have more than everybody else that I work with and I don't want to flaunt it. I always underplay what I have."

Despite efforts to be discrete about wealth while at work, word gets around and coworkers respond with a mix of emotions. Alexandra Jones, recently employed as a commercial mortgage broker, works in an office in which few of her coworkers are in the same socioeconomic group as she. "It produces a very odd situation. Most people are curious about my life. They clearly resist any kind of friendship with me. As soon as I started working, I knew I'd never be one of the gang."

Clearly, numerous women were sensitive to the messages they were getting from their coworkers about working when they "don't have to." In all these cases, not having to work is understood to refer to the financial security they enjoy. Anna Moore, who recently started working in real estate, was particularly indignant about this type of discrimination. "Since my husband is wealthy, people tell me that I don't need to work. I get very upset by such comments. I reply that everyone who works needs to work for some reason. Some work for money, others work for psychological reasons. My need is clearly psychological, but it's still a need! A need that is very important to me." Anna believes her needs are no less compelling than those of her coworkers, they are merely different.

Discrimination Against Appearance

Employers often make decisions pertaining to hiring, promotion, and pay on the basis of appearance. Even though it has been found that good-looking people earn 12% more than their plain colleagues, with the difference in pay being more acute for men than women,[12] women are certainly judged by their appearance. Indeed, Naomi Wolf and Wendy Chapkis, in their respective studies of beauty and appearance, provide a wide range of examples of appearance discrimination against women under many different conditions.[13] They claim that discrimination on the basis of looks and image works in two ways: women are discriminated against because they may be too feminine or because they are insufficiently feminine. Mona Harrington, in her study of women lawyers, described how if a woman is feminine in appearance and manner, it is assumed that she cannot be tough and therefore cannot be an effective lawyer.[14] Alternatively, women can be harmed if they are not feminine and pretty enough. The highly publicized Price Waterhouse case, when a woman was denied a partnership in the accounting firm, despite the fact that she was obviously the most qualified, is a case of appearance discrimination.[15] (She was told that her chances for promotion would have been higher if she had been more feminine in her dress, walk, and talk. She was also hurt because she didn't wear enough jewelry and makeup.) Similarly, women flight attendants are discriminated against when they cease to look as youthful and pretty.

What was the nature of the appearance discrimination that the sampled women in this study experienced or expected to experience? Some respondents focused on beauty. Abby Williams, a stunningly beautiful woman, expected a lot of discrimination in the labor market because of her striking blond hair. Sarah Bond, a vivacious and gregarious beauty, was told by a professor in her graduate program that she will have trouble getting a job because she is too pretty and women do not like to work with pretty women.

In addition to beauty, wealth is also a source of appearance discrimination. Women with choices tend to reflect their advantaged position in the image they project. They tend to look rich, they tend to dress in expensive clothing, they tend to be well groomed and their hair tends to be coiffed. Such an appearance is appropriate for some types of jobs while it is an impediment in others. Having learned about appearance discrimination the hard way, Ann Bowden said she purposefully takes her jewelry off before she goes to work in order to look less ostentatious.

Finally, clothing is also viewed as a source of discrimination insofar as it enhances beauty, conveys information about wealth, and contributes to overall image of the wearer. Elise Troy describes how "women who wear suits are treated differently from those who wear jeans. It happens in the supermarket and it happens in the office. It's just a fact of life." She adds that it is a fact that aspiring job candidates should never forget.

Discrimination Against First-Time Entrants into Labor Force

It is much harder for middle-aged women to find work if they have never worked before than if they are returning after a hiatus. First-time entry implies that there is absolutely no proven track record of paid employment and no formal proof of competency. Given that there is no universal measure by which to ascertain competence in childrearing (good mothers have screwed up kids and good kids happen to screwed up mothers), potential employers perceive themselves to be taking an enormous risk by hiring a first-time entrant.

All the women in the sample had at least some prior work experience and they all believe that if they didn't, they would be at a great disadvantage. One woman, claiming that the work she did was so insignificant that it qualifies her as a virtual first-time entrant, viewed her lack of substantive work experience as her greatest future obstacle. She expects to encounter consistent negative feedback from prospective employers when she reveals the nature of her past work.

Discrimination Against Returning Mothers

Returning mothers, also known as gappers or intermittent workers, have some tangible evidence to show that they have gotten on the treadmill before and have gotten off voluntarily. Their work experience conveys to potential employers that they have acquired experience with commitment, coming to work on time, being team players, and getting a job done (employers rarely realize that all of those characteristics are also required for running a household and thus that women would have gotten important and useful experience, whether they worked for pay or not).

Women who leave the labor market in order to be with their children encounter discrimination when they reenter. They lose seniority, they are less likely to receive on-the-job training, they are discriminated against because their job skills may have depreciated, and employers think that they are likely to take another leave in the future. More importantly, they return to lower wages than those women who never left (a study by Jacobsen and Levin found that the gap between workers who left and those who stayed remains over time, and although it decreases from 33% in the first year back to 10% after 20 years, it nevertheless remains.[16] Thus, they calculated, if a woman stays out seven years, she is paying for her hiatus with ten years of earnings).

Very few women believed this form of discrimination would be a problem for them. They felt that if they overcame some of the other obstacles, the fact that they were out of the labor force for a while would be less important than the fact that they had worked before, that they had been active volunteers during their years out of the labor force, and that they had updated their skills.

Discrimination Against Part-Timers

In a society that values work above all else, where people have experienced such work-creep that 60-hour weeks are considered easy weeks in some professions, and where the time workers spend in leisure activities has steadily decreased over the past two decades, there is likely to be discrimination against those who voluntarily choose to minimize their work hours. Part-timers are discriminated against because they are indicating that other activities are more important than their commitment to the workplace.

Many women with choices are convinced that if they a priori sought out part-time work, they wouldn't be taken as seriously as full-time workers. Roberta Martin, clear about her needs for a short workday, expects the worst but retains optimism in discussing her employment chances: "When I show up at an interview and say that I only want to work part time, the employer will think I'm not as interested as the women before or after me who will work any hours he assigns them. But what can I do? I either work those hours or I don't work at all. Hopefully, the employer will understand my constraints and will see that I can be a very good worker, even if only for part of the day."

Notes

1. Elizabeth Perle McKenna, *When Work Doesn't Work Anymore*, New York: Delacorte Press, 1997, p. 92.

2. Barbara Sher with Barbara Smith, *I Could Do Anything If Only I Knew What It Was*, New York: Bantam Doubleday Dell Publishing Group, 1994.

3. Rhona Mahony, *Kidding Ourselves: Breadwinning, Babies and Bargaining Power*, New York: Basic Books, 1995.

4. See, for example, Barbara Reskin and Heidi Hartmann, eds., *Women's Work, Men's Work; Sex Segregation on the Job*, Washington, D.C.: National Academy Press, 1986; Paula England, "Socioeconomic Explanations of Job Segregation," in Helen Remick, ed., *Comparable Worth and Wage Discrimination: Technical Possibilities and Political Realities*, Philadelphia: Temple University Press, 1984; Rosabeth Kanter, *Men and Women of the Corporation*, New York: Basic Books, 1977.

5. Shirley Burggraf, *The Feminine Economy and Economic Man*, Reading, Mass.: Addison-Welsley, 1998, p. 21.

6. Bernice Sandler, "The Classroom Climate for Women," in Susan Feiner, ed., *Race and Gender in the American Economy*, Englewood Cliffs, N.J.: Prentice-Hall, 1994, p. 166.

7. Gender differences in work-related characteristics are only part of the story. See Francine D. Blau and Marianne A. Ferber, ": Empirical Evidence from the United States," *American Economic Review*, 77, no. 2, May 1987, pp. 316–320. Also, see Janice

Madden, "The Persistence of Pay Differentials: The Economics of Sex Discrimination," *Women and Work*, 1, 1985, pp. 76–114.

8. The *New Yorker*, "How to Enjoy the Battle of the Sexes," February 26 and March 4, 1996, p. 177.

9. Arthur Emlen, *Employee Profiles: 1987 Dependent Care Survey: Selected Companies*, Portland: Oregon Regional Research Institute for Human Services, Portland State University, 1987, quoted in Arlie Russell Hochschild, *The Time Bind: When Work Becomes Home and Home Becomes Work*, New York: Metropolitan Books, 1997, p. 27.

10. Meryl Gordon, "Et Tu, Pat?" in *Mirabella*, March/April 1996.

11. Jeff Hearn, Deborah L. Sheppard, Peta Tancred-Sheriff, and Gibson Burrell eds., *The Sexuality of Organization*, London: Sage Publications, 1989, p. 82, cited in Naomi Wolf, *The Beauty Myth*, New York: Anchor Books, 1991, p. 42.

12. Natasha Walters, *The New Feminism*, London: Little Brown, 1998, p. 101.

13. Naomi Wolf, *The Beauty Myth*, New York: Anchor Books, 1991, and Wendy Chapkis, *Beauty Secrets: Women and the Politics of Appearance*, Boston: South End Press, 1986.

14. Mona Harrington, *Women Lawyers*, New York: Alfred Knopf, 1994.

15. The *New York Times*, May 16, 1990.

16. Joyce P. Jacobsen and Laurence Levin, "Effects of Intermittent Labor Force Attachment on Women's Earnings," *Monthly Labor Review*, September 1995.

Part V

BENEFITS

Chapter 10

Social Benefits: The Economic Contribution of Women with Choices

Secretary of State, Madeleine Albright, and Supreme Court Justice Sandra Day O'Connor both stayed at home when their children were young. Albright had never worked until her children reached school age, while O'Conner worked as an attorney and then left her law practice to care for her young children.[1] They both made the choice to stay home with their children and pursue careers only later in life. For all the cases of famous women who have entered the labor force in middle age there are thousands and thousands of unknown women who have taken the same path. They have believed that it is possible to have a meaningful and fulfilling work life even if it is postponed until their forties or fifties.

When women revisit their former employment choices and make the decision to start working for pay, benefits accrue to them personally as well as to society at large. Obviously, women pursue employment goals because doing so maximizes their personal benefits and not because it is good for society. However, their actions have enough economic consequences that social scientists should pay attention.

The purpose of this chapter is to explore these economic consequences. Questions are raised such as: What is the economic potential of middle-aged homemakers and what is the nature of the contribution these women can make to the economy? In order to answer those questions, it is necessary first to explore the occupational possibilities that exist for middle-aged women if they choose to pursue their aspirations in the labor market.

This focus on women's economic contribution in the labor force does not negate their enormous contribution to the economy in their capacity as homemakers. While the economic role of stay-at-home moms is often overlooked, there are three important ways in which they make a contribution to the economy. First, homemakers take care of the home and its members; they provide the glue that holds the family together and the oil that lubricates its hinges. On a more concrete level, they prepare the meals, drive the children, and pay the bills. As such, they are producers of goods and services. While these goods and services are not traded in the market, they nevertheless have economic value because, if they were not provided by the wife/mother for free, they would have to be purchased, for a price, in the open markets (Helen Barkey, mother, wife, and volunteer, reports that she often tells her husband, "If you had to pay for what I do, you couldn't afford me!"). Thus, contributions of stay-at-home women undoubtedly have a positive economic value.

Second, homemakers are often the principal consumers for the household. While they might not unilaterally decide about consumer durables such as automobiles and refrigerators, they are in charge of consumption decisions pertaining to goods such as the family's food, clothing, leisure goods, and so forth. As such, they contribute to the economy in their capacity as consumers by adding to the aggregate demand that fuels national production.

Third, by performing "home duties" (running the household and raising the children), stay-at-home women have enabled the release of men's time and labor for nondomestic economic activities and thereby provided an essential contribution to the economy. Men became enabled to work outside the home and thus to satisfy the manpower demands of growing economies only because they had someone else take care of their basic needs at home. This was the division of labor that fueled Western economic development during this century. Elise Troy, an attorney turned homemaker, describes how after she stopped working, she took over all the household responsibilities so that her husband could concentrate all his time and energy on his career. Ever since he stopped participating in household chores (he "doesn't even have to bring the mail in"), Elise says, "his law practice has taken off!"

Fourth, by producing children, women contribute workers to the future labor force. By dedicating themselves to raising those children, homemakers enhance the quality of that labor force. Every society depends on its labor force for economic growth, and women, in their capacity as mothers, are the cornerstone of that growth.

Thus, women are producers and consumers on the homefront, performing important functions in the micro- and the macro-economy. When they enter the labor force, women add yet one more dimension to their economic contribution.

WOMEN WITH CHOICES ARE HUMAN CAPITAL

When discussing the wealth of nations, economists have traditionally focused on their stock of physical capital. It was only in the post–World War II period that attention turned to the potential and the wealth embodied in the labor force. This wealth, which came to be called human capital, consisted of the education and the skills that workers accumulated over the years. According to economists such as Gary Becker and Theodore Schultz, a society's human capital stock is as important to its economic growth and development as its stock of physical capital.[2] Human capital is created by investing in human beings through a variety of schooling and training programs. As with any investment, it is expected to pay off in the future. The principal form of pay-back is embodied in worker productivity increases, which, in turn, result in both a personal benefit (in the form of higher earnings) as well as a social benefit (in the form of increased productivity and consequently higher rates of economic growth). As a result of such benefits, investment in education and training is viewed as crucial: families tighten their belts in order to provide their children with the best possible education, and societies universally allocate public funds in order to improve their educational systems. In more-developed Canada or less-developed Malaysia, in communist China or capitalist France, in big Russia or little Switzerland, education and training of the population undoubtedly make a country wealthier!

Women with choices contribute to America's stock of human capital in two ways—they produce it and they embody it. With respect to production, women produce the children who will participate in the future labor force. In fact, they do more than just produce them—they nurture them, educate them, instill them with values, and form their worldviews. It is women who rear the future engineers, teachers, and managers that will lead the world into the new century. Thus, women's role in the context of their families is not incidental or marginal to the economy. In the words of economist Shirley Burggraf, in terms of the human capital that it produces, the family "is actually the primary engine of economic growth."[3] As all sources of economic growth, human capital entails investments and American families have been making them. According to estimates, families invest a huge amount of money in their children: in 1995, the average family invested $140,554 in cash outlays and $270,000 worth of parent time.[4]

In addition to creating human capital in their children, women also embody it. They began to acquire skills from the time they learned to read and write and continued to do so throughout their secondary and higher education. During their first careers, they built upon their knowledge through work experience or skill-enhancing programs in their former workplaces. In their second careers, they acquired skills outside the formal schooling venues by living and juggling and managing life. The shadow skills described in Chapter 8 made an important contribution to their total capabilities as workers. Indeed, women who have learned to juggle lots of responsibilities, who have learned to manage a family and several hired helpers, and who have learned to handle responsibility in their volunteer activities have certainly increased their potential contribution to the economy, whether in the workplace or in the home. In the workplace, they can contribute skills of juggling, managing, working with people, and completing tasks. In the home, they can be more efficient and productive in their roles as producers and consumers. While unaccompanied by a formal diploma describing how, where, and when they were acquired, shadow skills nevertheless embody knowledge and experience. They are valid additions to the stock of human capital in society and should be universally recognized as such.

Shadow skills are an intriguing and compelling form of human capital because their social costs are zero while their social benefits are positive. How is that possible? How can the economy get a benefit without paying for it? The "free lunch" is evident if we analyze the concomitant social costs and social benefits inherent in the acquisition of the skills that homemakers acquire.

With respect to costs, shadow skills are acquired without any direct cost to the household or to the government.[5] Yes, shadow skills are acquired free of charge—there is no overhead, no expenditure on books and teachers, no tuition charges, and no state investment in school buildings. However, women who do not work in order to raise their children do incur an indirect cost, namely, the opportunity cost. This cost is measured by the value of their forsaken income, what they could be earning if they were working, in other words, their best alternative. During their child-rearing years, women who stayed out of the labor market gave up an income. Since that income was not zero,[6] the value of women's forsaken income is positive. It is only by observing the opportunity cost of women's time outside the labor force that the cost of acquiring shadow skills (and therefore investing in human capital) turns out to be positive. However, opportunity cost is not an out-of-pocket expense and so it is not a direct cost, and, therefore, everyone except economists overlooks it.

With respect to benefits, the acquisition of shadow skills represents a positive addition both for the individual as well as the overall economy. The individual woman with choices reaps benefits because shadow skills increase her chances of achieving her goals of entering the labor market. Society reaps benefits because shadow skills contribute to the overall human capital in a society.

Therefore, an analysis of the human capital embodied in middle-aged women with choices underscores the shortsightedness of overlooking them. Indeed, policymakers, academics, and the media should more carefully analyze the potential of these women and their possible economic contribution to society.

THE ACCOMMODATING WORK ENVIRONMENT AND WOMEN WITH CHOICES

In her study of working women, Judith Bardwick found that despite their employment, many women tend to (1) derive status primarily from their husband, (2) tie their identity primarily to being a wife and mother, (3) believe that their husbands' work is more important than their own, and (4) feel guilty about the effect of their career on their family.[7] It is likely that middle-aged homemakers who enter the labor force will continue to derive status primarily from their husbands, their primary identity will continue to be that of a mother and wife, and they will continue to believe that their husbands' work is more important than theirs. It is the fourth of Bardwick's conclusions that middle-aged women are trying hard to avoid—feeling guilty about the effect of their work on their families. Most will consider becoming employed only if the costs they incur are lower than the benefits they derive. Guilt is one of the costs they consider. In order to offset it or eliminate it altogether, women with choices seek out accommodations in the workplace that best satisfy their particular needs.

In an effort to find the most appropriate accommodating work environment, women with choices try to be introspective and identify what they want. Painful and confusing as this task may be, they ask themselves questions about the tradeoffs they are willing and able to make in their work lives. These questions fall into two general categories: What are they willing to give up and what are they willing to take upon themselves in order to be employed. With respect to the former, women ponder the following: How much of their freedom are they willing to forgo, how much loss in leisure can they take, how much family time are they willing to give up, and how much spontaneity can they live without. With respect to what they are willing to take on, women consider just how much time they are willing to devote to work-related activities, how much debt they are willing to incur in order to retrain or to set up a business, and how much responsibility they are willing to take on in their jobs. Women with choices also consider how much income they are willing to give up in order to have flexibility of hours. Alternatively, how much prestige will they give up if they choose to be on a mommy track and how many benefits will they forgo in order to work part time. Such painful introspection provides some measure of clarity to an otherwise fuzzy and confusing endeavor, that of embarking on a job search after a long hiatus.

The participants in this study were asked how much freedom they are willing to give up, how much responsibility they are willing to take on, and how important salary is to them. Possible answers included: a lot, some, little, and not at all. The emerging pattern was clear. The majority of women were willing to give up some freedom (58%), take on a lot of responsibility (71%), and put little or some emphasis on income (81%). In other words, women were willing to have jobs with responsibility as long as they could retain their freedom. Their salary was unequivocally the least important factor in their conceptualization of their future jobs. Anna Moore, a former banker who recently reentered the labor market as a real estate agent, explains this issue succinctly: "In real estate I work very hard. I often work 30 to 40 hours per week. However, it's the sort of work that always enables me to make it to my son's soccer game! That makes all the difference to me."

Women with choices operate under conditions quite different from those faced by the majority of women entering the labor force. Their distinguishing feature is their fundamental reason for working—satisfaction, not money, and satisfaction is embodied in freedom and flexibility. While female workers in other socioeconomic groups are bound by the income they must contribute to their households, the housework they must perform, and the working schedules they must abide by, women with choices have different constraints. They are bound by their desire to retain control over their time and flexibility in their working hours. They are unlikely to take a job unless it offers them some measure of flexibility. They are not desperate for employment so they can afford to be choosy. Such considerations distinguish their approach to the labor market, their willingness to negotiate, as well as their willingness to do what they don't like to do. Their free time vs. work tradeoff is different from that of most women, as is their tradeoff between free time and remuneration. This is not to say that women with choices are alone in their quest for free time. To the contrary, a majority of American workers, men and women alike, report that they are willing to trade time for money. Juliet Schor describes a 1989 poll of workers in which almost two-thirds said they would prefer to give up some of their salary, by, on average, 13% in order to gain time.[8] However, women with choices are likely to give up more money for time than the general working population, at least in part because they have the capacity to do so.

Given that women with choices have indicated a strong desire to retain flexibility and free time, even trading the possibility of money, power, and position for it, they are prime candidates for employment on the mommy track in their third careers. They cringe at the thought of full-time professional careers. The concept of the superwoman holds no appeal to them. The idea of a stressful job, in which the demands of the workplace are all consuming, is viewed with horror. The possible concomitant child neglect, marital distress, stress-related illnesses, and sleep deprivation hold no appeal to women with choices. At the same time, women with choices are prime candidates for exploiting all forms of accommodation in the workplace. They have all the right conditions to make demands in their workplace: they tend to have at least a college degree, an earning spouse, networking connections, and financial security. All of this enhances their ability to set the terms of their employment.

OCCUPATIONS FOR WOMEN WITH CHOICES

Middle-aged women who have acquired human capital during their second career need to determine how to exploit their skills in order to maximize their individual personal benefits. At the same time, society should consider how to exploit homemakers' cumulative human capital in order to maximize the benefits to the economy. At the level of the macroeconomy, this translates into finding the most appropriate occupations for the particular combination of shadow skills and formal training that have been acquired by middle-aged homemakers.

In the 1990s, American women have found the following occupations to be the most in demand: computer programmer, telecommunications manager, employee trainer, family physician, nurse-practitioner, physical therapist, diversity manager, ombudsman, environmental consultant, private investigator, and professional-temp placement specialist.[9] However, not all popular occupations are appropriate for middle-aged women with choices, especially those who rely primarily on their shadow skills. Realistically, what kind of occupations can these homemakers aspire to? A woman who lacks professional training and who has been out of the labor force for 25 years is unlikely to become the CEO of a Fortune 500 company. It is a waste of her time to aspire to such a goal. On the other hand, middle-aged women with choices need not despair and retreat from their employment goals altogether. Their options for employment lie between those two extremes.

Not all women with choices will embark upon identical occupational paths. While formal training, work experience, and personal characteristics all determine how prospective employers judge them, other less tangible and unmeasurable factors play a crucial role. For example, creativity is a must for middle-aged women. They, more so than other women, must be creative in terms of how they look for work, where they look for it, and what ideas they come up with for self-employment. Creativity is necessary since it enables women to create their own opportunities. As a result of the requirements that many of these women set for the sort of job they want and as a result of the obstacles they face with respect to their lack of recent work experience, creativity is second only to motivation in helping them succeed. Finding a niche for themselves is also crucial. Middle-aged women with choices need to identify a subfield of a sector in which there is a demand for their particular skills. Often this entails identifying a special interest group to whom to direct their services or products, such as finding special needs of a group in the population who could benefit from their particular knowledge (for example, single people, empty-nesters, animal lovers, etc.).[10] Finally, middle-aged women would benefit from having a passion. Passion motivates. Passion gives direction. If women have a passion, it should be reflected in their employment goals. If they do not have a passion for the activity they plan to pursue, they will have difficulty overcoming the initial inertia necessary for success. There are many options for producing goods or offering a variety of services that enable women to indulge their passion while simultaneously satisfying a market demand.[11]

While creatively channeling their passions into a niche, women with choices also have to determine if they prefer to be self-employed or to work for someone. Many women are attracted to self-employment because of the benefits it offers. For example, women can be their own bosses (and thus not have to tolerate directives they may disagree with) and they can have more flexibility with respect to worktime and location. Moreover, they can easily translate their passion, motivation, and love of an activity into a prestige occupation. At the same time, women with choices are often immune to the principal disadvantage of self-employment, namely, an overbearing concern with the bottom line. These women are more likely to have access to start-up capital without competing for loans, and they are more likely to have the ability to sustain a business in the red for a longer period of time than workers in other income brackets.

Self-employment is very popular among the respondents in this study: 52% of the sample reported that they would strongly prefer to work for themselves. Gloria Curran explained the reasoning behind her inclination toward self-employment. "I want to work at home and I want to set my own hours. I'd consider working for someone else, in an office, but only if the salary was so high so as to compensate for the loss in my freedom and flexibility." Isabel Gutierrez realizes she will have to work temporarily for someone else in order to gain experience in interior design, but "ultimately I want my own business. It's the only way I'll be able to set my own hours." Ann Bowden concurs with Isabel: "As an independent contractor, I have more control over my own lifestyle. No one tells me when I have to come in and when I can leave." Tory Cohen adds: "You have to work hard if you're self-employed, but at least you'll see the results of your labor. And anyway, you get a lot more choices and control over them when you're your own boss. What do you give up by not working for someone else? Only health care and the illusion of retirement benefits (I call it illusion, because you think they're enough to live on when you retire but they're not!)." Finally, Elise Troy wants to be on her own so that she can retain "the freedom to pick my own cases and my own hours" when she returns to practicing law.

Among those who are inclined toward self-employment, some women were exploring the possibilities for partnerships with others like themselves. Such a partnership enables women who share an interest to get together and pool their energies. They can complement each other in those areas in which they differ while strengthening each other in those areas in which they are similar. Shared family structures and socioeconomic backgrounds result in greater understanding for each other's work and nonwork constraints and demands. Women who shared volunteering experiences know how to work together. From experience, they know that teamwork, cooperation, and tolerance underlie a successful partnership.

Two mothers described how they came to pursue partnerships with other like-minded women. A few years ago, Gloria Curran discovered that she loved art and since then, it has been her all-consuming passion. It all began with a frustrating search for drape fabric. After reviewing mounds of materials from innumerable sources and finding nothing to her liking, Gloria took up her decorator's suggestion that she paint fabric herself. Together they set out on the laborious task of hand painting yards of material. Not only was the end result breathtaking but Gloria also discovered a new passion (and, she admits, a therapy for her problems). She would now like to channel that passion into a successful business. But it takes more than love of fabric painting to succeed in the competitive art world. Gloria is aware that there are numerous skills required for setting up a business that she altogether lacks. She is the first to admit that she knows little about budgeting, administration, or marketing. But she won't let her limitations get in the way of her goal. Her solution: She'd like to pool her resources with other women who have the skills she lacks. "Some of us are talking about opening an art store that will sell various forms of art. We are identifying our strengths and weaknesses, and we're hoping to combine our energies and set up a business together. I know what I do well, and I also know what I can't do at all. If we each manage to complement our weaknesses, then we have the right conditions to start a partnership."

Amanda Adams, a former computer analyst and group project manager at a major Miami firm, is also very good with her hands. During her second career, she worked on innumerable art projects in her child's school. Because she was good at it, she was repeatedly asked to help out with crafts. She and others who spent their days by the potter's wheel, with crayons in hand and papier-mache up to their elbows, are exploring ways to make a business out of their activities. "We want to open a store that will sell art and teach art and make commissioned art. We'd like it to also be a site for entertainment related to art, both for children and adults." While Amanda is drawn to the creative aspects of an art store, as well as the flexibility she thinks is associated with it, she remains apprehensive about the numerous unknowns. These include the intricacies of running a business and the nature of her relationship with her friends once they become business associates, all valid concerns, she feels, and none with easy answers. While she is very excited about the idea of the art store, Amanda has made contingency plans if it fails to materialize (she has explored self-employment opportunities, specifically for part-time work as a computer consultant).

Partnerships do not appeal to every woman considering setting up a business. Helen Barkey, a former nurse, plans on starting a party planning service or opening a boutique. While she has considered going into partnership with women with similar interests, she is skeptical about the success of such an endeavor. "I've been burned in the past during volunteering, so I'd be very careful if I went into business with others. I put 200% of myself into whatever I do and I only want to work with others who do the same. I've started keeping lists in my mind of women with whom I want to work with as well as those I never want to work with again. This list applies to my volunteering efforts as well as a possible future business." The list of people she thinks she could develop a partnership with is too short to be encouraging.

While self-employment is not a panacea for middle-aged women, it is certainly the option that accommodates the greatest number of their constraints, addresses the greatest number of their concerns, and, in the process, satisfies the greatest number of their needs. In that sense, the emergence of self-employment possibilities in the late twentieth century opens new doors for late entrants into the labor force. The benefit of self-employment transcends age, gender, and socioeconomic background. It even transcends culture. It is because of its positive aspects that self-employment has also been touted as a solution for the employment crisis of women in many developing countries. Evidence from across Asia and Africa shows that creative and entrepreneurial women have transformed their family and village lives by taking on the opportunities offered by self-employment possibilities (and, of course, sustained by the institutional changes that have turned those possibilities into realities).

This does not imply that there are no benefits to women with choices derived from working for someone else. To the contrary, there are many. By becoming a hired worker, set-up costs are avoided, and responsibilities are lowered, not to mention that it is easier to learn by doing under the guidance of more experienced workers. The advantages of working for someone else are so great that 16% of the women sampled said they would not even consider anything else. Denise Bentley, a 49-year-old former journalist, was clear about her future employment goals: "I'd never want to be self-employed in any way. You work twice as hard for half the money. And anyway, I don't want a solitary job—I've had that for years at home." Jessica James was also clear about her inclination against self-employment (an inclination that is rooted, she thinks, in her former career as an attorney): "It takes a tremendous number of hours to open and sustain a successful law office, I know this from experience. It just wouldn't meet my current needs to spend so much time, energy, and capital on my job." Clearly, in her third career, Jessica prefers a less-consuming job—in her mind that cannot be achieved by working for herself. Another respondent, Roberta Martin, had a particular type of constraint that precluded self-employment: "I'm trained as a math teacher. If I were to be self-employed, that would mean tutoring students. Such tutoring can only take place after school, in the evenings, and on weekends. Those are exactly the times when I don't want to work, those are the times I want to be with my family. With my particular skills, in order to work in the mornings, I have to work for someone else." Finally, Abby Williams, with ample experience working for herself before her 10-year hiatus, said, "I want to work for someone else—it's just so much easier!"

I have divided occupational possibilities of middle-aged women with choices according to the shadow skills women acquired informally during their second careers. Within each occupational category listed below, middle-aged women could apply the knowledge and experience they already possess. Most occupations are in the service sector (only the few that entail production of finished products are classified in the manufacturing sector). That is no wonder, given that the American economy is essentially a service economy in which over 70% of the national income is derived from services and in which some 80% of the jobs entail the provision of services.[12] Women with choices have for years been providing just that—services. They have provided a wide variety of services to a wide array of recipients: their children, their spouses, their parents, their children's schools, their religious organizations, and their volunteer institutions. If it is services that are in demand by the economy, women with choices have the experience to provide them.

A few words of caution are in order. First, by identifying occupations for middle-aged women with a long hiatus or with little work experience, I am not characterizing certain jobs as either male or female, or as upper class or lower class. Instead, I am offering a realistic assessment of what motivated middle-aged homemakers can do. The occupations listed below are relevant for those women who lack prior professional training or who do not want to work in the fields they were previously trained in. Few of the occupations listed require major retooling or retraining although some require certification courses. Clearly, those women who are currently embarking on law, architecture, or Ph.D. degrees will have different options from the ones listed below. So too will those women who hope to return to the highly skilled professions they once had. Since these women know exactly what they want, they will not be the focus of the following.

Second, the descriptions of shadow skills in Chapter 8 have touched upon a very sensitive subject in both the academic literature and the popular press, namely, the role of gender characteristics in leadership skills. It is sensitive because there are those, both males and females, who claim and disclaim that there are inherent and immutable differences in style between men and women on the grounds of their sex. I do not propose to enter that discussion here. Suffice it to say there will always be stereotypes of women in leadership positions and there will always be women who shatter those stereotypes. Finally, the occupations listed below are appropriate both for self-employment as well as working for others.

Occupations Using Skills in Human Interaction

Ann Bowden and Sarah Bond both started their graduate studies in social work when they were well over forty. Both are convinced that they could not possibly do meaningful social work without the life experience that age has given them. "I simply didn't have the same understanding and empathy when I was in my twenties as I do now," said Ann. Sarah adds that "life experience should be a prerequisite for social work!" During their second careers, Ann and Sarah, as well as numerous other women, acquired skills in human interaction, loosely known as people skills. Those who have them are said to get along with people. They can apply an understanding of human nature to their interpersonal relationships. Women who have stayed at home to rear children or who have worked as volunteers in service organizations have often learned these people skills in order to thrive and survive in the many life circumstances they faced. What can they now do with those skills?

Women who are nurturing and loving, who can sympathize and empathize, who are willing to listen and to understand, and who are capable of providing attention and care are prime candidates for positions in human services. These include services for children or for the elderly. When these nurturing skills are further combined with management skills, women can offer services as professional mothers: they can set up nursing care, arrange for medical assistance for relatives far away, or arrange creative children's transportation. When nurturing is further combined with a mission, possibilities abound in services such as helping heal the grief of loss, ending drunk driving, or preventing teenage pregnancy.

Moreover, women's nurturing experiences often convey an ability for occupations that require some measure of empathy and sympathy. These include services for any of the following: weight control; sleep disorders; depression; stress; emotional problems; in-home health care; holistic medicine and health; nutritional information; addictions such as drug, alcohol, or smoking; allergies; terminal illness; sexual dysfunction; marriage problems; divorce; physical handicaps; physical fitness; and physical abuse. Women's vast responsibilities for the lives of several individuals gives them the experience that they need for some of these services. Moreover, particularly empathetic women with a talent in art have found art therapy to combine their interest in both art and healing.

Women's experience in managing the household finances gives them financial skills to apply to business—theirs or other people's. The fact that many women regularly paid the bills, dispensed family money, and allocated household expenditures is valuable in positions such as financial officers. Their budgeting skills make them adept at fundraising (especially if combined with effective people skills). Their experience and skills gained in the organization of household finances enables them to pursue options such as how-to services for the following: bill paying, medical claims, recovering from debt, acquiring credit, negotiating fees with lawyers, collecting child support, preparing taxes, personal economics, getting the most from your ex-spouse, recovering from bankruptcy, coordinating estate sales, or applying for financial aid. Those with a particularly strong sense of finance and business may be motivated to venture into business, for example, open a cafe, a boutique, beauty salon, or a catering service.

Women's experience with people and interpersonal relationships makes them adept at providing services in the form of personal shopper, reunion planner, wedding consultant, image consultant, matchmaker, couples enrichment group leader, and errand service organizer. Moreover, the years women spent organizing their children's birthday parties and their own social functions predispose them for employment as party planners (for both adults or children) as well as social events organizers.

Their experience in their own home gives them the ability, if so inclined, to be interior designers and decorators, collectibles dealers, or antiques finders. If they traveled extensively during their hiatus from the labor force, they can combine a passion (i.e., antiques) with sources overseas to provide a service focused on identifying sources for clients. Alternatively, they may be interested in some form of import or export of goods from countries they have special links to. Those interested in homes might like selling real estate; those interested in their gardens might be interested in some form of horticultural services, including garden planning or floral retail.

The insight into human nature that women have attained during their child-rearing years, coupled with their supervisory skills, the ability to arbitrate among people, and the patience they have developed, enable middle-aged women to manage groups, judge situations, and oversee activities. As such, they had practice as, for example, personnel managers.

Mothers know how to get people to behave in the way that they want, a skill that predisposes them for jobs in politics. Women's flexibility and adaptability are suitable for those occupations in which decision making is not predetermined but allows a lot of spontaneity, an essential for jobs in politics. Finally, women have learned, with experience, to inspire, to motivate, and to persuade. In their communication, they have had to give, guide, help, and intuit, skills that are also useful for jobs in politics.

Occupations Using Skills in Conveying Information

In order to communicate with their children, household helpers, and volunteer staff, women with choices have learned to speak in a way that conveys information. They learned techniques for telling that are effective and efficient and simultaneously sensitive. They have also learned to influence, to motivate, and to inspire while conveying information. In order to explain, to define, to help others discover, imagine, and learn, they have developed the skills of teachers.

However, just because they have raised children and taught them many things does not mean mothers are qualified to be grade school teachers. Indeed, teaching children, reaching out to them effectively, and holding their attention require formal skills and training that raising a child does not necessarily impart.

However, short of teaching in the school system, women with choices may extend their teaching skills into a wide variety of other endeavors.

What kind of information can women convey? Women have not only acquired skills in conveying information, they have also acquired information that has value. Their own particular interests may determine into what direction that information can be channeled. Women may be information providers by, for example, teaching busy people how to organize their lives, how to dress (fashion consulting), how to arrange their furniture (home/office interior design), or how to behave (etiquette consulting). According to their inclination, they may teach dancing, cooking techniques, or resume writing; they may also conduct exercise classes or instruct yoga. Moreover, if their own experience is augmented with precise and up-to-date information, women can successfully advise by providing services such as camp consulting, outdoor survival skills, or nanny placement services.

Women who seek occupations founded on conveying information have the choice of several mediums. They may convey their expertise through a verbal method, written method, visual method or, for those with computer skills, through the CD-rom. Verbal efforts take the form of consultant, storyteller, or singer. In the publishing industry, women might write books, stories, romance, diaries, fiction, poetry, and how-to books. The visual method includes the use of photography or videos, while a home page on the Internet spreads their message rapidly and reaches across the globe.

Occupations Using Skills in Producing Tangible Products

The skills women have acquired while producing concrete and tangible products are useful in occupations in which consumer goods are produced. The days women have spent helping their children make the science fair poster, the hours they contributed to making the backdrop for the school play, and the energy they expended on the table decorations for the annual museum auction have all come to fruition: women know how to begin with unrelated inputs, how to combine them in the most efficient proportions, and how to end up with a tangible finished product. In other words, they have mastered the production function for a good that can be sold on the open market. This economic activity, also known as manufacturing, has been performed by women in factories, in cooperatives, and in homes for centuries. Moreover, to the extent that women were involved in purchasing for the household, they have developed the skills of purchasing agents, indispensable for the acquisition of inputs used in the manufacturing process.

A combination of women's manufacturing skills and their interests may yield business activity in the following areas: garden (landscape, flowers), clothing (sewing, patterns, dyes, knitting), foods (catering service, breads and baked goods, personal chef, canning gourmet food, health foods, vitamins, winemaking), arts (painting, sculpture, photography, jewelry), and amusement (toys, kits, making party favors, make baskets, dried flower wreaths).

Occupations Using Skills in Juggling and Managing

Women have managed numerous activities and projects and have juggled responsibilities and demands throughout their lives. They have managed their own lives as well as those of others. In doing so, they have performed several tasks simultaneously. The multitasking experience they have thus acquired is useful in service jobs that are executive, administrative, and managerial in nature. Women with such experience are particularly adept at working as managers, especially of their own business. To their job they can bring to bear their skills in organizing, alloting responsibilities, administering, and allocating scarce resources among competing ends. Indeed, running a family is like running a small business. It requires skills such as problem solving, leadership, guidance, responsibility for a group, as well as the ability to make quick decisions and to learn by doing. These are all skills that predispose women to some form of management. It is thus no wonder that a survey of 270 female and 645 male executives polled by the Foundation for Future Leadership showed that women are better managers than men. They scored higher than men in problem solving, planning, managing employee relationships, leading and communicating (the only area where men scored higher is managing themselves, including handling pressure and coping with frustration).[13]

Women's experience in controlling and exercising power predisposes them to jobs in management (and politics). Their ability to think quickly (due to their skills in responding instantaneously to situations as they arise), to be flexible and adaptable, to negotiate, and to think on their feet also prepares them for jobs in management. Moreover, their experience in organization and juggling can help them provide the service of professional organizers. They can organize lives, wardrobes, desks, children's activities, and children's summers.

THE DEMAND FOR MIDDLE-AGED FEMALE LABOR

It is easy to understand why some women with choices want to enter the labor force in middle age. It is also relatively easy to identify what sort of jobs they could perform and what occupations might be right for their particular skills. However, these are both supply-side considerations that focus on the conditions and desires of the suppliers of labor, that being the women. What about the demand side? What about the employers, the ones who demand women's labor? For any market to function properly, there must be both a supply and a demand. What is the nature of the demand for middle-aged homemakers? Specifically, why would employers hire a middle-aged woman who has been out of the labor market for many years? Why take the risk? What is the perceived benefit?

Alexandra Jones has years of experience both inside and outside the labor force. Recently, she started working again and plans to stay employed until retirement. Her current job requirements include active participation in the company's hiring process. She had some interesting and encouraging views on the demand for middle-aged female labor. "When I interview prospective employees," she said, "I take into consideration their life experiences (as well as their credentials). As a woman who hasn't worked for many years, I appreciate how important that life experience is. So, when a middle-aged mother walks into my office, I'm thrilled. I know right away what she had to go through and what she had to learn in order to survive. Unfortunately, there just haven't been enough middle-aged mothers looking for work!"

What is it that employers such as Alexandra are seeking and what is it that they might be finding in women with ample life experience? While Alexandra might have a heightened awareness of shadow skills given her own life experience, all employers examine the total package embodied in prospective employees. They compare the value of that package with its cost, in other words, they perform a cost/benefit analysis. They identify the expected value of what the worker will produce and compare it to the cost of hiring that worker. Since they do not know with accuracy the future value of the worker's output, they infer it by assessing properties of prospective workers that will determine their productivity. These include credentials, shadow skills, personality, as well as evidence of creativity, perseverance, and motivation. They estimate the value of all indicators of worker productivity, however imperfect they may be. With respect to the cost of hiring the worker, the employer estimates the sum of the salary, the value of the accompanying benefits (social security, health care, etc.), as well as the cost of any training that might have to take place to enable the worker to perform her duties.

In order to understand the benefit and cost to employers of hiring middle-aged women with choices, it is helpful to refer to the above discussion of how much freedom women are willing to give up, how much responsibility they are willing to take on, and how important salary is to them. The responses indicate a unique tradeoff between work and free time among middle-aged women with choices. This tradeoff gives them an advantage in the current labor market because employers are attracted by their willingness to trade income (compensation) for more leisure (less than full-time work). By hiring advantaged middle-aged women, employers can get more for less. They get women who are motivated, intelligent, creative, yet who do not demand a high salary and who, often by accepting part-time employment, are willing to forgo benefits such as health care and pension plans. Employers get a wealth of experience and a breadth of skills at a lower cost than they would otherwise spend on equivalent labor. In economics jargon, the marginal product of such workers exceeds their wage (in other words, the value of women's labor exceeds what they are paid). How can that be? It might be because of the particular nature of supply and demand for middle-aged women's labor. Women with choices are motivated to get into the workforce and they are relatively insensitive to wage as long as the work they do is of interest to them and the conditions of their work life are to their liking. In other words, financial remuneration is not the crucial determinant of the supply of their labor (again, in economics jargon, the labor supply with respect to wage is elastic, as is the income elasticity of labor supply). Since employers are concerned with the bottom line, they are more likely to take a risk with an individual who will cost less than one who will cost more, especially if the risk is perceived to be only short term (indeed, risky workers are not hired with contracts that cannot be easily terminated).

The greatest challenge lies in getting employers to see past the lack of recent work experience, the age, and the hiatus. How can a woman ensure that her human capital is actually recognized by potential employers? Especially under conditions of tight labor market conditions, when unemployment rates are low and the market seems saturated, under what circumstances will employers take note of the advantaged, middle-aged woman? Women's ability to successfully compete for a position in such a labor market will depend not only on their prior formal skills but also on their current ability to convince a prospective employer of the relevance of their shadow skills. In so doing, the three characteristics (introduced above) of a successful middle-aged job seeker are once again invoked: creativity, passion, and finding a niche for herself.

POTENTIAL ECONOMIC LOSSES TO SOCIETY

When middle-aged women with choices enter the labor market, the economic benefit to society is embodied in the human capital that they contribute. That human capital in turn is responsible for increasing the aggregate supply of goods and services, thus propelling the macroeconomy into cyclical growth. Yet, the prospect of middle-aged homemakers entering the labor force in droves is often viewed with disdain by policymakers, labor market analysts, and working people at large. Their negative response is rooted in the fact that women with choices do not need to work for pay. If they have stayed home so long, the argument goes, why rock the boat now, especially when they have so little productive time left? The crux of this view is the belief that women who have not been in the labor force for economic necessity would, by starting to work, in some way negatively intervene and thus disrupt the functioning of the labor markets (the skeptical view might be as follows: these women would be taking the place of those who do need to work for pay merely to satisfy their upper-class yearning for something new and meaningful!). The argument against women's reentry makes use of the following discomforting statistics of a general downsizing across America: since 1979, more than 43 million jobs have been lost.[14] While new jobs have been created during this period, they tended to be at less than middle-class pay (indeed, one generation ago those who got laid off subsequently found work that paid as well. Today, two-thirds work for less pay than before). Therefore, why increase the competition for jobs and thereby hurt those who have to work for a living?

Is there any economic justification to this argument? Are there any ways in which entry into the labor force by middle-aged women with choices might have negative ramifications and thereby offset the positive benefits to the economy of their entry? Some of these possible ramifications are explored below.

Displacement of More "Deserving" Workers

Tory Cohen, a 42-year-old homemaker and volunteer, described the universal response she encountered whenever she voiced her desire to work for pay. "People keep asking me why I want to work. I feel as though they are resentful, as though they're condemning me for taking work away from someone who really needs it." The argument that middle-aged women will compete with male (read: heads of household) and female (read: women who work for economic necessity) workers and, in the process of competition will displace them, is simply flawed. When working for others, middle-aged women with choices, on the whole, tend to prefer part-time employment and flexibility in time and location. As such, they do not compete for the same jobs as those held by professional males who are heads of households. For the same reasons, they are not in competition with career women who are full-time workers, who have dedicated years of service to their jobs, and who are not on a mommy track. Middle-aged women are also not in competition with unskilled and underprivileged women since they are not competing for jobs in their occupational categories. Indeed, women with choices are unlikely to engage in factory assembly work or to flip hamburgers at a fast-food restaurant. They would pose no threat to men or women who have been working without a hiatus and thereby have accumulated the experience and the expertise that would tilt the competition in their favor. Thus, whether they are trained professionals or untrained returning moms, women with choices are not in direct competition with any other labor category except other women like themselves.

To the extent that women with choices begin to work for themselves and create their own business, the economy is open to anyone with drive and creativity. To the extent that their socioeconomic background helps them in the creation of their own business, it provides them with an advantage in the competitive struggle for survival in the small business area. But it is just that, one advantage, one of many that exist among the general population. Some people have the advantage of superior intelligence, others have the advantage of superior physical strength. Inbred characteristics are not cause for disqualification from economic competition, so why should socioeconomic advantage be?

Displacement of More "Deserving" Products

If consumer income is finite at any point in time and if consumers allocate their income among the goods and services they buy, then income spent on one good implies there is less income to be spent on another. If consumers purchase goods produced by women with choices, it follows that they will have less income to allot to more "deserving" products, namely, those produced by people who have to work out of economic necessity. In that way, "deserving" or worthy products become displaced by "undeserving" ones in the marketplace. This argument is senseless on several grounds. First, women with choices have as much right to compete in the marketplace and to market their products among consumers as anyone else. Second, the initial assumption pertaining to fixed income is valid only in the very short run. Therefore, for all intents and purposes, consumption is not a zero-sum game. To the contrary, as total income rises (or falls) over time, so does the possibility of purchasing more (or less) of all goods. American economic history reveals that workers are motivated to work ever longer hours in order to increase their income so as to consume more of the ever increasing supply of goods. There is no reason to believe that this trend will not continue into the future. Third, the principle of consumer sovereignty bestows upon the consumer the right to decide what good to buy. If consumers do not want to purchase goods produced by women with choices, they will simply vote with their wallets and decrease their demand for such goods. In a market economy, such consumer behavior will result in producer bankruptcy, as it would for any business, irrespective of the gender, age, and socioeconomic background of the owner.

Loss of Women's Contribution to the Household

If women with choices leave their households in order to take up employment, the ensuing vacuum will plunge the household into a free fall! In the process, the basic needs of the household will not be met so the productivity of all its members will decrease and thus the household will incur an economic loss. This argument rests on the assumption that women mind the children and the home, and as such perform a crucial economic function. But questions of who will rear the children and who will mind the home are no longer pertinent for middle-aged women as they were some ten years earlier. The children are older and tend to require less constant attention. Many have already left their parental home. In their capacity as homemakers, women's overview of household affairs remains necessary and desirable, although it no longer requires full-time attention since the wheels of the household machinery have been set in motion and are well greased from years of successful operation.

Moreover, when women with choices enter the labor market, they are likely to hire additional household help, thereby contributing to the employment of low-skilled labor and thus directly stimulating economic growth.

Negative Demographic Effects

Working women tend to have fewer children. They have fewer children because each child is more expensive than it would be if they didn't work: according to Gary Becker and others who uphold this microeconomic theory of fertility, mothers who are employed earn an income and as such have a positive opportunity cost of time (in other words, their time is worth more than zero dollars).[15] When they bear children and become homemakers, they cease earning and therefore incur a loss of income. The opportunity cost of their time is then added to the explicit costs of having children (resulting in a higher total cost of children to working mothers than to unemployed moms). It follows from this theory that when women enter the labor force and thereby increase the opportunity cost of their time, they will bear fewer children (in other words, if the cost of having children rises, fewer will be demanded). Fewer children translates into a smaller pool of workers for the future labor force, a fact that could have serious long-term manpower repercussions and disastrous demographic consequences.

This microeconomic theory of fertility is used to explain demographic changes in countries around the world: across levels of development (in more developed countries as well as in the Third World), across political systems (in democracies as well as in dictatorships), and across economic systems (in capitalism as well as in socialism).[16] However, it is not valid for women past their childbearing years! Women in their third careers are unlikely to bear any more children, therefore, their entry into the labor market will have no demographic effect at all.

In conclusion, there are no economic losses to society incurred by middle-aged women entering the labor force. There are also no moral grounds on which these women can be discouraged from entering the labor force. Women with choices have as much right to enter the labor force as anyone else. They must have equal access to jobs as well as equal opportunity to get them, based on equal rights, civil rights, and human rights legislation in this country. Gender equality was the cornerstone of the women's movement: its goals were that women have choices and that they should be able to exercise those choices as long as they harm no one. While the women's movement did not have women of privileged socioeconomic backgrounds in mind during its struggle for equality, surely its basic principles are as valid to intragender discrimination (on the basis of class and privilege) as they are to discrimination between genders. Equality is related to fairness (as pointed out by economist Amartya Sen), and equal opportunity for middle-aged women with choices to compete in the labor market is clearly fair.

CONCLUSIONS

There was a time when help wanted ads in newspapers were divided by gender. A look at the *New York Times* classified section of the 1950s indicates that employers were very clear about the gender they wanted to hire for particular jobs. While such discrimination on the basis of sex is outlawed in the 1990s, it is a fact that not all occupations are equally suited for all men and women. It follows that not all occupations are equally suited for middle-aged women with choices who desire flexibility in their work lives. It is not the employer who is discriminating, rather it is the women with choices who are discriminating by being choosy about the job for which they will give up their current lifestyles. It is not society that is holding these women down in shackles nor is institutional discrimination to blame. Rather, a realistic overview of what is available to them, coupled with their ability to make choices, drives them toward certain types of employment.

Indeed, women with choices tend not to have the same work vs. family considerations that are shared by the vast majority of women. They are often willing to work for less pay, they are willing to tolerate being underemployed, and they are willing to work without many benefits. In other words, they are often willing to work for a total remuneration package that is not only lower than one of comparably aged women but also lower than the marginal product of their labor.

Is it exploitation to pay women less than the value of their product? This question was answered by one of the sampled women, Elise Troy, a former high-income attorney turned homemaker who knows exactly where she wants to work in the future. When her children leave home, she is hoping to work part time in an organization whose goals and values she holds in high esteem. Her pay there, she knows, will be minimal. "Should I be insulted by what I know they will offer me? I've thought about it and my answer is no. It's more important for me to do work that is compelling than to earn a high salary." Another respondent, Rebecca Miller, concurs: "It's simply not important how much I get paid, as long as I do what I like."

It cannot be exploitation to pay women less than the value of their product since both employees and employers are rational, informed, and are maximizing their utility. Women are voluntarily accepting to work at lower wages than they would receive had they worked all their lives.[17] The difference may be viewed as the price they pay for the luxury of staying out of the labor market and for getting on the labor treadmill while it is moving. Also, to the extent that women are doing work they like to do, they are willing to accept a wage lower than they would if they were doing distasteful work. So the wage differential between what they are paid and what they might be paid may be viewed as the price women pay for doing what they like. Moreover, they are willing to accept a lower wage because, in many cases, they are not fundamentally changing their lifestyles: they enter the labor force only under conditions that enable them to combine work and home in a comfortable way. Under those conditions, women are happy because their job gives them satisfaction and employers are happy because they are getting more for less (more output at a lower cost).

If women are being paid below the marginal product of their labor, what happens to the residual? In other words, if there is a discrepancy between the value of women's pay and the value of the product they produce, then who benefits from the difference? The employers benefit. The existence of this benefit (known as producer surplus in economics literature) is not evidence of exploitation since the residual may be viewed as additional inducement to the employer to hire women who otherwise might not be hired. Women, as rational individuals who make informed choices, can simply choose to reject an arrangement in which the residual is accrued by the employer. Indeed, they do not have to work for economic necessity and they have the power to make choices, so if they exert their free will and accept such an arrangement, it cannot be called exploitation.

Of course, there are women with choices for whom this discussion about the tradeoff between wages and freedom does not apply. They are the ones who are highly trained and skilled. Possibly they were professionals before embarking on their hiatus and their demands upon returning to the labor force include maximum payment for services rendered. Their demands are more stringent and their willingness to compromise less obvious. While these women might seek flexibility in their positions, they will not turn away from the labor force if they do not receive it. They are the returning professionals, committed to a career (albeit with a hiatus) from the start.

Notes

1. Katherine Wyse Goldman, *If You Can Raise Kids, You Can Get a Good Job*, New York: HarperCollins, 1996, p. 9.

2. The literature on human capital is vast. See for example, Theodore Schultz, "Investment in Human Capital," *American Economic Review* 51, no. 1, March 1960 and Gary Becker, *Human Capital: A Theoretical and Empirical Analysis*, With Special Reference to Education, Chicago: University of Chicago Press, 1975.

3. Shirley Burggraf, *The Feminine Economy and Economic Man*, Reading, Mass.: Addison-Wesley, Publishing Co, 1998, p. ix.

4. These numbers are for the first child. It is clear from these data that parents, especially stay-at-home moms, are not small players in the economy. See Burggraf, p. 173.

5. Furthermore, since shadow skills were acquired while another social and economic function was performed (i.e., rearing children and managing a household), they represent a positive by-product derived from staying-at-home (in economics jargon, a positive externality).

6. In neoclassical economic theory, wage is determined by the marginal product. For most women in industrial societies, and especially those who are educated and advantaged, the marginal product of their labor is not zero, hence their wage is not zero but rather it is positive.

7. Judith M. Bardwick, *In Transition: How Feminism, Sexual Liberation, and the Search for Self-fulfillment Have Altered America*, New York: Holt, Rinehart and Winston, 1979, p. 41.

8. Juliet Schor, *The Overworked American*, New York: Basic Books, 1992, p. 164.

9. Goldman, p. 49.

10. Moreover, potential demand of their services or the goods they produce might come from the following social subgroups: those married without children, parents, single parents, female head of households, two-career parents, housewives, gay singles, couples, step-families, battered wives, battered lesbians, grandparents, etc.

11. For example, if they are animal lovers, women can organize and provide the following: pet sitting service, groom pets from van, breed pets, photograph pets, counseling to grieving pet owners, cook gourmet foods for pets, dog walking service, etc.

12. Encyclopaedia Britannica, *Book of the Year*, 1997, Chicago: Encyclopaedia Britannica, Inc., pp. 756, 801.

13. As cited in *Working Mother*, June 1997, p. 10.

14. The *New York Times*, March 8, 1996.

15. Gary Becker, Kevin Murphy, and Robert Tamura, *Human Capital, Fertility and Economic Growth*, Chicago, Ill.: Economic Demography Group, Economics Research Center, NORC/University of Chicago, 1989.

16. This is true not only of those who already have children, but also of those that plan to have children.

17. Capitalist society values people according to their wage, which is determined by the market value of the good they produce. If the market value of homemaking is zero, then the wage is viewed by society as zero, and therefore the value of the person

performing such an economic activity is zero. In the neoclassical tradition, homemakers are thus worthless.

Chapter 11

Individual Benefits: Personal Fulfillment and Goal Achievement

Elise Troy was an accomplished multitasker, I knew it the moment I walked into her home. There were so many visible signs of ongoing projects and tasks simultaneously performed without a hint of stress. Elise had gotten up from her desk to greet me at the door and had left evidence of bills partially completed and envelopes as yet to be stamped. The living room sofa and armchairs were covered with strips of sample upholstery awaiting her choice and decision. The dining room table was barely visible under copies of matted 12 x 16 enlargements of photographs she had taken (and developed) of her son's sports team, one for each boy in the picture. A journal where she documents her thoughts and feelings lay on the coffee table for excerpts to be read to me. The housekeeper went about her business, flowing silently from room to room, obviously well versed in her duties; the yardman's mower buzzed outside the window; I pushed the tape recorder closer and probed deep into Elise's past. She seemed completely unfazed by the number of ongoing activities. Her cool energy permeated the room and her ability to keep numerous balls in the air simultaneously was obvious. I was duly impressed.

But it was Elise's genuine happiness that made the greatest impression on me. She was happy with a vengeance. She admitted that it took her a long time to achieve happiness and now that she has it, she wasn't letting go. Elise described her past, a seemingly distant past in which she was frustrated, tired, snappy, and unhappy. At that time, she tried to be a good attorney, a good mother, a good homemaker, and a good wife, all at once. "I was frustrated because I tried to do everything and so I couldn't do anything. The more I tried, the more I failed. I'm a perfectionist, yet I found myself being a mediocre lawyer, a mediocre wife, and a mediocre mother. I was tired all the time, I was under a lot of stress and as a result, my disposition was not very pleasant. I was unhappy because in my self-evaluation, I was giving myself a C in everything." Elise realized that she had to make some choices. She chose quality over quantity. She decided to do fewer things but to do them well. Ever since she gave up her law practice and devoted herself to her family, Elise feels that she raised her grade as a mother and wife to an A! And that has made her very happy.

Elise knows that her life circumstances are going to change in the near future. Her children will grow up and leave home, and then her extensive school involvements will cease. She welcomes that upcoming period because she views it as an exciting, new phase of her life in which she hopes to be just as fulfilled as she is now. While her children will no longer be the primary source of her fulfillment, she has no doubt that something else will. In fact, Elise knows exactly what she'd like that something else to be: legal work in a center for abused children. In this endeavor, she could combine her skills as an attorney with her passionate battle against child abuse. If this specific plan fails to materialize, Elise believes that there are other options that could equally fulfill her. With such confidence and clarity of vision, Elise expects a smooth transition into the empty nest stage.

Elise, I realized, embodies a different version of a superwoman. She is a super happy woman, proud to be a mom and cognizant of the importance of being with her children in this most important period of their lives. She is aware of how lucky she is to have had the choice of staying at home while her children were growing up. Moreover, she is confident about her past career accomplishments as well as her future potential. In her midforties, she feels as though, in a way, her life is only beginning. She has experienced a lot, and she wants even more in the future—more experiences, more fun, more fulfillment. As the superwoman of the 1990s, Elise wants it all! She wants a professional career, she wants to volunteer for meaningful causes, she wants to be a soccer mom, she wants to be an affectionate and supportive wife. Unlike the superwomen of the 1980s, she recognizes that she cannot do all this simultaneously but must do it in steps. In other words, she will pack it all into her total life span, just not all at once. And so, Elise is confident that she will always be fulfilled, only the principal source of her fulfillment will change over time.

THE THIRD CAREER

Middle age may manifest itself in the urge to purchase a convertible automobile, indulge in bright red suitcases, or dye dark hair blond. It may also produce an urge to change one's life in a more fundamental manner. This may include trading in an old career for a new one, perhaps one that has been a fantasy all along but was never pursued due to a variety of financial, social, or personal constraints. Trading in an old career in middle age may have an overall positive effect. In discussing productivity and production, psychologists and economists have suggested that it is desirable for workers to shift gears every 10 to 15 years. Such a change in the work one does is invigorating and refreshing, and it serves to eliminate the boredom and complacency that set in when repetitive activities are performed over a period of years. The same argument may be applied to women's lives. After raising children and running a household for some 15 years, middle-aged women with choices are due for a new beginning. They are ready to invigorate and stimulate and infuse excitement into their comfortable but familiar lives. They are ready to shift gears; they have been full-time mothers and homemakers for so long, they now yearn for a refresher. The comparison with a business firm is compelling. To the extent that women view their role as homemakers as the dominant expression of themselves and the job that they performed in the workplace of life, then a change of course may be viewed as a change in employer. They spent some 15 years at one type of endeavor and most can count on spending at least that long in another. Elise Troy called this new endeavor a third career:

In my first career, I was unmarried, childless and working full time as an attorney. Then I became a full-time homemaker, tending to my home, raising my children, and volunteering in my community. That was my second career. Now I look forward to yet one more career, my third, in which I hope to fuse the previous two. I'd like to go back to work, but I don't want to have a full-time, demanding career as I had before; I'd still like to tend to my home, but my children will be grown up or gone so I won't be as needed as before. My third career will, I hope, be a balanced combination of so many things I enjoy in life.

The third career, a blend of the first two, is possible for middle-aged women with choices because neither work nor home require their full attention anymore. Indeed, women in third careers usually do not opt for all-consuming careers; women in third careers usually have grown children. In a sense, these women are "half-backs": while reentering the workforce, they are only half going back to the sort of work life they had before they became homemakers. Elizabeth Perle McKenna described her leaving her demanding career in order to be a full-time author at home; "When I quit my job, I had no sense that I was part of a growing movement of women who were trying to figure out a new way to doing work and living life."[1] In middle age, women with choices are also part of a growing group of women trying to figure out how to integrate employment into their lives.

The shift in gears that is embodied in this new life, this third career, is not motivated by women's fears that their marriages will disintegrate and that they will need to support themselves (indeed, only one of the married women said that her marriage was not good and her motivation to work was in preparation for a possible divorce). The desire to shift gears is also not motivated by the fear that their source of livelihood (be it their husbands or their own) will fail to support their lifestyles in the future (indeed, only 16% of the women professed to be worried about their spouse's future ability to provide for them). Instead, the motivation for shifting gears in midlife lies in a desire to achieve a new and different type of fulfillment. For those who have reached middle age without ever feeling fulfilled, it represents an attempt to pursue what has to date eluded them. A recent article about women and work in the *New York Times* applies aptly to these middle-aged women: "Although a second income helps pay the bills, working really is not about money for some of these women. . . . Instead, going to work becomes similar to an illicit pleasure, almost akin to sneaking off to have an affair."[2]

Women with choices strive to achieve fulfillment because it feels good to be fulfilled. It feels good to set a goal, to work toward that goal, and to achieve it. To the extent that women with choices are setting working for pay as their goal, they are doing so because it makes them feel good. Most participants in this study already feel good about themselves and their past choices. Overall, they are happy with their former decision to leave the labor market and to raise children (indeed, only 13% reported that they regretted their choice). To the extent that they made other bad decisions, took wrong turns, compromised, and failed, they seemed able to bounce back successfully, further reinforcing their feelings about themselves.

The drive to feel good is not unique to women with choices. It is, in fact, an important dimension of the current times. The 1990s are a decade in which people have become in touch with their feelings and in which value is placed on those feelings. The proliferation of literature on how to feel good about oneself clearly attests to this. It has been said that people in the 1990s are looking for fulfillment rather than money: "very few people are talking about increasing their wealth or being nicer to people." Rather, "the '80s were about what you own and what you bought, the '90s are about what you feel."[3] Moreover, today women believe they have a right to feel good and be happy. Unlike their mothers and grandmothers, for whom the focus was on satisfaction rather than happiness, women today have shifted their emphasis away from mere satisfaction. While they have retained traditional values including duty, discipline, and commitment to family, they have acquired a sense of entitlement to spiritual, emotional, and intellectual happiness, and the prevailing mood in society is supportive of that entitlement.

It is the pursuit of this self-fulfillment and the concomitant "feel-good" factor that best explains why the participants in this study are trying to enter the labor force when they can choose not to work for pay. Helen Barkey is an example of a woman who has it all yet who wants more. She is a professional woman who left her career out of choice in order to be a full-time homemaker for her husband and three children. She describes her marriage to a physician as "wonderful." They have "a lot" of money and can afford "to do all those things that money can buy." Helen is "very happy" and is seeking to increase that happiness even further. She is looking forward to entering the workforce for the fulfillment it will provide her. She says "my work would be only for enrichment and for feeling good about myself." Julia Schuman is also seeking to feel good. Her background is similar to Helen's: she is happily married (to an attorney). Although she wishes he worked fewer hours, she understands the time demands of his profession. She has healthy and well-adjusted children, she has sufficient wealth to satisfy her family's needs. Yet, she too wants to feel good about what she'll be doing in the future. "When I worked as an attorney, I felt that what I did was important. That felt good. As a full-time mother, I feel that being available to my children is important, and that too feels good. By going back into the workforce, I again expect to feel good. I won't work unless I feel that way. In my profession and for my particular inclinations, that means taking on cases that I think are important."

Helen and Julia have both identified what will make them feel even more fulfilled and even better about themselves than they already do. So too, for most middle-aged women in the sample, self-fulfillment is the underlying basis for their aspirations to "do something new in their lives," in stark contrast to desires by numerous working women to decrease their workload and thus improve the balance between work and home.

TO DREAM THE POSSIBLE DREAM

In their twenties and thirties, women with choices pursued the activity they believed would be the most self-fulfilling, that of staying at home. Now, in middle age, they plan to pursue new goals and seek fulfillment with the same determination, dedication, and commitment that they previously extended to their husbands, their children, and their communities.

The majority of women with choices believe that they can set goals for themselves and that they can achieve those goals. With remarkable consistency, the middle-aged respondents expressed their conviction that they would achieve the dreams they dreamed. During the interview, women were asked to explain in detail how they envisioned their lives ten years from now. They were first asked to describe the fantasy, that is to describe what they would like to happen with respect to their marriages, their children and most importantly, the way in which they spend their days. Then they were asked to describe the reality, in other words, what they actually think their lives will be like ten years from now. With the exception of three respondents, women's fantasies were remarkably close to their expected reality. It was clear that women overwhelmingly dreamed possible dreams, at least, dreams that they believed were possible.

What were those fantasies? Not surprisingly, they were very similar. Not one of the women hoped to win the lottery, not one envisioned herself in a jet-set life gallivanting around the world, not one dreamed of leaving her family for a prince on a white stallion. Instead, they focused on their health and that of their loved ones. Without fail, those who had children first calculated how old their children would be in ten years and then wished for them to have completed their education and to be happily settled down. Those who were not married hoped for a loving relationship with a man; those who were married hoped for endurance and happiness within their marriages. Some hoped the stock market wouldn't crash or that their husbands would continue earning as much as they currently do (or more). Then women described how they hoped to spend their days: "I want to become a party planner"; "I want to complete my architecture degree and design homes"; "I want to be a psychologist in private practice"; "I want to open a boutique"; "I want to open an art shop with my girlfriends"; "I want to practice law part time"; "I want to go back to nursing"; "I want to become a wedding consultant"; "I want to write a book"; and on and on. Those who were not clear in their goals merely said, "I want to be working at something that gives me pleasure."

When women were asked to set aside the fantasy and describe the way they envisioned their future reality, most repeated more or less the same words. When asked how many components of their fantasies they actually thought might be realized, women overwhelmingly responded "all!" The response I heard over and over was, "I see no reason why all that can't happen." If women hoped to be employed in ten years, they thought they actually would be; if they hoped to have a business or a practice, they believed they would succeed; if they were divorced and hoped to remarry, they expected that would happen; if they had hopes about their children's futures, they saw no reason why these hopes couldn't be realized.

More revealing than the content of women's fantasies is their conviction that they will actually live out those fantasies. Such confidence with respect to their ability to achieve the goals they set for themselves is quite remarkable and in part explains their determination in their drive for self-fulfillment.

IF I'M OK, YOU'RE OK

There is no doubt that it is easier for women to achieve their goals if they have family support, especially that of a spouse or partner. As mentioned in Chapter 8, professional women listed the support of their husbands as one of the three most important sources of their success.[4] Moreover, in her study of accomplished women, Elsa Walsh found that for women to strike a balance between work and family, the relationship with a man is one of the crucial components, especially if that relationship is defined by friendship, love, and support.[5]

Middle-aged homemakers were aware that they need that support in order to pursue their aspirations. Many believed that spouses, as well as children, need to understand that their interests are best served if their wives, or mothers, are happy and fulfilled. Indeed, if women feel good about themselves, that positive feeling will permeate the entire household. There will be a trickle-down effect to all members of the social unit. A woman who feels good about herself will be a better mother. Happy and fulfilled women are better mothers to their children because they are more serene, more tolerant, and more giving. As such, they also become better role models for their children. Alternatively, if women are unhappy, they will be short-tempered, sad, snappy, angry, and depressive. Children are unlikely to derive great benefits from such a mother.

A similar argument applies to spouses. A wife who is happy is one who will greet her husband with a genuine smile and who will be tolerant of his idiosyncrasies. A wife who is confident and has high self-esteem will also be a more giving partner. The benefits to a husband of a happy and fulfilled wife are extensive and certainly outweigh the costs entailed in providing her the support, the freedom, and the latitude to pursue her goals and her own routes to self-fulfillment, whatever those may be. This point was emphasized by Elise Troy.

She spoke about how her husband's career as an attorney took off once she implemented the life choice that made her happy: "It was only after I stopped working and became a full-time homemaker that I felt better about myself and my life. I became happy and my entire family benefited. My husband keeps saying that the reason *he's* doing so well is because *I'm* doing so well."

It is believed that when women are accommodating to men, then men will feel good about themselves, which tends to give them a surge of energy and elan. Consequently, they will increase their productivity and thus also their economic contribution to society. According to Susan Ostander's study of upper-class women, "When women stroke and soothe men, listen to them and accommodate their needs, men of every class return to the workplace with renewed energies."[6] Why should the argument be any different for women? Women who are supported by their husbands or partners are able to take off. Their energies become boundless. Understanding and tolerance from their immediate families serves to propel women toward their goals. By analogy, women who are met with disparaging comments, bullying hostility, and condescending attitudes from their husbands are likely to expend precious stamina and effort protecting themselves. Thus, women whose husbands create obstacles will have greater difficulty in achieving their goals.

CHOICE OF APPROPRIATE GOALS FOR WOMEN

In formulating their future goals, women with choices emphasize personal satisfaction. To maximize that satisfaction, they must harness their passions and make passion the focus of their goals. Passion was mentioned in Chapter 10 as a crucial component in a woman's occupational choice. It is once again invoked, this time because of its prominent role in personal satisfaction and fulfillment. However, passion alone is insufficient in the formulation of goals. Rather, it must be accompanied by an assessment of the limits within which that passion can be realized. The upper limit defines just how high women can aspire in their goals while the lower limit defines their limitations. The role of passion in setting goals, the desirability of aspiring high (the upper limit), and the assessment of limitations (the lower limit) are discussed below.

The Role of Passion

There are jobs, there are careers, and then there are callings. These differ in fundamental ways. A job is simply employment for pay, usually the kind workers flow in and out of. It does not entail consistency in the field, or long-term commitment, or skill acquisition. A career is work in a profession that requires special preparation and is undertaken with commitment. It entails the long term. People invest time and energy in building and nurturing a career, so they have more to lose by leaving it. A calling is an inner urge, a strong impulse. A calling is what one does because one feels it in one's bones. A calling comes about from an internal drive that tells a person what they should be doing. They feel that they want and can do it. A job is taken for practical reasons while the soul receives sustenance from the calling (hence the pianist who drives a taxi, the artist who doubles as a cook, the cook who works as a secretary). For the truly fortunate woman, a career or job coincides with a calling. For most, it does not. Women with choices go for the calling, if they can identify it.

How does one know what one's calling is? In Native American cultures, discovering one's calling is part of coming of age. Among the Dakota Sioux, young males purify themselves and then deprive themselves of food, drink, and sleep until their vision arrives to them.[7] Without going to such lengths, women with choices may have already identified their passion by the time they reach middle age. Whether it happened when they painted their drape fabric (as in Gloria's case) or when they tried a meaningful case in court (as Elise did), the identification of a calling imbues passion into women's future goals.

While women have many goals throughout their lives, only some are driven by intense passion while most are driven by sheer survival. Those that are based on passion are especially satisfying. Middle-aged women with choices will maximize their utility by pursuing whatever goals stir them and whatever they love to do and feel a passion toward. Their passion should be their guide. The more passion women feel about an activity, the greater the energy they will receive from it—energy that is indispensable to overcome the numerous obstacles that stand in the way of achieving their goals. When they are excited about getting up in the morning and embarking upon a task, not only will they feel happier but a sense of empowerment will permeate their endeavors. No mountain will seem too high, no hurdle too big.

The Desirability of Aspiring High

Many women with choices have read to their children Watty Piper's book *The Little Engine That Could.*[8] Its message is highly inspirational, stating that when an individual aspires to something (even as seemingly impossible as successfully climbing over a mountain was for an overloaded, small-motored train), it can be achieved if the person really tries. If this were applied to women with choices, the message would be that women can do so much that seems beyond their capacity, if only they put their minds to it. If they believe in themselves, they have the possibility of achieving lofty goals. Those women who lack lofty aspirations have no possibility of ever achieving them. If they are satisfied with little, then they will only have little.

An Assessment of Limitations

Despite the desirability of aspiring high, women's goals must be grounded in reality. Nobody can do everything and be everything, all women have constraints they cannot alter, they all have obstacles they cannot overcome. With respect to personal achievements, it is not true that the sky is the limit.

In order not to waste their energies on pursuits that are beyond their limits, women with choices must conduct a careful reality check when they set their goals. Such a reality check must be repeated periodically while they are working toward their goal. They must stop and assess whether the goals they have set for themselves are attainable, appropriate, and desirable. They must analyze with honesty who and what they are, and then they must ask themselves, "Is this goal right for me, given who I am *now*?" Knowledge and understanding of themselves is important because it serves as an anchor and a compass. It is an anchor because it keeps women from straying too far from what they are and can be. It is a compass because it points out to them the possibilities they can explore in the future. In the absence of such a reality check on their current life position, women may develop illusions about their capacities, making it harder to achieve the goals they set for themselves.

FULFILLMENT AND CHOICE IN MIDDLE AGE

Anna Quindlen, author and former *New York Times* columnist, describes how she expects to feel on her deathbed when she reflects about the course of her life. She said that the most important question she would ask herself at that time was whether she did what she had wanted to do.[9] Pondering that question helped her decide to leave her job and become a full-time author. Women with choices who want to pursue an alternative path in middle age are acting as though they have asked themselves the following deathbed questions: "Did I do what I wanted before it was too late?" "Did I go to graduate school, or open my business, or get a job after my kids left home?" "Did I pursue my passion?" Their answers to those questions might lead them to try to change their lives by leaving their home and entering the workplace.

The possibility of a venture outside the home imbues women with excitement and hope. They look forward to experiencing a new type of competence and assertiveness in society. They want to lead and make decisions within a nondomestic environment. They are ready to cope with new circumstances and in a new way. Moreover, they are demanding the opportunity to earn success, to acknowledge their ambition, to develop competencies, to assume leadership, to acquire power, and to take new risks. They want to earn an income even if they had the choice not to. In her study of women, work, and feminism, Natasha Walters found that in the 1990s, more women than men say that they would work even if they didn't have to.[10] Middle-aged women with choices are clear examples of such women.

These women had employment choices in the past and they now have them again. It took courage in the 1980s to be "just a mom." Similarly, it now takes courage to break out of their life patterns, to explore uncertain options, and to ultimately find a new life for themselves. In this new life, many middle-aged homemakers will have a third career in which they will have one foot in the labor force, in flexible, accommodating, and creative positions they will have carved out for themselves. Those positions will be creative and they will also be fulfilling, otherwise they won't be filled by women with choices. Chances are these women will love what they do, or else they won't do it. If they love it, it will simultaneously be work and leisure for them, possibly even a calling. In this way, women with choices in their third careers may be the rare workers who succeed in combining a job with a calling. They will thus have achieved the personal fulfillment they are pursuing in their middle age.

Notes

1. Elizabeth Perle McKenna, *When Work Doesn't Work Any More*, New York: Delacorte Press, 1997, p. 258.

2. The *New York Times*, November 11, 1997.

3. The *Miami Herald*, January 1, 1994.

4. CATALYST, cited in the *Philadelphia Inquirer*, February 28, 1996.

5. Elsa Walsh, *Divided Lives, The Public and Private Struggles of Three Accomplished Women*, New York: Simon and Schuster, 1995.

6. Susan Ostander, *Women of the Upper Class*, Philadelphia: Temple University Press, 1984, p. 146.

7. Mary Morris, "Hello, This Is Your Destiny Calling," *New Woman*, February 1993, pp. 80–82.

8. Watty Piper, *The Little Engine That Could*, New York: Platt and Munk Co., 1954.

9. Cited in McKenna, p. 91.

10. Natasha Walters, *The New Feminism*, London: Little Brown, 1998, p. 2.

Appendix I

Method

The aim of the survey was to achieve a cross-sectional sample of middle-aged women who had been out of the labor force for at least six years and who were exploring future employment possibilities (or who had just recently reentered the labor force). The aim was to further understand how they perceived their choices in middle age, what their goals were with respect to the labor market, what obstacles and constraints they foresaw, and what advantages they perceived themselves to have. I tried to understand how they felt about their hiatus outside the workforce, how they thought their families would react if they started working, and what concrete expression their goals had taken. Thus, my aim was to peek into the window of both their perceptions and their actions in order to understand their current choices in light of their past ones.

SELECTION OF RESPONDENTS

In the sample, respondents were identified through the snowball method. This entailed finding a handful of initial (or seed) women who fit the profile requirements and asking them to produce other subjects. They in turn were asked to provide others still, and so on.

Subjects were first contacted by telephone and the project was described to them. They were asked several questions and if they satisfied the broad requirements, they were invited to participate. The positive response rate to that initial invitation was quite high: indeed, 81.1% accepted. A time for the interview was agreed upon (an interview was chosen rather than a questionnaire— given the nature of the questions and the effort to solicit open-ended responses, it was not realistic to expect women to write long and time-consuming answers). Although the response rate was high, the number of actual interviews was lower since a few women canceled (and declined to reschedule) or failed to show up at prearranged times. The effective response rate was higher among English-speaking women than among the Hispanic population.

Snowball sampling is problematic since biases exist in the choice of respondents. Indeed, the choice is highly subjective. A random sample within census tracts might have been preferable, although it is likely that in the location where the interviews were conducted, it would have yielded a similar sample. In the end, snowballing proved adequate in providing a sample because women tend to associate with others like themselves (a woman who is middle-aged and unemployed will tend to know others like herself).

The sample focused on a cohort of women who shared the following characteristics: they were not in the labor force as a result of a conscious decision not to be there and their hiatus was at least six consecutive years in length;[1] they were middle-aged; they were of a socioeconomic background that they felt enabled them not to work. Moreover, they were thinking about entering the labor force (or had just done so within the past year) because they want to, not because they had to. These requirements imply that the respondents are not representative of women at large, nor of all middle-aged homemakers.

The women in this study reside in metropolitan Miami and some surrounding pockets of Dade County.[2] With a population of some 2.01 million people, Miami is atypical insofar as its foreign-born population is higher than in the average American city. Its upper-income population is also higher than the U.S. average.[3] Moreover, Miami is a city with a high turnover of residents and high rates of economic growth and thus is unique by several indicators of demographic and institutional change. Miami has extensive ethnic diversity in its population, including large Jewish, Anglo, Black, and Hispanic components.[4] A study of a cross section of women in these ethnic/cultural/racial categories provides a view of the role of cultural and religious/ethnic traits on behavior. The choice of a major metropolitan area for this study introduces a clear urban bias in the sample. As a result, there are limitations to generalizing the conclusions in this book across the entire geographical spectrum of American society.

THE NATURE OF THE SURVEY

Susan Ostander interviewed 36 upper-class women for her study, Patricia Houck Sprinkle interviewed 23 across income and geographical boundaries, Elizabeth Johnson interviewed 39 women in one city, and Myra Dinnerstein interviewed 22 middle-aged women.[5] This too is a small-scale research project, entailing the participation of 31 women. There is a tradeoff between size of sample and statistical reliability. The sample was relatively small because all the interviews were long and conducted exclusively by the author. I might have focused on a larger sample, but then I would have sacrificed the in-depth exploration. While the ideas expressed and explored here would warrant a follow-up by a wider and larger survey, I was nevertheless able to gain a comparative perspective by interviewing only 31 women.

Several pretests helped transform vague questions into a structured interview. Questions on the questionnaire were exploratory, meant to discover, not verify existing theory. The interview was open-ended, enabling me to explore ideas that I had not incorporated into the questionnaire. The interview guided the respondents through what was often chaotic in their minds. For many, the interview served to organize their thoughts. I was told by women on numerous occasions that the interview helped them crystallize their ideas. It also helped them verbalize feelings that had to date not been verbalized. For a few, the interview opened the gates of pent up feelings and released both resentment and pain.

The interviews took place from May 1996 to June 1997. All interviews were taped and subsequently transcribed to facilitate analysis. All names have been changed to ensure anonymity and any identifying characteristics were omitted. Every effort was made to protect the privacy of the respondents in the descriptions. The quoted material in the text may have been condensed and edited for clarity purposes only, without altering the gist of the response.

THE BIASES

There is an unequivocal bias in retrospective reporting. Interviews by definition introduce bias into research especially when people say and answer in ways that they desire to be true rather than that are true. This problem is compounded by another one, much harder to account for. I was dealing with a very sensitive subject, one that many homemakers feel defensive about, namely their choice to forgo or give up professional careers. All women in the sample, consciously or subconsciously participated in the mommy wars. I, the interviewer, had obviously chosen to have a professional career, interviewing women who had chosen not to have one. The fact that I was on the other side of the divide, so to speak, might have elicited a knee-jerk response. That response might include elevating their choice to stay home to greater heights than they might otherwise. Maybe women who had doubts about their choices were less willing to share those with an employed woman; maybe they portrayed a home-life happiness that they did not feel. The responses of women to questions posed by a woman who had made a choice different from theirs might have been adversarial.

To best address this issue, I had to establish a relationship of trust with the respondents. I appealed to women by telling them that there was so little information about middle-aged homemakers like themselves and the dilemmas that they face. I told them that so many other women struggle to figure out what to do with their lives, that this is a study of that struggle, and that whatever they feel is normal. I also pointed out that the grass is always greener on the other side of the employment divide. In that way, I believe that the adversarial air in the interview, to the extent that it existed at all, was quickly dispelled and that the sampled women did not feel there was a right and wrong answer to any of the questions.

Given my proximity to the subject under study, that of choice among middle-aged women, it is impossible to claim that I am 100% objective. While I am not personally involved in the home vs. work decision, so many of my friends and acquaintances are. I would be dishonest to pretend that their views and their dilemmas did not mold and color my opinions and therefore the focus of this research.

Notes

1. Six was chosen arbitrarily because it is the age at which children begin school.

2. It includes Coral Gables, South Miami, Miami Beach, Key Biscayne, and Unincorporated Dade.

3. Florida ranks twentieth in the United States by income per capita.

4. In 1995, 56% of the population was Hispanic (Bureau of Economic and Business Research, *Florida Statistical Abstract*, Gainsville: University of Florida, 1996).

5. Susan Ostander, *Women of the Upper Class*, Philadelphia: Temple University Press, 1984; Patricia Houck Sprinkle, *Women Home Alone*, Grand Rapids, Mich.: Zondervan Publishing House, 1996; Elizabeth Johnson, "Suburban Older Women," in Elizabeth Markson, ed., *Older Women*, Lexington, Mass.: Lexington Press, 1983; Myra Dinnerstein, *Women Between Two Worlds*, Philadelphia: Temple University Press, 1992.

Appendix II

Empirical Overview: Women with Choices in America and in the Sample

Statistics are crucial for providing an insight into the way things are and the way in which they operate. As a result of their descriptive value, selected statistics pertaining to women with choices are introduced to provide the framework for this study.

In 1994, there were 260 million people residing in the United States of which 51.2% were women (some 133.5 million).[1] Of these, 24.9 million women were between the ages of 40 and 55 years (amounting to some 25.3% of all women). Within this age category, 73.4% were married, 15.9% were divorced, and 3.4% were widowed.[2]

Out of the total female civilian labor force of 50.3 million, 33 million are between the ages of 35 and 64 years. While the overall participation rate of American females is 66.6%, it is highest in the 35–44 age bracket (77.1% of those are employed), followed by the 45–54 age bracket (74.6%), and is the lowest in the 55–64 age bracket (48.9%). The labor force participation rate is lower for married than for single women, irrespective of their age bracket (for example, among women aged 45 to 54, single women's labor force participation rate is 68.8% while that of married women is 61.9%).

However, it would be misleading to think that it is only the younger middle-aged women who are active in the economy. In fact, about 80% of the nearly three million women aged 50–60 who are college educated are presently in the workforce. Of these, nearly three-quarters hold full-time jobs.[3] Employment among women without college degrees in the 50–60 age bracket has reached 8.1 million women (65% of the age group, up from 54% in 1984).

Married middle-aged women living in households with gross assets over $600,000 total 3.4 million, and a breakdown of women holders of those assets reveals that 1.4 million women have gross assets of that amount or more.[4]

Taking into consideration the middle-aged population of women, coupled with data on employment, it is estimated that there might be some 3–5 million women across the country who fit the profile of women with choices.

What about the women who participated in this study? What are they like, what are their characteristics? A background of the participants is provided below in order to more easily place their life anecdotes into an appropriate context.

AGE

The average age of the women was 44.2 years while the median age was 45. The average was skewed by the inclusion of one respondent who was 31 at the time of the interview. She was one of four women under 40 (the others were 38 or 39). Some women in their thirties had children early and others in their late forties had children late so the age of the mother was not necessarily a good indicator of the age of their children and therefore of their own propensity to reenter the labor force.

MARITAL STATUS

The majority of women (84%) in the sample were married at the time of the interview (this high number coincides with national data that indicate affluent couples have a divorce rate that is less than half the norm).[5] Five women were divorced, one of which was cohabiting with a partner.[6] None were widowed. Women were married on average for 18.3 years.

EDUCATION

All the women in the sample had college degrees. Two of them had received their bachelor's degrees as adults. The majority had majored in liberal arts or business. In addition, 43.3% of the women had a postgraduate or professional degree while 10% had two. The most common degrees were in law, business administration, and social work. One woman had completed most courses toward her MBA degree.

Generally, educated women tend to have spouses with comparable or superior education. Susan Feiner pointed out how people tend to marry within their own social and educational class.[7] This was also true in the sample under study. While all but 6.6% of the husbands had college degrees, 73.3% had postgraduate or professional degrees. The most common professional degree was law (33% of the husbands were attorneys), followed by business administration (23.3% had MBA degrees, although 30% reported to be businessmen), and finally medicine (13.3%). Others had a variety of master's degrees, while 6.6% of the husbands had two professional degrees, usually law and business. In addition to lawyers, businessmen, and doctors, the sampled women were also married to writers, managers, and bankers, among others.

WEALTH AND INCOME

Direct questions pertaining to household wealth and income were excluded from the questionnaire. In the absence of concrete data, financial status was discerned by the analysis of a variety of indicators, however, the choice of appropriate indicators of wealth is complicated. While visible signs of conspicuous consumption (such as luxury automobiles and expensive watches) are often associated with wealth, they may only be a mirage. Stanley and Danko have found that the majority of American millionaires do not exhibit wealth in such ways.[8] In fact, they do not exhibit wealth at all: they tend to live frugally and hold their assets in accounts that are not visually apparent. In the absence of direct questions about wealth and income, the following seemed the best measurable indirect indicators of household wealth: the number of hired domestic helpers, children's enrollment in private schools, the number of automobiles, and the frequency of vacations in the past year. None of these indicators alone connote wealth, but taken as a group they provide sufficient and convincing evidence of an above-average standard of living.

All but 10% of the respondents had household help (those who had none at the time of the interview indicated that they did have help in the past and they plan on having it again in the future). The most common configuration was three or four part-time workers. Indeed, 36.7% of the sample had a part-time housekeeper, gardener or yardman, poolman, and occasionally a laundress.[9] Another 10% of the sample had live-in housekeepers while 6.7% of the sample had between five and seven part-time workers in help.

Among the respondents who had children, 65.5% enrolled them in private schools, 6.9% had children in both private and public schools, while the remaining women had children only in public schools. However, all but one of the women with children in public schools expressed concern about the quality of public school education and planned on moving their children into private schools when they reached high school.

Within the past year, the sampled women took an average of 2.2 vacations. Only one woman responded that she took no vacation, while 13% took four or more. Although most of the vacations were to destinations within the United States, one-half of the women reported visiting Europe, Asia, or the Caribbean during the past year. Skiing was also popular, with a minority of the women taking a mountain holiday at least once in the past winter.

The average number of automobiles per household was 2.5. Ten percent of the women owned only one automobile, however, their households consisted of only one adult. None of the married women owned only one automobile, while 47% owned two, and 17% of the women reported owning four or five automobiles (note that the low driving age in states such as Florida in part explains this high number).

According to these indicators of wealth, women in the sample enjoy a standard of living that is well above the U.S. average. This coincides with their own perceptions of their lifestyles; women were asked if they considered themselves to be advantaged relative to the general population and 80% responded affirmatively. Yet, when asked if they thought they belonged to the upper class, only 50% said yes. This subjective interpretation of their position within society both confirms their privileged status and underscores the difference between upper income and upper class.

Finally, while the women in the sample clearly enjoy an above-average lifestyle, it is not one that they are sustaining with their own earnings. So what is the source of the wealth that enables the consumption described above? The majority had derived wealth from their husband's income. However, 43% reported also having independent wealth. Some qualified that statement by saying that "it was little," others said "it was a lot," some said it was inherited, while others specified that it was brought into the marriage.

CHILDREN

Of the participants surveyed, 97% had children. The average age of the children was 13 years. All women with children had at least one child living at home, although some 10% expected to have none within one year, 35% of the mothers had at least one child living outside the home (having left for college or work rather than living with their divorced father) and 55% had at least one child in high school.

Despite the widespread use of hired help, women in the sample consistently strove to play the most prominent role in their children's lives. When asked who cared for their children, 17% of the respondents answered that they alone did, with no assistance. Only a minority claimed to have (or to have had) full-time hired childcare helpers including nannies (14%) or au pairs (7%). The majority (66%) claimed to have occasionally received childcare assistance from their housekeepers. Among the Hispanic women in the sample there was some evidence of motherly and grandmotherly input in childcare. Among all ethnic groups, it is clear that women with choices tended to choose a housekeeper, a laundress, a gardener, a poolman rather than a full-time nanny.

EMPLOYMENT

All the women in this study had previously worked for pay. Sixty-one percent had worked only full time, 3% had worked only part time, while some 35% of the women had done both. The average working period prior to their hiatus was 8.7 years, although some 39% of the women worked for ten or more years and 26% worked for five or less. Women varied with respect to how long they had been outside the workforce at the time of the interview. On average, their hiatus was 11.8 years long, although some 30% of the women were out for 15 years or more.

Women had performed a wide variety of jobs during their working lives. While the most popular careers were in business (including accounting, management, and finance) and in law, women also worked in nursing, retail, real estate, travel, computer programming, interior design, journalism, public relations, and teaching.

At the time of the interview, participants were in one of three phases with respect to their work intentions. They were either unemployed but fantasized about entering the labor force (35%), they were in the process of actively searching for employment (16%) or they had just recently begun working (32%). The remainder were retooling and reeducating.

Returning to their old careers was not a very popular option. While few women expressed a desire to work in their previous jobs, 58% said they expected to use their old skills in some way. Women who formerly worked in business or law were most likely to consider returning to their field. The majority, however, were looking for work that was entirely different from what they had previously done (these goals and aspirations are the topic of Chapter 3).

PARENTS AND IN-LAWS

All women in the study had either living parents or in-laws. While only two were actively caring for an elderly relative at the time of the interview, approximately one-half of the sample expected to care for a parent or an in-law in the future.

RELIGION AND ETHNICITY AND RACE

Several religions were represented by the sample. Most women were Catholic (37%), Jewish (27%), or Protestant (13%). The remainder were Congregational, Episcopal, or expressed no religious orientation. Some of the women were married to men who espoused a religion different from theirs (17%). Twenty percent of the sample was Hispanic and all remaining respondents were Caucasian.

Notes

1. These statistics are from the U.S. Bureau of the Census, *Statistical Abstract of the U.S. 1995*, Washington, D.C.: GPO, 1995.

2. The U.S. census contains data by the following age categories: 45–54 and 55–64. Given the ages of the respondents in this study, it seemed more appropriate to limit the study to women up to their mid fifties.

3. These statistics from the Department of Labor Statistics were published in the *New York Times*, November 28, 1994.

4. *Statistical Abstract of the U.S.*, 1995, op. cit., p. 485.

5. Thomas J. Stanley and William D. Danko, *The Millionaire Next Door, The Surprising Secrets of America's Wealthy*, Atlanta: Longstreet Press, 1997, p. 182.

6. Once widowed or divorced, older women are less likely to remarry. There is only one bridegroom for every nine brides 65 and over— not only are older men in short supply, but they are more likely to marry a woman who is younger. Elizabeth Markson, "Without and Within the Family," in Elizabeth Markson, ed., *Older Women*, Lexington, Mass.: Lexington Books, 1983, p. 151.

7. See Susan Feiner, *Race and Gender in the American Economy*, Englewood Cliffs, N.J.: Prentice-Hall, 1994.

8. Stanley and Danko, chapter 1.

9. In Florida, where the number of homes with swimming pools is undoubtedly above the national average, hiring a poolman is not the luxury that it is elsewhere.

Appendix III

The Survey

I.D. # _____

Name _____

Address _____

_____

Phone Number _____

Date of Interview _____

Location of Interview _____

Date Transcribed _____

NOTE: for the purposes of this questionnaire, working outside the home is defined as working for pay, not volunteering.

PERSONAL BACKGROUND INFORMATION

I want to begin by asking you some personal questions about your background. Your answers will enable me to get to know you and to put your subsequent responses in an appropriate context. Some questions are in parentheses— please skip those if you wish.

Demographic Information

PB 1. How old are you?
PB 2. a. Do you have children?
    b. If so, how old are they?

c. What grades are they in?

d. Male/female?

PB 3.   a. Who cared for your children when they were young?

b. If you, did you receive any help? from whom?

PB 4.   a. Are you married?

b. If not, are you widowed, never married or divorced?

c. If you are not currently married, is there a "significant other" who partakes in your life and your decisions?

PB 5.   a. How long have you been married? if divorced or widowed, how long?

b. Have you been married before?

c. How many times?

(d. Would you describe your marriage as good, bad, or so-so?)

PB 6.   a. What does your husband do?

b. What is his age?

PB 7.   Who lives in your household other than yourself?

PB 8.   a. Do you have living parents?

b. Do they live near you?

c. Do you partake in their daily lives?

d. Are you directly involved in their care or do you expect to be involved in the future?

PB9.   a. What is your religion, your ethnic group, your race?

b. Same questions for your husband

PB 10.   Do you consider yourself very religious, somewhat religious, or not religious?

PB 11.   a. Where did you grow up?

b. What part of the world do your ancestors come from?

PB 12.   Do you have any major health problems (yes or no)?

PB 13.   a. If you have children, do you expect them to leave home in the near future?

b. How soon?

Education Information

PB 14.   a. Did you attend university?

b. Where?

c. What was your major?

d. Did you attend graduate or professional school?

e. What was the highest degree attained?

PB 15. Same questions about your husband

a. Did he attend university?

b. Where?

c. What was his major?

d. Did he attend graduate or professional school?

e. What was the highest degree he attained?

PB 16.   a. Did you stop your education because you got married?

b. Because you had children?

Employment Information

PB 17. a. Have you ever worked for pay?
        b. Part time or full time?
PB 18. What did you do?
PB 19. For how long?
PB 20. Why did you stop?
PB 21. a. Did you like or dislike working for pay?
        b. Were you satisfied with your earnings?

Income Information

Income information is pertinent to this study because socioeconomic backgrounds determine the ability to choose not to work. I need to understand your socioeconomic background so I need to ask indirect questions about indicators of wealth and income.

PB 22. If you have children, do they attend private or public schools?
PB 23. a. Do you have household help?
        b. How many?
        c. In what capacity? (e.g.. housekeeper [full time or part time?], nanny, babysitter, cook, gardener, poolman, laundress, other)
PB 24. a. Have you taken a vacation in the past year?
        b. Where?
PB 25. a. How many automobiles does your household have?
PB 26. Who manages the financial affairs of your household?
        a. Regular bills?
        b. Investments?
PB 27. Do you and your husband keep separate financial accounts?
PB 28. Do you have a source of income independent of your husband (just yes or no)?

Miscellaneous

PB 29. Would you define yourself as being advantaged?
PB 30. Would you define yourself as belonging to the upper class?

Thank you. We will now begin the taped interview.

YOUR PAST CHOICES

I would like to understand how you perceive the options that you have had in your life. I would like to know how you feel about the choices you have had and the choices you have made.

C 1.   a. Do you think that you have more choices than most women?

          b. What women do you think have more choice than you?

C 2.   a. Do you think that you have more choices in your decisionmaking than women who are less wealthy than you?

          b. Less educated than you?

C 3.   a. Did you marry out of choice?

          b. Were you educated out of choice?

          c. Did you exercise choice in staying out of the labor force? Probe.

C 4.   a. Tell me about your decision to stay out of the labor force. How did you decide it?

          b. Was it easy or hard?

          c. Did you ever regret it? If so, when?

C 5.   a. Do you feel that you have more choices *now* than you did in the past?

          b. Why or why not?

          c. Has your age given you more or less choices?

WHAT DO YOU THINK PEOPLE EXPECT OF YOU?

I would like you to tell me what you think people expect of you. I am trying to understand if women believe that the expectations their family and friends have of them *now*, in middle age, are different from what they were in their twenties and thirties (or, if they have children, when their children were young). NOTE: I am making a distinction between entering the labor market and "doing something with one's life." The latter does not necessarily involve pay for labor.

Husband

(if divorced or widowed, describe situation in the past)

E 1.   What does your husband expect of you *now* (what does he expect you to do, to be, how does he expect you to spend your time)?

E 2.   When you first got married, what did your husband expect of you with respect to employment and childcare?

E 3.   Did he convey different expectations of you *before* you were married?

E 4.   If his expectations changed, why do you think that happened?

E 5.   How do you think your husband would react if you wanted to join the labor force (does he want you to work, does he want you not to work)?

E 6.   Does he ever tell you that you should be employed?

E 7.   If you think he would object to your working, why would he do so?

E 8.   How would he react if you found a job that had flexible hours or if you worked only part time?

E 9.   a. Does he admire women who work?

          b. Does he make fun of men whose wives work?

E 10.   Does your husband come into contact with women in his job at his level or close to his level?

E 11. Do you think that he wants to have you available to him and for his needs all the time?

E 12. a. Does your husband partake in any household activities and chores?

b. What about children, does he spend time with them, does he share in the raising of them?

c. How many hours per week would you say that he devotes to the children?

Children

If you have no children, please skip to next section.

E 13. What do your children expect you to do for them now (that they are teenagers)? Probe.

E 14. How do you think they would feel if you "did something with your life"?

E 15. How would they feel if that something was working in the labor force?

E 16. a. Do you think that your children respect you?

b. Admire you?

c. Are you a role model for your daughters?

E 17. Do you think you would be more respected and more admired if you were in the labor force?

E 18. Do your children ever ask you why you do not work outside the home when other mothers do?

Peer Group

E 19. Think of your five closest girlfriends. How many of them work outside the home for pay?

E 20. How would your girlfriends who work react if you joined the labor force?

E 21. How would your girlfriends who do not work react if you joined the labor force?

Parents and In-Laws

E 22. What do you think your parents and your husband's parents would say if you were to begin working outside the home?

E 23. I have a few questions specifically about your mother's life and her attitudes.

a. Did your mother work outside the home? part time or full time?

b. Did she stop working when she had children?

c. Did she have help with childrearing?

d. Was she involved in any activities outside the home?

e. While you were growing up, did she convey to you that she thought you should work outside the home or not?

Miscellaneous

E 24.   What are the three things that you think would change the most in your household if you entered the labor force?

E 25.   I would like to talk about the expectations people have of you now, and to what extent you think those expectations are pressures.

    a. Do you feel that any of the above people are pressuring you to do something with your life? Probe.

    b. To enter the labor market? Probe.

YOUR ASPIRATIONS

I am trying to understand what you want to do for the next two decades of your life. I am trying to understand what you feel you want to keep the same and what you want to change. Your answers will help me understand what middle-aged women are aspiring to and how they expect to achieve those aspirations.

A 1.   How do you feel about your age?

A 2.   I have a few questions about how you view your life *now*.

    a. Would you describe yourself as happy?

    b. Would you describe yourself as fulfilled?

    c. Are you happy with your role as a full-time mother?

    d. Do you think your husband and children appreciate your efforts on their behalf?

    e. Is something missing from your life? If so, what?

A 3.   a. What do you like the most about your life? list three things

    b. What do you dislike the most about your life? list three things

A 4.   a. Do you feel that you have achieved what you wanted to achieve at your age?

    b. Do you feel that there is still a lot more that you need/want to do?

A 5.   How often do you see a doctor?

A 6.   Have you ever been depressed?

A 7.   Are you ever bored? When?

A 8.   Please fantasize for a moment. Tell me what you would *like* your life to be like in ten years?

A 9.   Now tell me what you think your life will actually be like in ten years?

A 10.   Do you feel that you would like to do something new or different in your life now?

A 11.   If so, which of the following are relevant in your desire to do something with your life? Tell me about them.

    a. Do you want more fulfillment

    b. Do you want more structure in your life

    c. Do you want to give your life more purpose

    d. Do you want more respect and status

    e. Do you want to expand your social circle

    f. Do you want to expand your intellectual horizons

    g. Do you want financial independence

h. Do you want more excitement in your life

i. Do you want greater control over your life

j. Do you want security (insurance) for the future

k. Please pick three from the above list, and if you can, rank them in order of importance.

A 12.   If you want some of the above, how do you think you can get them?

A 13.   Do you think that working outside the home may provide some of them?

A 14.   a. Do your current aspirations have anything to do with your previous education and training?

b. If yes, do you think that you will need to do something to update your skills?

c. If no, why don't you want to pursue what you were educated in?

A 15.   What is the effect of the following on the pursuit of your aspirations?

a. the fact that your children no longer really need you

b. the fact that you have the money to pursue them

c. the fact that you have the self-confidence that comes with wealth

d. the fact that you have the domestic help to enable you to be away from your household

e. marital disharmony

f. need for money

ACTIVITIES

I would like to get a glimpse of your life. What you do every day, how you feel about what you do? How much of what you do would you describe as leisure, how much is work, how much is drudgery?

AC 1.   Describe a typical day in your life. For example, please describe what you did yesterday.

AC 2.   In your typical day, what sort of activities do you consider to be leisure and which ones do you consider work or chores?

AC 3.   Which of the following activities do you do on a regular basis?

a. cook

b. clean

c. food shopping

d. drive children

e. oversee homework

f. yard work

g. mend and sew

h. laundry and ironing

AC 4.   Are you involved in the following activities, and how much time do you spend on them, on average, per week?

a. socializing, partying and entertaining, also talking on the phone

b. shopping

c. sports and exercise

d. clubs

  e. visual entertainment (TV, VCR, movies, theater)

  f. reading (books, newspapers, magazines)

  g. hobbies

  h. volunteering

  i. grooming (do you have a regular hairdresser appointment? a regular manicure? other)

  j. sleeping (Do you nap during the day?)

AC 5.   Do you belong to any organized leisure programs (sports, exercise clubs, political organizations, clubs, religious organizations, etc.)?

AC 6.   a. Would you describe your life as full?

  b. Complex?

  c. Are you too busy?

  d. Are you stressed out?

  e. Do you feel that you have to juggle a lot of activities? Probe.

AC 7.   Do you ever wake up in the morning and have nothing to do that day?

AC 8.   a. Has there been a change in your involvement in your leisure activities in the recent past?

  b. Do they hold as much interest for you as they did when you were younger or, if you have children, when they were small?

  c. Do you foresee shifting out of them and perhaps taking on new interests?

  d. How do you think your leisure activities will be affected if you join the labor force?

AC 9.   Please read the following paragraph and comment on it. What elements of it resemble your life?

The advantaged middle-aged woman with choices wakes up to the smell of coffee brought to her bedside on a sterling silver platter by her uniformed housekeeper. She stretches leisurely across her satin sheets while the housekeeper draws open the heavy brocade curtains and awaits instructions for morning activities. In turn, the woman inquires about her children: did they have a nutritious breakfast and did the chauffeur get little Johnny to school on time. She proceeds to eat, bathe, and carefully groom herself. Then she tackles the complex task of choosing the most appropriate outfit to wear. Her rotating clothes rack, operated by the push of a button, reveals the hundreds of ensembles suitable for her numerous moods and occasions. She dresses, at times interrupted by telephone chats with her girlfriends. Later she emerges from her quarters to give further instructions to the various hired help who have by now shown up and then speeds away, along her winding driveway, in her convertible Mercedes. She valet-parks in front of her beauty salon, where the staff await her. She emerges two hours later, confident and satisfied with the image she is projecting. She proceeds to a fundraiser luncheon with other socialite women, all donned in hats and Parisian couture, to raise money for the construction of a new wing at the local museum (of which her husband is a trustee, of course). The lunch ends, she returns to her automobile, chatting with friends on her mobile phone as she makes her way home. Should she rest for a while or should she go work out at her gym, she wonders? "I think I'll stay home, take it easy, and catch up with my daughter!" On route, her teenage daughter speeds by in her Range Rover and they wave to each other as they drive in opposite directions. "Oh well, I guess it'll be the gym, after all." In the evening, a shower is followed by yet a new choice of clothing and a peck on the cheek by her husband as they meet on their grandiose stairway. The evening ends with a lavish dinner with his business associates at the club. On the way there, husband and wife talk about their upcoming cruise and Junior's future enrollment at Princeton. After much champagne and ballroom dancing, the woman with choices settles into her oversized bed to sleep the deep and restful sleep reserved for the advantaged woman with not a care in the world.

VOLUNTEERING

I would like to ask you some questions about your volunteering activities and how you feel about them.

V 1.   Do you volunteer your time and energy and service without pay?
        If not, please move on to the next section. If so, approximately how many hours per week?
V 2.   What kind of volunteering activities are you involved in (are you involved in schools, religious organizations, cultural institutions, health organizations, etc.)?
V 3.   a. Do you hold office in any of them?
        b. Are you sitting on any boards?
V 4.   How do you think your volunteer work differs from the work you might do in the paid labor force?
V 5.   a. What do you value most about volunteering?
        b. What does it do for you?
        c. Why do you do it?
V 6.   How would you rank the following reasons for volunteering:
        a. I like to help people
        b. it is a status symbol
        c. I get to meet other people
        d. it is the least I can do for society, given that I am so privileged
        e. I become involved in activities I otherwise would not be involved in
V 7.   What skills have you acquired during your volunteer work?
V 8.   a. Do you expect to continue volunteering over the next two decades of your life?
        b. To the same extent as you do now?
        c. If you think you will decrease your volunteering commitments, why do you think you will do so?
V 9.   Has the nature of the fulfillment that you derive from volunteering changed or is it the same as it was when you first started volunteering?

YOUR ADVANTAGES IN THE LABOR FORCE

I now want to ask you some questions pertaining to how you feel about positioning yourself to search for and to find work for pay.

AD 1. a. Do you think you have any advantages (relative to other women) when entering the labor force?

b. What do you think your advantages are?

AD 2. Do you think that the skills that you acquired in your previous training or education are obsolete or are they still useful?

AD 3. Do you think that you have acquired any skills during your childrearing years? (if you had no children, during your adult life when you were not employed) If so, what are they?

AD 4. I have called the skills that women acquire while juggling all the responsibilities and demands that they have (i.e., household, children, volunteer work) shadow skills. I have divided them in four categories. Please think about each category, and tell me if you feel that your skills in any of those categories have been increased during the past decade or so.

a. skills in human interaction

b. skills in conveying information

c. skills in producing final products

d. skills in managing and juggling

AD 5. Do you think any of these skills are marketable? Probe.

AD 6. In your efforts to enter the labor market, do you think that you have any of the following advantages?

a. financial security so you are not desperate to find a job

b. confidence that comes with status and privilege

c. the possibility to reeducate and to retool

d. a society that encourages women to work

e. an accommodating work environment

f. children who can teach you a lot (e.g., computer skills)

g. you know how to manage your time

h. a husband who is well connected in the working world

i. pick the three advantages that are most relevant in your case and rank them, if you can.

YOUR GOALS

I will ask you some questions about your future goals, what they are, and how you hope to achieve them.

G 1.   Are you clear about your goals for the future? Do you know exactly what you want to do or do you know vaguely what you want to do?

G 2.   a. What are your goals? please describe what you want to do with respect to future employment?

b. What are your goals with respect to your family, if you have one?

G 3.   Please describe how you plan to achieve your goals

G 4.   Do you think that you will stay focused on those goals until you achieve them or might you change your mind and try something else?

G 5.   Do you intend to reeducate yourself and to acquire new skills?

G 6.   What sort of jobs do you think you can do?

G 7.   Are you inclined toward self-employment or working for others?

G 8.   In the following categories of jobs, which might you be interested in?

a. working with people

b. conveying information

c. producing goods

d. managing

G 9.   In the list above, which jobs do you think you would be capable of performing?

G 10.   How do you think you will decide what kind of job to try to get?

G 11.   a. How much freedom are you willing to give up in order to be employed (a lot, some, little, none)?

b. How much responsibility are you willing to take upon yourself in order to be employed (a lot, some, little, none)?

c. How important is salary to you (a lot, somewhat, little, not at all)?

G 12.   What role do you think the following will play in your ability to attain your goals?

a. previous training

b. your interest and passion for something

c. chance and luck

d. family support, especially spouse if you have one

G 13.   What role do you think the following will play in your ability to find employment?

a. previous training

b. your interest and passion for something

c. chance and luck

d. family support, especially spouse if you have one

THE OBSTACLES YOU MIGHT ENCOUNTER

I would like to ask you some questions about what obstacles you think you might encounter when you try to get a job.

O 1.   I have listed below some common obstacles that women face when they begin their job search. These are obstacles that come from themselves. Please comment on them and say whether they apply to you.

a. lack of self-confidence

b. lack of clear goals

c. initial inertia

d. procrastination

e. fear of failure

f. fear of collapse of safe environment (home?)

g. fear of recrimination (by family and friends)

h. perception of limited options due to class background

i. please rank the above in order of importance

O 2.   What kind of obstacles do you think you will encounter in the workplace?

O 3.   Do you think you will be discriminated against in the workplace? On what basis?

O 4.   Please comment on the following forms of potential discrimination, and say if you think you will encounter them?
a. against women in general
b. against mothers
c. against middle age
d. against wealth and social position
e. against appearance
f. against first-time entrants into the labor force
g. against returning mothers or returning women
h. against part-timers and flexible workers

We have reached the end of the interview. Is there anything that you would like to say about your choices, your goals, and your employment aspirations that I have not covered in my questions? OK then, that is all. Thank you so much.

Selected Bibliography

Amott, Teresa, and Julie Matthaei, *Race, Gender and Work: A Multicultural Economic History of Women in the United States*, Boston: South End Press, 1991.

Baltzell, E. Digby, *Philadelphia Gentlemen: The Making of National Upper Class*, Glencoe, Ill.: Free Press, 1958.

Bardwick, Judith M., *In Transition: How Feminism, Sexual Liberation, and the Search for Self-Fulfillment Have Altered America*, New York: Holt, Rinehart and Winston, 1979.

Barnett, Rosalind C., and Carol Rivers, *She Works, He Works*, New York: Ford Foundation.

Barrett, Nancy, "Obstacles to Economic Parity for Women," *The American Economic Review*, 72, May 1982, pp. 160–165.

Berkun, Cleo S., "Changing Appearance for Women in the Middle Years of Life: Trauma?" in Elizabeth Markson, ed., *Older Women*, Lexington, Mass.: Lexington Books, 1983.

Bianchi, Suzanne, and Daphne Spain, *American Women: Three Decades of Change*, Washington, D.C.: U.S. Dept. of Commerce, Bureau of the Census, 1983.

Blau, Francine D., and Marianne A. Ferber, *The Economics of Women, Men and Work*, 2nd Ed., Englewood Cliffs, N.J.: Prentice-Hall, 1992.

Burggraf, Shirley, *The Feminine Economy and Economic Man*, Reading, Mass.: Addison-Wesley, 1998.

Coontz, Stephanie, *The Way We Really Are: Coming to Terms with America's Changing Families*, New York: Basic Books, 1992.

Daniels, Arlene Kaplan, *Invisible Careers, Women Civic Leaders from the Volunteer World*, Chicago: University of Chicago Press, 1988.

Deem, Rosemary, *All Work and No Play? The Sociology of Women and Leisure*, Milton Keynes: Open University Press, 1986.

Dinnerstein, Myra, *Women Between Two Worlds*, Philadelphia: Temple University Press, 1992.

Dornhoff, G. William, *The Higher Circles*, New York: Random House, 1970.

Feiner, Susan, ed., *Race and Gender in the American Economy*, Englewood Cliffs, N.J.: Prentice-Hall, 1994.

Gerson, Kathleen, *Hard Choices, How Women Decide about Work, Career, and Motherhood*, Berkeley: University of California Press, 1985.

Gognalons-Nicolet, Maryvonne, "The Crossroads of Menopause: A Chance and a Risk for the Aging Process of Women" in Elizabeth Markson, ed., *Older Women*, Lexington, Mass.: Lexington Books, 1983

Goldman, Katherine Wyse, *If You Can Raise Kids, You Can Get a Good Job*, New York: HarperCollins, 1996.

Hand, Jennifer "Shopping-Bag Women: Aging Deviants in the City," in Elizabeth Markson, ed., *Older Women*, Lexington, Mass.: Lexington Books, 1983.

Harris, Louis and Associates, *Families at Work, Strengths and Strains*, General Mills American Family Report, 1980–81, Minneapolis: General Mills, 1981.

Hayes, Cheryl D., and Sheila B. Kamerman, eds., *Children of Working Parents: Experiences and Outcomes*, Washington, D.C.: National Academy Press, 1981.

Heynes, Barbara, "The Influence of Parents' Work on Children's School Achievement," in Sheila Kamerman and Cheryl Hayes, eds., *Families that Work: Children in a Changing World*, Washington, D.C.: National Academy Press, 1982.

Hochschild, Arlie Russell, *The Time Bind: When Work Becomes Home and Home Becomes Work*, New York: Metropolitan Books, 1997.

Jacobsen, Joyce P., *The Economics of Gender*, Cambridge, Mass.: Blackwell, 1994.

Josselson, Ruthellen, *Finding Herself: Pathways to Identity Development in Women*, San Francisco: Jossey-Bass Publishers, 1987.

Lopata, Helena Z., *Occupation: Housewife*, New York: Oxford University Press, 1971.

Mack, Dana, *The Assault on Parenthood: How Our Culture Undermines the Family*, New York: Simon & Schuster, 1997.

Margolis, Maxine, "In Hartford, Hannibal, and (New) Hampshire, Heloise Is Hardly Helpful," *MS* 4, no. 12, June 1972, pp. 28–32.

McCarthy, Eugene, and William McGaughey, *Non-Financial Economics: The Case for Shorter Hours of Work*, New York: Praeger, 1989.

McKenna, Elizabeth Perle, *When Work Doesn't Work Anymore*, New York: Delacorte Press, 1997.

Miles, Rosalind, *The Women's History of the World*, London: Paladin Grafton Books, 1988.

Minton, Michael H. with Jean Libman Block, *What Is a Wife Worth*, New York: McGraw-Hill 1983.

Ostander, Susan A. *Women of the Upper Class*, Philadelphia: Temple University Press, 1984.

Schor, Juliet, *The Overworked American*, New York: Basic Books, 1992.

Simpson, Ida Harper, and Paula England, "Conjugal Work Roles and Marital Solidarity," *Journal of Family Issues* 2, June 1981, pp. 180–204.

Stanley, Thomas J., and William D. Danko, *The Millionaire Next Door: The Surprising Secrets of America's Wealthy*, Atlanta: Longstreet Press, 1997.

Walters, Natasha, *The New Feminism*, London: Little Brown, 1998.

Wolf, Naomi, *The Beauty Myth*, New York: Anchor Books, 1991.

Index

About the Author

MILICA Z. BOOKMAN is Professor of Economics at St. Joseph's University in Philadelphia. She was educated at Brown University, the London School of Economics, and Temple University. She is the author of five books on economics as well as numerous articles.

ISBN 0-275-96811-1

EAN

9 780275 968113

HARDCOVER BAR CODE